Mudras
Seals of Yoga

By the same author:

Ashtanga Yoga: Practice and Philosophy

Ashtanga Yoga: The Intermediate Series

Pranayama The Breath of Yoga

Yoga Meditation: Through Mantra, Chakras and Kundalini to Spiritual Freedom

Samadhi The Great Freedom

How To Find Your Life's Divine Purpose – Brain Software For A New Civilization

Chakras, Drugs and Evolution – A Map of Transformative States

Mudras
Seals of Yoga

Gregor Maehle

Published by Kaivalya Publications
PO Box 181
Crabbes Creek, NSW 2483
Australia

First published 2022

 A catalogue record for this
book is available from the
NATIONAL
LIBRARY
OF AUSTRALIA
National Library of Australia

Maehle, Gregor
Mudras: Seals of Yoga/by Gregor Maehle;

ISBN (pbk.) 978-0-6488932-5-7
Includes bibliographical references
Includes index

Hatha yoga

Dedication

To the ancient sages of India who blazed a trail, which even
today can still be traced.

Disclaimer

This book does not constitute medical advice. Contact a medical practitioner to determine whether you are fit to perform these yogic exercises.

NOTES

If not otherwise stated *Hatha Yoga Pradipika* quotations refer to the standard 4-chapter edition, rather than the 10-chapter edition. Similarly, if not otherwise stated quotations from the *Gheranda Samhita* are from R.B.S. Chandra Vasu's translation.

Acknowledgements

My gratitude to Shri B.N.S. Iyengar who with his instruction on the *mudras* of the *Gheranda Samhita*, which he himself had received from Shri T. Krishnamacharya, kindled my interest and research. My gratitude to my wife Monica, who continues to support me in my outlandish lifestyle, where little is happening outside from yoga. To my curious students who force me to develop further.

To the literary divisions of the Kaivalyadhama and the Lonavla Yoga Institutes for their continued effort in making *shastras* available, particularly to the late Dr M.L. Gharote and his son Dr M.M. Gharote.

Preface

I am hereby presenting the eighth volume or my series of yoga textbooks, *Mudras – Seals of Yoga*. I began writing this book over eleven years ago, and it was to be the first volume in a *Mudra, Pranayama, Meditation* trilogy. Instead, I changed course and focussed on *Pranayama The Breath of Yoga* and subsequently *Yoga Meditation – Through Mantra, Chakras and Kundalini to Spiritual Freedom*. Although to a large extent supported and informed by the *mudra* material, the methods in these two volumes proved so potent that I neglected the original project. After my fifth volume *Samadhi, The Great Freedom,* interest in my work grew and I spent more and more time presenting my material to audiences worldwide. Being by nature a recluse-level introvert, I had to change my personality to rise to that challenge. For a number of years, I had the privilege to connect with students worldwide and see them transform through the work. On the downside, this led to my writing falling by the wayside. While further volumes condensed in my head, I wondered how I would ever find the time, introversion, and muse to write them.

This opportunity came during the COVID pandemic. With Australia closing its borders for almost two years, I completed two important long-term projects, *How to Find Your Life's Divine Purpose*, containing my teachings on the yogic process of *sankalpa* (affirmation, resolution) and *bhavana* (cultivation of thought processes in alignment with the Divine) and *Chakras, Drugs and Evolution – A Map of Transformative States*, my response to the current reboot of the psychedelic revolution, including a topography of mystical experiences. After completing both, the path was now free to return to the long-neglected *Mudras – Seals of Yoga*. This project kept lingering in the back of my mind because the *chakra*-Kundalini meditation described in *Yoga Meditation* is a demanding and complex method that demands a certain readiness of mind. This readiness is often achieved through the long-term practice of *asana* and *pranayama*, but it can still be a taxing process despite these. Apart from other important subject matter, this current volume describes how *mudras* can supercharge and accelerate one's *asana*, *pranayama* and meditation practice so that success in *chakra*-Kundalini meditation is achieved more quickly. May the *mudras* lead to swift success!

Contents

List of Shastras consulted in this text:

Amanaska Yogah
Amrita Nada Upanishad
Aparokshanubhuti of Shankaracharya
Bhagavad Gita
Brhad Aranyaka Upanishad
Brhadyogi Yajnavalkya Smrti
Chandogya Upanishad
Dattatreya's Yogashastra
Dhyanabindu Upanishad
Gheranda Samhita
Goraksha Shataka
Hatha Ratnavali of Shrinivasayogi
Hatha Yoga Pradipika (10-chapter edition)
Hatha Yoga Pradipika (4-chapter edition)
Hatha Yoga Pradipika with the Commentary Jyotsna of Brahmananda
Hatharatnavali of Shrinivasayogi
Hathatatva Kaumudi of Sundaradeva
Hathayoga Manjari of Sahajananda
Jogapradipyaka of Jayatarama
Kapalakurantaka's Hathabhyasa-Paddhati
Khechari Vidya of Adinatha
Kumbhaka Paddhati of Raghuvira
Maitri Upanishad
Mandala Brahmana Upanishad
Nadabindu Upanishad

Nathamuni's Yoga Rahasya
Ramayana
Shandilya Upanishad
Shiva Samhita
Siddha Siddhanta Paddhati
Trishikhi Brahmana Upanishad
Vasishta Samhita
Yoga Bhashya
Yoga Chudamani Upanishad
Yoga Kundalini Upanishad
Yoga Makaranda
Yoga Rahasya
Yoga Sutra
Yoga Taravali
Yoga Yajnavalkya
Yoga Tattva Upanishad
Yuktabhavadeva of Bhavadeva Mishra

Introduction

WHAT IS MUDRA

Writing about *asana, pranayama,* meditation or *samadhi* is relative straightforward. They are sequential limbs of yoga with clear demarcations. Even within those demarcations there are reasonably clear rules in which order, for example, *pranayama* techniques or *samadhis* are practised. They are usually performed in ascending order of difficulty. Writing about *mudras* is a more complex challenge. *Mudra* is not one of the eight limbs of yoga, which according to Yoga Sutra II.28 are restraints, observances, postures, breath extension, independence from external stimulus, concentration, meditation and revelation. So, what are *mudras* if it is not a yogic limb? Aren't they just fancy hand positions?

Hand *mudras,* so-called *hasta* mudras are a feature of *tantric* Buddhism and in Indian classical dance, but in yoga really only a small part of the subject of *mudra.* Although the term *mudra* is not explicitly mentioned in the Yoga Sutra, the medieval *Hatha*[1] texts usually devote an entire chapter to them. The term *mudra* is translated as seal in the sense of *pranic*[2] seal or energetic seal.

---

1 The term *Hatha* refers to yoga that is primarily (but not only) physical in nature and mainly comprises of *asana* and *pranayama. Hatha Yoga* is not an end in itself but is to prepare for higher or *Raja Yoga.* So says the *Hatha Yoga Pradipika,* "This *Hatha Yoga* is a ladder for those who want to climb the heights of *Raja Yoga*".

2 The term *prana* primarily refers to a subtle life force which is not perceptible to the senses, and only secondarily it refers to the breath. The breath is the main tool to influence this life force for the better.

1

A *mudra* often involves a particular posture, application of *bandhas*[3] and regular breath retention (*kumbhaka*) to achieve a particular *pranic* outcome. The *Siddha Siddhanta Paddhati* states that the root *mud* means to delight, whereas the root *rā* means to bestow[4]. This *shastra* (scripture) therefore defines *mudra* as that which bestows delight. Delight, however, the *Paddhati* does not find in sensory or aesthetic stimulus, but in realizing the union of the individual self with the cosmic self. *Mudra* then is loosely what leads us to self-realization or to use a more flamboyant term, cosmic consciousness. Stanza VI.30 of the *Siddha Siddhanta Paddhati* then gets even more exulted by saying that *mudra* causes delight to the multitude of gods and causes terror to the hordes of demons. I'm interpreting the shastric terms 'gods' and 'demons' metaphorically as the luminous and dark aspects of our own psyche. If we apply that reading, then *mudra* is that which enables us to embrace the loftier aspects of ourselves and to not yield anymore to our dark side. While at first impression, this appears to be a very vague definition, as you will keep delving into this book, you will eventually come to perceive this definition as quite accurate.

The late *tantric*[5] scholar Sir John Woodroffe describes *mudra* as what gives fortitude to the body, creates health, protects

---

3 *Bandhas* are a sub-category within *mudras*. They are muscular locks from which an outward directed *pranic* force rebounds back into the body to prevent *prana* loss.

4 Siddha Siddhanta Paddhati VI.29

5 *Tantra* is an extremely complex term but according to Arthur Avalon's own definition it means the re-interpretation and re-application of *Vedic* knowledge for an increasingly materialistic and technological society during the last 1000 years.

from injury through the elements and activates Kundalini[6] (in Section 4 of this book, the complex term Kundalini is treated extensively). Other effects of *mudras* include the redirecting of *prana* back into body that normally would be lost thus enabling *pratyahara*[7]. Swami Niranjanananda Saraswati confirms[8] that *mudras* redirect *prana* and store it by blocking the flow in certain areas[9]. *Dattatreya's Yogashastra* in stanzas 31-32 lists the *mudras* and calls them *Hatha* practices[10]. *Mudras* even found entry into the lofty *Upanishads*[11]. So describes the *Mandala Brahmana Upanishad* in stanza II.i.9 *Shambhavi Mudra* and its powers of giving mind and intellect stability[12].

LISTS OF MUDRAS

While most medieval *Hatha* texts contain a list of *mudras*, the most influential ones are those from the *Goraksha Shataka*, the

---

6 Sir John Woodroffe, *The Serpent Power*, Ganesh & CO, Madras, 1995, p. 206

7 *Pratyahara* is the fifth limb of yoga. It stands for independence from sensory stimulus.

8 Swami Niranjanananda Saraswati, *Prana and Pranayama*, Yoga Publications Trust, Munger, 2009, p. 325

9 Swami Niranjanananda Saraswati, *Yoga Darshan*, Yoga Publications Trust, Munger, 2009, p. 420

10 Dr M.M. Gharote (ed.), *Dattatreyayogasastram*, Lonavla Yoga Institute, Lonavla, 2015, p. 17

11 The ancient *Upanishads* contain the mystical doctrines of the *Vedas* and in Hinduism are considered divinely revealed scriptures.

12 Dr M.M. Gharote (ed.), *Mandalabrahmanopanisad and Nadabindupanisad*, Lonavla Yoga Institute, Lonavla, 2012, p. 92ff

Hatha Yoga Pradipika and the *Gheranda Samhita*. Not a single hand *mudra* made either of those three lists.

1. The *Goraksha Shataka*, the oldest of the three texts in stanza 32 lists five *mudras*: *Maha Mudra, Nabho Mudra, Uddiyana-, Jalandhara-* and *Mula Bandhas* [13].

2. The *Hatha Yoga Pradipika*, after the *Yoga Sutra* and the *Bhagavad Gita* probably the most influential yoga text, has one of its four chapters devoted to *mudras*. In stanza III.6-7 gives us an expanded list of ten *mudras*: *Maha Mudra, Maha Bandha Mudra, Maha Vedha Mudra, Khechari Mudra, Uddiyana Bandha, Mula Bandha, Jalandhara Bandha, Viparita Karani Mudra, Vajroli Mudra*, and *Shakti Chalana Mudra*[14].

3. The *Gheranda Samhita*, the youngest of the three texts but no less important, expands this in stanzas III.1-3 to 20 *mudras*[15]: *Maha Mudra, Nabho Mudra*, the three *bandhas, Maha Bandha-, Maha Vedha-, Khechari-, Viparita Karani-, Yoni-, Vajroli-, Shakti Chalana-, Tadaga-, Manduka-, Shambhavi-, Ashvini-, Pashini-, Kaki-, Matangi-*, and *Bhujangini Mudras*.

We can see from this list that none of the *mudras* have been abandoned but that the list gradually expanded. One could consult other lists, but they largely constitute copies of these

---

13 Swami Kuvalayananda (ed.), *Goraksasatakam*, Kaivalyadhama, Lonavla, 2006, p. 40

14 Pancham Sinh (transl.), *The Hatha Yoga Pradipika,* Sri Satguru Publications, Delhi, 1991, p. 28-29

15 James Mallinson, *The Gheranda Samhita*, YogaVidya.com, Woodstock, 2004, p. 60

three main lists. The *Yoga Tattva Upanishad*, for example, lists in stanzas 26-27 *Maha Mudra, Mahabandha-, Khechari-,* and *Vajroli Mudras* and *Jalandhara-, Uddiyana-, and Mula Bandhas*. These are all *mudras* in the *Hatha Yoga Pradipika*, but three are missing from the list. We could surmise this list is an in-between stage of the *Goraksha Shataka* and the *Pradipika* lists. The *Shiva Samhita* in stanza IV. 15 also extols a list of 10 *mudras*, which it claims are the best, but then simply copies the list of the *Pradipika*, if only in changed order [16]. As a peculiar sidenote, before this passage, the *Shiva Samhita* praises the extraordinary power of *Yoni Mudra* but then does not include it in its list. This tendency we find replicated in other texts, too, i.e. the tendency that in odd locations *mudras* are described as very important, which are not reflected in the main list. It appears that *shastra*[17] authors and scribes sometimes simply chose an elegant number such as 5, 10 or 20, but in the actual text did not feel limited by the *mudras* contained in that number. *Jayatarama's Jogapradipika* finally offers 24 *mudras*[18]. It is difficult to analyse *Jayatarama's* list because one of his past times was to change the names of the *mudras* and make the descriptions opaque. Nevertheless, we see a certain overlap with the list of the *Gheranda Samhita*.

The foundation of the current volume was laid in 1996 when I took a two-month course with B.N.S. Iyengar (do not mistake

---

16 R.B.S. Chandra Vasu, (transl.), *The Shiva Samhita*, Sri Satguru Publications, Delhi, 184, p. 44

17 The term *shastra* directly translated means path to truth but as a single word the English 'scripture' captures the meaning best. Yoga *shastra* is the class of writings that includes all historical, authoritative texts on yoga.

18 Swami Maheshananda, et al. (eds & transl.), *Jogapradipyaka of Jayatarama*, Kaivalyadhama, Lonavla, 2006, p.110-133

with B.K.S. Iyengar) that dealt exclusively with *mudras*. Iyengar taught from lecture notes he had taken when studying with T. Krishnamacharya during the 1940s. He showed me the notes on several occasions and as far as I remember, these classes took place in Mysuru from 1945-1948. The course was based strictly on the list of the *Gheranda Samhita*, with the exception of the five *dharanas* also in this list, which according to T. Krishnamacharya were *dharanas* (concentration exercises) and not *mudras* (*prana* diversion techniques). I have added a further 11 common *mudras*, which brings the total to 31. The added *mudras* are *Yoga Mudra*, a commonly used but misunderstood *asana mudra*, *hasta mudras* including *Shanka-*, *Akasha-*, and *Jnana Mudras*, and finally, *mudras* that appear in *shastra* but have not made the common lists such as *Jihva Bandha, Agochari-, Matsyendra-, Jyoti-, Dhyana-,* and *Bhramari Mudras*. Ambiguity is sometimes difficult to avoid, but I have explained my reasoning as clearly as possible why a particular *mudra* appears in the list. *Vajroni Mudra* is a different technique to *Vajroli Mudra*, but sometimes both are listed as variations of *Vajroli Mudra*, which makes little sense as both versions have nothing to do with each other. I have listed them as two different methods. *Bhramari Mudra*, I have listed as a *mudra,* although often it is listed as a *pranayama* method. If it is practised without *kumbhaka* (breath retention) it is more akin to a *mudra. Yoni Mudra* and *Shanmukhi Mudra*, finally, are exactly the same technique that occurs under two different names; hence it is listed here under one name only, *Shanmukhi Mudra*.

PURPOSES OF MUDRAS

In this section, I will describe the manifold purposes of *mudras*. They are much more diverse than the purposes of the yogic limbs of *asana, pranayama* or meditation, which lend themselves to be sorted into descriptive categories. Why that is the case will be covered in the next section. The *Hathatatva Kaumudi of Sundaradeva* states that if the yogi practices *mudras*, fear of death is overcome[19]. This is the case because *mudras* support realizing oneself as the immortal and eternal, i.e. the consciousness (*purusha*) as it is called in yoga, or the self (*atman*) as the *Upanishads* would have it. But the *Kaumudi* also says that without *mudras*, *prana* (life force) does not enter *Sushumna*[20] (the central energy channel)[21]. This is confirmed by the *Yuktabhavadeva of Bhavadeva Mishra,* which states that for raising Kundalini *mudras* need to be practised[22]. The ten-chapter edition of the *Hatha Yoga Pradipika* holds[23] that Kundalini forms the very foundation of the entire science of yoga and that the yogi needs to put all effort into practising the *mudras* to raise Kundalini[24].

While the *Pradipika* sees the focus of *mudras* on Kundalini raising, the *Gheranda Samhita* sees their aim as *sthirata*, i.e.

19 M.L. Gharote et al (eds. & transl.), *Hathatatvakaumudi,* The Lonavla Yoga Institite, Lonavla, 2007, p.18

20 One of the main goals of physical yoga is to induce life force into the central energy channel where it powers spiritual revelation and peak experiences, instead of scattering *prana* in extravert pursuits.

21 M.L. Gharote et al (eds. & transl.), *Hathatatvakaumudi,* The Lonavla Yoga Institite, Lonavla, 2007, p. 141

22 *Yuktabhavadeva of Bhavadeva Misra,* Lxxiv

23 M.L. Gharote et al (eds. & transl.), *Hathapradipika of Svatmarama (10 chapters)*, Lonavla Yoga Institute, Lonavla, 2006, p. 98

24 M.L. Gharote et al (eds. & transl.), *Hathapradipika of Svatmarama (10 chapters)*, Lonavla Yoga Institute, Lonavla, 2006, p. 101

fortitude[25]. T. Krishnamacharya, being a Vaishnavite[26], was primarily interested in this aspect of mudra, while he relied on *pranayama* as the main means for Kundalini raising. Dr M.L. Gharote, translator and editor of many yoga texts, explains that in *mudra* one tries to control semi-voluntary muscles (such as the anal sphincter, thoracic diaphragm, ocular muscles etc.) with the aim of integrating the central and autonomous nervous system[27]. Ultimately, I see *mudras*, particularly those in the *dharana mudra* section, as an alternative for those who shy away from extensive *pranayama* and *chakra*-meditation. Please note the term extensive in the previous sentence. *Mudras* can reduce the time necessary spent on those practices but cannot replace them entirely. Long-term commitment to *chakra*-meditation seems easy for those with a more visual and auditory orientation, but it can be challenging for those more kinaesthetically inclined.

---

25 The different outlook of these two important texts is based on differences in their underlying theology. While both texts belong in a wider sense to the category of *tantras*, the underlying theology of the *Gheranda Samhita* is Vaishnavism, with its attached tendency to piety and puritanism. The *Hatha Yoga Pradipika* on the other hand is built onto a more radical Shaivite *tantrism*, with its own attached possible sets of problems, such as debauchery and ocultism. This does not mean that one text is inferior to the other. Both texts need to be taken serious by modern yogis by taking into account their cultural settings and problems. One needs to navigate these with caution without falling for extremes. The reader will see this principle at work when studying the current text.

26 Vaishnavism is a religious movement within Hinduism that puts Vishnu centreplace. It's characteristics are very different from Shaivism, which revolves around Shiva. The *Hatha Yoga Pradipika* is a Shaivite text.

27 M.L. Gharote et al (eds. & transl.), *Hathapradipika of Svatmarama (10 chapters)*, Lonavla Yoga Institute, Lonavla, 2006, p. xxi

With the *mudra* approach, an avenue fulfils to a greater extent the needs of the kinaesthetically inclined, i.e. the need to feel body sensations as a confirmation that something is happening spiritually.

WHEN TO PRACTICE MUDRAS

We are now turning to the question when in relation to other yogic practices are *mudras* to be practiced. This means we are discussing whether they should they be learned and integrated into one's practice before or after *pranayama*. It seems an early point to turn to such a detailed question, but as we will see, there are far-reaching repercussions to the answer that need to be addressed this early in our study. T. Krishnamacharya stated that *mudras* prepare for *pranayama*, hence *mudras* should be practised first [28]. We find this view also supported in the *Yoga Rahasya*, handed down through Krishnamacharya's family lineage. The *Yoga Rahasya* allocates both *asana* and *mudra* to the first *ashrama* (*Vedic* stage of life), called *brahmachary*, whereas it allocates *pranayama* to the second stage of life, called *grhasta*. This order of techniques is also corroborated by Acharya Bhagwan Dev who opined that *pranayama* should follow *mudras* [29]. However, *shastra* author Jayatarama argues that *pranayama* facilitate *mudras*, hence *pranayama* should be practised first [30]. This is also the order espoused by the *Hatha Yoga Pradipika*,

---

28 T. Krishnamacharya, *Yoga Makaranda*, Media Garuda, Chennai, 2011, p. 111

29 Acharya Bhagwan Dev, *Pranayama, Kundalini & Hatha Yoga*, Diamond Books, New Delhi, 2008, p. 34

30 Swami Maheshananda, et al. (eds & transl.), *Jogapradipyaka of Jayatarama*, Kaivalyadhama, Lonavla, 2006, p. 98

which says that the sequence of yogic practices is *asanas, kumbhakas* (*Hatha* texts generally refer to *pranayama* by the term *kumbhakas* – breath retentions), *mudras* and *nadanusandhana* (hearing inner sound, *Hatha*'s main avenue towards *samadhi*)[31]. But the *Goraksha Shataka*, the mother of all *Hatha* texts, describes *mudras* first, and then only *pranayama*[32]. Summarizing, we say that although authorities feel compelled to make a statement about the order of these techniques, reaching agreement they cannot.

Let's look into some of the rationales to see whether a conclusive view is possible. *Mudra* is often defined as a combination of *asana, bandha* and breath. In this view of *mudra*, it is a way of slowly introducing *kumbhaka* (breath retention). Most *mudras* do contain breath retentions. The reason these breath retentions do not constitute *pranayama* proper is because the count is missing, i.e. the length of each retention is not precisely measured. The breath retentions during *mudra* are always held "to capacity", rather than to a determined count. Additionally, there are few repetitions and rounds either, whereas once one has entered into formal *pranayama* practice count, ratio (the relation of the length of inhalation, exhalation and *kumbhaka* relative to each other) and the number of repetitions become paramount. *Mudras* are usually done either once or repeated several times, but one will not usually engage in the practise of one and the same mudra for a whole practice session, as this is the case with *pranayama*. Another important aspect of *pranayama* is *bandha*. Once breath retentions are commenced, a high level

---

31 Dr M.L Gharote, *Yogic Techniques*, Lonavla Yoga Institute, Lonavla, 2006, p. 92

32 Swami Kuvalayananda, (ed.), *Goraksasatakam*, Kaivalyadhama, Lonavla, 2006, p. 40

of *bandha* proficiency is necessary. This proficiency is learned through *mudra*, combining *asana*, *bandha* and *kumbhaka* in the absence of count. The absence of count enables us to focus on the intricacies of the *bandhas*, which prepares for practising *pranayama* proper (i.e. *kumbhakas* with count) later down the track. The type of *mudras* addressed so far should be performed during or right after our *asana* practise. Some, as we will see, are taking place within relatively advanced asanas and, therefore, it is necessary to be prepared and warmed up. If not warmed up properly one could easily get hurt in *mudras* such as *Vajroni-*, *Pashini-*, *Maha-*, or *Viparita Karani Mudras*.

On the other side, however, as this text will reveal, there are clearly many *mudras*, which constitute advanced elements of meditation or even *samadhi*, such as *Khechari Mudra* or *Shakti Chalana Mudra*. It would be nonsensical and even counterproductive to practice *mudras* such as these before attaining proficiency in *pranayama*. When looking at the above statements from *shastras* and authorities regarding as to when practice *mudras*, the problem is that any answer will treat *mudras* as if they were one uniform category, such as with *asanas* or *pranayamas*. However, *mudras* are not that at all. We will analyse this more closely in the next section.

ORDER AND CATEGORIES OF MUDRAS

In the *shastras mudras* are often listed in no particular order, which makes the understanding of the whole category of *mudra* difficult. There have been attempts to define groups of *mudras* through their location applied, such as hands, head, postural, pelvic, etc. I worked with this method for a while and found it unsatisfying because the location does not say much about the function. I then looked into ordering *mudras* according to function. This would lead us to the groups of *bandhas* (energetic locks), *mudras* that are combinations of posture, *bandhas* and *kumbhaka*, *mudras* engendering longevity, those associated with increasing strength, *mudras* designed to raise Kundalini, and *mudras* designed to trigger samadhi. The order would then look like this:

1. *Bandhas*:
   Mula Bandha, Uddiyana Bandha, Jalandhara Bandha, Jihva Bandha, Maha Bandha

2. *Mudras* that are combinations of posture, *bandha* and *kumbhaka*:
   Yoga Mudra, Tadagi Mudra, Maha Mudra, Maha Bandha Mudra, Maha Vedha Mudra, Kaki Mudra, Vajroni Mudra, Shanmukhi Mudra, Shakti Chalana Mudra, Matsyendra Mudra

3. *Mudras* promoting longevity:
   Tadaga Mudra, Viparita Karani Mudra, Ashvini Mudra, Manduka Mudra, Bhujangi Mudra, Vajroli Mudra, Matanga Mudra, Maha Mudra, Kaki Mudra

4. *Mudras* for raising Kundalini
   Khechari Mudra, Pashini Mudra, Ashvini Mudra, Bhujangi Mudra, Vajroni Mudra, Vajroli Mudra, Shakti Chalana Mudra

5. *Mudras* creating strength:
   Matangi Mudra, Pashini Mudra, Vajroni Mudra

6. Meditation and *samadhi mudras*
   Shambhavi Mudra, Shanmukhi Mudra, Jyoti Mudra, Bhramari Mudra, Khechari Mudra

The problem with this approach is that it makes *mudras* in one group lacking connection with each other. The categories of strength, longevity, meditation, *bandhas,* combination of…, etc. are from different levels of structural hierarchy. Many *mudras* need to appear in several categories, which makes the above table clumsy. To find a solution to systematize *mudras,* we need to hark back to the *Yoga Sutra*. Patanjali, the author of the *Sutras,* ordered limbs according to function and outcome. And that is exactly why he didn't treat *mudras* as a separate limb. The function and outcome of the *mudras* are already explained through their association with the limbs. There are *mudras* primarily related to *asana, pranayama, pratyahara, dharana* and *samadhi.* Primarily here means they can have aspects related to several other limbs, but usually, the *mudra's* primary function is easily discernible. That easily discernible primary function determined the order in which I have presented the *mudras* here. The view that *mudras* are allocated to certain limbs is corroborated by *Hatha Yoga Samhita* which states that *mudras* are techniques that support practices like *pranayama, pratyahara, dharana, dhyana* and *samadhi* [33]. These are the categories in which I have ordered the *mudras,* with omitting *dhyana* because I could find only one *mudra* primarily relating to *dhyana,* even then not clearly.

Here then are the categories and their allocated *mudras:*

---

33 Dr. M.L. , *Yogic Techniques,* Lonavla Yoga Institute, Lonavla, 2006, p. 91

1. Asana Mudras

These *mudras* are primarily *pranic* (this anglicized term means energetic or related to life-force) modifications of *asanas* and are inserted into one's existing *asana* practice. *Mudras* in this group include *Tadaga-, Viparita Karani-, Vajroni-,* and *Yoga Mudras.* Alternatively, they are techniques whose purpose, similar to *asana,* is primarily to strengthen the body and increase health and longevity, such as *Nabho-, Matsyendra-, Bhujangi-, Manduka-,* and *Matangi Mudras.* The purpose of this group is the *sthirata* (fortitude) of the *Gheranda Samhita,* which was also T. Krishnamacharya's focus. Authorities who believed this group of *mudras* to be the quintessential one concluded that *mudras* should be practised before *pranayama.*

2. Pranayama Mudras

In this group, you will find *mudras* primarily associated with the limb of *pranayama* or they are ancillaries to *pranayama.* These are *Mula-, Uddiyana-,* and *Jalandhara Bandhas,* as well as *Shanka-,* and *Kaki Mudras.*

3. Pratyahara Mudras

Pratyahara, the fifth limb of yoga, is often translated as sense-withdrawal, but it is better understood as independence from external (sensory) stimulus. The *mudras* in this group are primarily designed to project sensory *prana* (*prana* that powers the various senses, such as audio, visual, etc.) back into the body, therefore making us independent from sensory stimulus[34]. These include *Jihva Bandha, Shambhavi-, Akasha-, Jnana-,*

---

34 Sage Vyasa argues in his *Yoga Bhashya,* commentary on the Yoga Sutra, that the mind settles on what the senses settle. Freedom of mind therefore is

Agochari-, and *Dhyana Mudras*. Two special cases here are *Shambhavi-*, and *Dhyana Mudras*. *Shambhavi Mudra* would also deserve to be listed under *samadhi mudras*, but it is so important as a *pratyahara mudra* I have included it in this earlier category. *Dhyana Mudra* could have deserved a separate category of meditation *mudras*, but because this *mudra* is something of an anticlimax and has been treated like an orphan by *shastra*, I have refrained from this step and included it in this present section. Please also note that the English term meditation is ambiguous. It is sometimes used to translate the Sanskrit *dhyana*, but in yoga, it is the combined process of *pratyahara, dharana* and *dhyana* (yogic limbs five through seven).

4. Dharana Mudras

This is by far the most important section of *mudras*[35]. They are all *mudras* designed to raise Kundalini. In his 1905 seminal textbook *The Serpent Power*, Sir John Woodroffe states that *mudras* are keys for opening the door to Kundalini[36]. The connection between the term *dharana* (the 6th limb of yoga, often translated as concentration) and Kundalini is: With Kundalini raised, success in *dharana* is guaranteed. With Kundalini dormant, success in *dharana* is hard to come by. The *mudras* in this section are *Maha-, Maha Bandha-, Mahav Vedha-, Ashvini-, Vajroli-, Pashini-*, and *Shakti Chalana Mudras*. These *mudras* represent the

---

dependent on sensory freedom.

35 From a birdeye view this could be seen as a tendentious statement as it reveals the present author to be more intersted in Kundalini-raising than in *sthirata* (fortitude).

36 Sir John Woodroffe, *The Serpent Power*, Ganesh & CO, Madras, 1995, p. 206

main focus of the *Hatha Yoga Pradipika*, i.e. raising Kundalini. Authorities who believed this group of *mudras* to be the quintessential one necessarily concluded that *mudras* should be practised after *pranayama*.

5. Samadhi Mudras

These are *mudras* designed to trigger *samadhi* (revelatory ecstasy, the 8th limb of yoga). They cannot cause *samadhi* alone by themselves but only trigger it in a mind that already gravitates towards *samadhi*. Such gravitation is brought about through the long-term practice of *asana*, *pranayama* and yogic meditation. This category of *mudras* includes *Bhramari-*, *Shanmukhi-*, *Jyoti-*, *and Khechari Mudras*. As earlier stated, *Shambhavi Mudra* could have been included in this category, too, but its presence in the *pratyahara* category is too important and I didn't want to list *mudras* twice.

HOW TO PRACTICE MUDRAS

Sir John Woodroffe in *The Serpent Power* explains that not all *mudras* need to be exercised by each person, but only as many as required in that particular case [37]. With the order of categories created in the previous section, we can now easily analyse to which category Woodroffe's statement applies. It applies to the categories 1 *asana mudras*, 4 *dharana mudras*, and 5 *samadhi mudras*. Of these three groups, we would select and add on only as many *mudras* as we need to achieve our respective goal. We would not learn them simultaneously but would focus on each

---

37 Sir John Woodroffe, *The Serpent Power*, Ganesh & CO, Madras, 1995, p. 206

16

one typically for 14 to 28 days before adding on the next [38]. If we learn too many of the *mudras* in these groups simultaneously, we will create confusion. A typical example would be *Maha Mudra, Maha Bandha Mudra* and *Maha Vedha Mudra*. During the learning period, we would focus on each *mudra* individually and only eventually, once integrated, would we execute them all in sequence. Similarly is the situation with the *asana mudras*.

Different to that are the *mudras* in the classes 2 *pranayama*, and 3 *pratyahara*. Of these, most are practiced simultaneously as ancillaries to *pranayama* and meditation (the term meditation here again used in a general way for the compound of *pratyahara, dharana* and *dhyana*). This means these *mudras* are to be integrated as ancillaries into our *pranayama* and meditation practice without allocating extra timeslots to them. A case in point here is the group of the *bandhas*. The *bandhas* are all executed as a compound during our *kumbhaka* practice; application of all *bandhas* during *kumbhaka* is part of the definition of *kumbhaka*. Besides some initial experimental and tuition sessions, there will be no dedicated *bandha* time slot in our practice.

WHY SHASTRA ANALYSIS?

Similar to my book on *pranayama* so also this present text relies on scriptural research. When I was young and travelled through India looking for teachers, I, as most young seekers would do, hoped to meet the one great teacher that would reveal all the secrets. This person never eventuated. While I am indebted to several teachers, when it comes to the subject of *mudra*, mainly to B.N.S. Iyengar, I did not meet a single person that had mastered

---

38 As taught by B.N.S. Iyengar, the 28-day period is refered to as a full mandala, because it reflects a complete moon cycle.

this subject comprehensively. Possibly T. Krishnamacharya was the last person to have done so. Theos Bernard faced a similar situation a few decades before me. When he kept probing his teacher, whom he called the Maharishi, for more details on a wide variety of yogic subjects, the Maharishi finally pointed out to him that yoga was in decline in India for 500 years, and that many details he would only find in *shastra*. For this reason, already early on, I embarked on a comprehensive review of *shastra*, and for decades, this was a good part of my work. Many details of yogic technique could only be unearthed and reconstructed through *shastric*[39] analysis. Because we are holding on to this somewhat naïve hope to meet that elusive *maha-yogi* (great yogi), many yogic methods today are taught in watered-down and impotent form. Great improvement could be achieved if the voice of *shastra* would be listened to more.

---

39 Anglified term meaning "pertaining to *shastra*"

Section 1:

Asana Mudras

This group of *mudras* consists of those who predominantly deal with the body. Some are modified *asanas* that prepare for *pranayama*, i.e. creating the conditions for *pranayama* to succeed. They also help with the transition from a practice that solely relies on *asana*, to one that consists of *asana* and *pranayama* practices. This is an important aspect of *asana mudras*. Another sub-group in this category includes *mudras* that extend the life span and increase health and strength.

For various reasons, some students are stuck on an exclusive *asana* practice. *Asana mudras* lower the threshold to start the transition towards a more integrated, wholistic yoga approach, beginning the graduation from *asana* to a compound *asana/pranayama* practice. *Asana mudras* largely form an in-between stage, in that regard, breath retention (*kumbhaka*) is often involved but is applied here without count. *Kumbhaka* in *pranayama* proper is counted, i.e. each breath retention has a pre-prescribed length. This can make the entry into *pranayama* quite challenging for those not used to such a regimen. *Asana mudras*, involving *kumbhaka*, but no count, lower the threshold for introducing *kumbhaka* in a similar way as *Nauli* does this, too[40].

An exception here is *Viparita Karani Mudra*, which does not involve *kumbhaka*. This *mudra*'s main effect is nevertheless of *pranic* nature, in that regard that it arrests or fixates *prana* in the throat *chakra* (in the case of the shoulder stand) and the third eye *chakra* (in the case of the headstand), respectively. In this way, it establishes important prerequisites for both *pranayama* and meditation. *Mudras* described in this section are:

1. *Tadaga Mudra*
2. *Viparita Karani Mudra*
3. *Vajroni Mudra*
4. *Yoga Mudra*
5. *Nabho Mudra*
6. *Matsyendra Mudra*
7. *Bhujangi Mudra*
8. *Manduka Mudra*
9. *Matangi Mudra*

---

40 *Nauli* is a *kriya*, a purification technique that takes place during external *kumbhaka*, i.e. a breath retention after exhaling, yet without count. One of the side effects of *Nauli* is that it gradually builds resilience and tolerance towards being in the state of external *kumbhaka* (breath retention after exhaling). This is due to the fact that, due to the absence of count, we can abort the *kumbhaka* whenever we need to.

Chapter 1

TADAGA MUDRA
(TANK SEAL)

Tadaga Mudra (alternative spelling *Tadagi Mudra*) means Tank *Mudra, and* it is so-called because the abdomen during this *mudra* is hollowed, or basin-shaped, like a receptacle for water. The term *Tadaga Mudra* is also colloquially used in Ashtanga Yoga for the ten breaths of lying on your back, after the back-bending sequence, and before the cool-down sequence. The ten breaths here are utilized for separating the vigorous series of postures, during which breath is faster, from the finishing *asanas*, during which the breath is slowed down. However, the term *mudra* here is only justified when *kumbhaka* is added. The entire cool-down sequence is supposed to be of *mudric*[41] nature, that is *prana* mobilized during the vigorous series is now sealed in the body. For this effect to occur in the supine position, *kumbhaka* is necessary. *Tadaga Mudra* is placed in a very strategic position in the series and is supposed to signal that all postures after this point are to be made *mudric*, i.e. to be used as pranic seals.

Let's look at the evidence of why external *kumbhaka* is necessary here. *Tadaga Mudra* has been classified by M.V. Bhole M.D., one of the key researchers at Kaivalyadhama Institute, as a form of *Uddiyana Bandha*[42]. Dr Bole specifies there are five types

---

41 Anglification, meaning "of mudra-like nature"

42 Yoga Mimamsa - A Quarterly Research Journal, Kaivalyadhama, Lonavla, 1924-2004, 15.2

of *Uddiyana*, of which I have described four in *Pranayama The Breath of Yoga*, i.e. inhalation *Uddiyana Bandha*, internal *kumbhaka Uddiyana Bandha*, exhalation *Uddiyana Bandha*, and external *kumbhaka Uddiyana Bandha*[43]. This last *bandha* is an atypical *bandha* in that regard that it does not constitute a muscular contraction from which a *pranic* force rebounds and is projected back into the body. Instead of that, suction is utilized to suck *prana* into the desired direction. Because of its atypicality, this technique is simply often called *Bahya Uddiyana* (external-kumbhaka *Uddiyana* or more colloquially external-*Uddiyana*), leaving out the term *bandha*. Due to its supine position *Tadaga Mudra* provides the ideal platform to slowly integrate external-*Uddiyana* and external breath retention into one's practices.

External breath retention (exhaling and then retaining the breath outside) should always be accompanied external-*Uddiyana*. The reason for this is that the exhalation increases *tamas*[44] in the mind and at the end of the exhalation, the mind has reached peak-*tamas*. To hold the breath at the end of the exhalation (i.e. to perform external breath retention/*kumbhaka*) means to keep the mind as its most *tamasic*, of itself a very negative state. However, this can be turned around by engaging external-*kumbhaka Uddiyana*. The technique works like this: exhale completely and lock the throat. This is achieved by swallowing saliva and sustaining the grip of the throat muscles brought about by the swallowing reflex. Once the permanent contraction of the throat is achieved, perform a so-called faked or

---

43 Gregor Maehle, *Pranayama The Breath of Yoga*, Kaivalya Publications, Crabbes Creek, 2012, p. 146-172

44 One of the three elementary particles (*gunas*) of natue (*prakriti*). Best translated as mass particle or inertia.

false inhalation. This means while keeping the throat contracted, you engage the secondary respiratory muscles as if you would inhale, i.e. lifting and expanding the ribcage. A vacuum in the thorax is thus created, which sucks the diaphragm and with it the abdominal contents up in the thoracic cavity, creating the hollowed-in, tank-like appearance of the abdomen.

The abdominal muscles need to be kept relaxed. If they are contracted, this will impinge on the ability to suck the abdominal contents into the thoracic cavity. Students of yoga often mistake the significance of why the technique is sometimes named *Uddiyana Bandha* and at other times just *Uddiyana*. Even shastras rarely spell out the difference because this was considered a part of individual, oral instruction. Shrinivasayogi, the author of the *Hatha Ratnavali*[45], to my knowledge, initiated the tradition to label the passive suction-type external-*Uddiyana* as *Bahya Uddiyana*. This text was probably set down during the 17th century, and its author was well aware of the need to disambiguate external-*Uddiyana* from *Uddiyana Bandha*.

CONTRAINDICATIONS FOR EXTERNAL KUMBHAKAS

External-*Uddiyana* exerts a powerful suction on the brain and the cerebrospinal fluid. External-*Uddiyana* must be learned slowly during *Nauli*, *Tadaga Mudra* and *Yoga Mudra*. Beginners should initially perform not over 2 or 3 repetitions per day and then slowly increase the rate over weeks and months. Due to the intense pressure exchange, External-*Uddiyana*, like *Nauli*, should not be practised by women when they wish to conceive, during menstruation or pregnancy. However, it is very beneficial for the female reproductive system at all other times.

---

45 *Hatha Ratnavali of Shrinivasayogi*, II.56

The practice of *kumbhaka* rarely is advised for anyone suffering from high blood pressure or heart disease. The same must be said about peptic ulcers. It also should not be practised if hyperacidity occurs and not for at least six weeks after giving birth. *Kumbhaka* practice should never be combined with psychedelic drugs. There are inhibitors in our nervous and endocrine systems that prevent us from tampering with our respiration and heart rate. Through years of skilful practice, the yogi learns to suspend some of these inhibitors and venture into areas not accessible to the untrained person. There are reasons these areas are inaccessible to the untrained. However, these very same inhibitors may be suspended through some psychedelic drugs, and anything can happen if you practise *pranayama* under their influence. These contraindications apply for all external *kumbhakas*, independent of the *mudra* during which they occur.

Tadaga Mudra is sometimes also performed in *Pashimottanasana*, it is combined with external breath retention and external-*Uddiyana*. So says T. Krishnamacharya in *Yoga Makaranda* that *Tadaga Mudra* is to pull the stomach backwards as to make it hollow in *Pashimottanasana*[46]. But a well-known video depicting T. Krishnamacharya during the 1940s shows him lying on his back when performing the *mudra* with external *kumbhaka*. He was familiar with both versions. The *Pashimottanasana*-variation is more advanced as it demands proficiency in forward-bending and a strong, supported low back.

Some teachers have misinterpreted the name Tank *Mudra* by suggesting expanding the belly tank-like, thus pushing it

---

46 T. Krishnamacharya, *Yoga Makaranda*, Media Garuda, Chennai, 2011, p. 109

out [47]. This is an erroneous description. Neither in external nor internal *kumbhaka* are yogis pushing the belly out. Particularly in *Pashimottanasana* this would destabilize the low-back, especially if these instructions, as sometimes observed, are accompanied by suggesting releasing at the same time the *bandhas*. This instruction should therefore be ignored.

Nathamuni's Yoga Rahasya lists *Tadaga Mudra* in verse II.13 and shows it as reclining on your back[48]. *Yoga Rahasya* also states this mudra is to be practised by *brahmacharys* (students, the first Vedic *ashrama*/ stage of life). This makes this *mudra* with most *asanas* a preparation for *pranayama*. *Pranayama,* according to the *Yoga Rahasya*, is a *grhasta* practice (householder, the second Vedic *ashrama* or stage of life). According to the Vedic teaching, *brahmachary* (student) practices are integrated into one's life before tackling *grhasta* (householder) practices.

The *Gheranda Samhita,* in stanza III.50, lists this *mudra* with the alternate spelling of Tadagi Mudra, and confirms that the pond-like appearance is achieved by drawing the belly in and up (i.e. produced by external-*Uddiyana*)[49]. Sage *Gheranda* further states that the *mudra* destroys decrepitude and death. Bahadur Chandra Vasu's translation of the *Gheranda Samhita* has this stanza at II.61, but also confirms to make the stomach hollow

47 Swami Satyananda, *Asana, Pranayama, Mudra and Bandha*, Yoga Publications Trust, Munger, 1969, p. 450

48 T.K.V. Desikachar (transl.), *Nathamuni's Yoga Rahasya*, Krishnamacharya Yoga Mandiram, Chennai, 1998, p. 102

49 Swami Digambarji et al (eds. & transl.), *The Gheranda Samhita*, Kaivalyadhama, Lonavla, 1978, p. 88, also James Mallison's translation, p. 77

like a tank, rather than pushing it out [50]. *Shastras* were hand-copied in days of yore, and modern translations are often based on manuscripts sometimes differing in their order or number of stanzas.

The *Yoga Chudamani Upanishad* describes *Uddiyana Bandha* in stanza 48-49[51]. However, after initially quoting the *Hatha Yoga Pradipika* verbatim, the *Upanishad* then says that the drawing back towards the spine below the navel in *Pashimottanasana* is called *Uddiyana Bandha*. This is an error in the manuscript (because this type of *Uddiyana Bandha* is typically practiced when practising *pranayama* in a sitting posture) or it does refer to *Tadaga Mudra*, without mentioning in name. If this were the case, this fact would provide food for Dr Bhole's assertion that *Tadaga Mudra* must indeed be looked at as the fifth category or type of *Uddiyana Bandha*.

TECHNIQUE

After completing the backbending sequence, lie down on your back to perform *Tadaga Mudra*. Completely exhale and then contract and lock your throat. Now perform a faked inhalation by expanding your chest. A faked or false inhalation means to execute the muscular actions to inhale. Due to the contracted and locked throat, however, no air can enter the lungs. A vacuum is created, and this vacuum will now suck the abdominal contents into the thoracic cavity. You are now in the state of external *kumbhaka* with external-*Uddiyana*. Hold

---

50 R.B.S. Chandra Vasu, (transl.), *The Gheranda Samhita*, Sri Satguru Publications, Delhi, 1984, p. 29

51 Sw. Satyadharma (transl.), *Yoga Chudamani Upanishad*, Yoga Publications Trust, Munger, 2003, p. 121

this state to capacity, i.e. as long as you are comfortable. Then release your throat and gently inhale. Do so before the breath-holding becomes uncomfortable. You can repeat this several times but for somebody proficient in external *kumbhaka*, once or twice is sufficient.

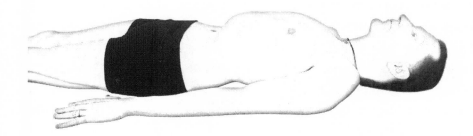

Tadaga Mudra, **supine**

Once you are comfortable with the supine version of *Tadaga Mudra*, perform it in *Pashimottanasana* as well. In the Ashtanga method, you would do so only in your second *Pashimottanasana*, which takes place after your backbending sequence. *Tadaga Mudra* is not performed during the first *Pashimottanasana* early in the Primary Series, as we are not properly warmed up yet. When performing *Tadaga Mudra* in *Pashimottanasana*, you need to be well progressed in forward bending (i.e. reasonably flexible), and your low back must have gained support strength. This is so because during forward bending you are to contract your abdominal muscles to support the low back. You are using your transverse abdominis muscles to tuck the lower abdomen inwards towards the spine. Because the fluid-filled abdominal cavity cannot be compressed, it will compensate by elongating in the longitudinal direction, pulling your lumber vertebrae apart from each, thus protecting the intravertebral discs of the lumbar spine. While this sounds complicated, it is what every competent weightlifter or athlete would automatically do.

During the *Pashimottanasana*-version of *Tadaga Mudra* we cannot contract the transverse abdominis. We cannot do this because it needs to be relaxed to allow the vacuum action of *Bahya Uddiyana*, which sucks the abdominal contents into the thoracic cavity. The *Pashimottanasana*-version of *Tadaga Mudra* is therefore not suitable for beginners, but only for those who already are very competent forward benders. If you experience any strain in your low back discontinue the posture.

Once you held the external *kumbhaka* in *Pashimottanasana* to capacity, release the contraction of your throat and gently inhale. Do not gasp for air but release the breath retention before the need for gasping to occur. In either case, whether you are performing *Tadaga Mudra* supine or in *Pashimottanasana*, it is a signal to the body that now the *mudra* phase of your *asana* practice has commenced. From *Tadaga Mudra* onwards, all remaining postures, i.e. those of the cool-down or finishing sequence, are to be made *mudric*. This is the connecting theme of the descriptions of the next three *mudras*.

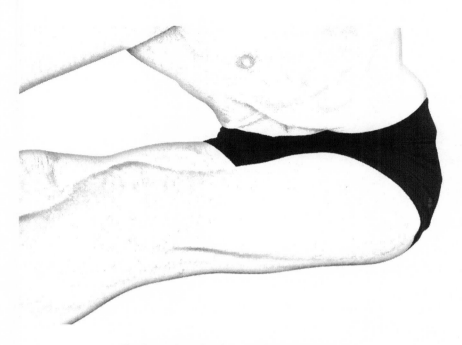

Tadaga Mudra in *Pashimottanasana*

Chapter 2

VIPARITA KARANI MUDRA
(Inverted-Action Seal)

For whatever reason this fashion started, *Viparita Karani Mudra* is often taught as a watered-down, mellow version of the shoulder stand. This is an error. *Viparita Karani* refers to conferring on all inversions a *mudric* nature, i.e. turning them into energetic seals. The *siddha* Gorakhnath explains in *Yoga Gorakshataka*, stanza 55, that pratyahara (the 5th limb of yoga, independence from external stimulus) is achieved by placing the sun in the navel on top of the moon, which is above the palate. This so-called moon, a *pranic* storehouse in the centre of the cranium, is the repository of the so-called lunar *prana*, *prana* that powers introversion and everything that comes with it. In the normal, day-to-day order of things, the navel (seat of gastric fire) is below the moon, so *amrita* (another name for lunar *prana*) oozing from the moon is burnt by the sun. Saving this nectar of the moon from being burnt by the sun is, according to Gorakhnath, *pratyahara*[52], and *Viparita Karani* is how to achieve it[53]. The *Gheranda Samhita*, in stanzas III.33-35, confirms that the moon has to be placed below the sun (by inverting the body) and this is called *Viparita Karani Mudra*. According to sage *Gheranda*, it is done by placing the head

---

52 Swami Kuvalayananda (ed.), *Goraksasatakam*, Kaivalyadhama, Lonavla, 2006, p. 42

53 Goraksha Shataka, stanza 59

on the floor with hands supporting, and then raising the legs up while remaining steady, i.e. by performing the headstand[54].

Similarly, in the *Yoga Makaranda* T. Krishnamacharya describes this *mudra* as placing the head on the ground and the lifting of the legs into an inverted position[55]. He emphasises that the body must be absolutely straight, i.e. the spine perfectly aligned against gravitation, for the *mudra* to be worthy of this name. Here we are getting a picture of *Viparita Karani Mudra* as a high-class headstand, an understanding of this *mudra* radically different from the often-taught, watered-down, half-inversion or legs-up-the-wall posture. A.G. Mohan confirms[56] that T. Krishnamacharya taught that the headstand (*Shirshasana*) was not just an *asana* but a *mudra*, and to do justice to that name, the breath needed to be substantially slowed down, ideally to only two breaths per minute[57]. The notable Western yoga pioneer Theos Bernard, in his 1950 publication *Hatha Yoga* agrees that

---

54 R.B.S. Chandra Vasu (transl.), *The Gheranda Samhita*, Sri Satguru Publications, Delhi, 1984, p. 25, Kuvalayanada's and J. Mallinson's translations have the stanza at III.31, although Mallinson accompanies it with an image of *Sarvangasana* (shoulder stand)

55 T. Krishnamacharya, Yoga *Makaranda*, Media Garuda, Chennai, 2011, p. 107

56 A.G. Mohan, *Krishnamacharya: His Life and Teachings*, Shambala, Boston & London, 2002, p. 27

57 This would make the average *Ashtanga* headstand of 25 breaths a staggering 12 minutes long. Please note that when I am suggesting to aim for a headstand of 70 to 80 breaths, I am applying a much faster breath ratio. 12 minutes to me seems the upper limit of a reasonable headstand. Even such practice would be medically sound only if one was capable of placing very little weight on the head for that entire period. A veritable feat.

Shirshasana is not a true *asana* but indeed the *mudra* known as *Viparita Karani Mudra*[58].

Other texts rightfully claim that *Shirshasana* (headstand) and *Sarvangasana* (shoulder stand) constitute *Viparita Karani*. This means that both inversions, the headstand and the shoulder stand, need to be transformed into *mudras*. So states Brahmananda's commentary *Jyotsna* on the *Hatha Yoga Pradipika* in stanza 6 that before practising *kumbhaka* (breath retention) one needs to perform *Viparita Karani Mudra* so *Jalandhara Bandha* can be executed properly[59]. *Jalandhara Bandha* (to be described in painstaking detail later) constitutes an extreme neck-flexion, to which the neck must be warmed up and prepared using the shoulder stand. T. Krishnamacharya agreed that the practice of the shoulder stand should precede the execution of *kumbhakas*, the rationale here being that a *kumbhaka* proper needs to be accommodated by *Jalandhara Bandha*. Sahajananda's *Hathayoga Manjari* states that one needs to enter *Viparita Karani Mudra* from the supine position and raise the legs vertically. The arms are then used to support the torso, raised until the chest touches the chin[60]. If more clarity was needed, then this passage makes it clear that *Viparita Karani Mudra* can indeed take place in the shoulder stand, too. Sahajananda follows this with a description of the headstand, which he also considers *Viparita Karani Mudra*.

---

58 Theos Bernard, *Hatha Yoga*, Rider, London, 1950, p. 29

59 Pancham Sinh (transl.), *The Hatha Yoga Pradipika,* Sri Satguru Publications, Delhi, 1991, p. 22

60 O.P. Tiwari (publ.), *Hathayoga Manjari of Sahajananda,* Kaivalyadhama, Lonavla, 2006, p. 51

Jayatarama's *Jogapradipyaka* treats *Viparita Karani Mudra* in stanzas 561- 577[61]. The *shastra* suggests placing the shoulders and head on the floor, raising the legs up to the sky and placing the chin at the jugular notch. It thus clearly refers to the shoulder stand rather than the headstand. Jayatarama considers gazing to the navel important, which is possible only in the shoulder stand and not in the headstand. Yogeshvaranand Paramahansa argues in *First Steps to Higher Yoga* that both *Shirshasana* and *Sarvangasana* constitute *Viparita Karani*[62]. This view may be taken from the *Hatha Yoga Pradipika*, a *Shaivite shastra*, which states that the *Viparita Karani* concept can be extended to any inversion[63]. We find this view that *Viparita Karani* is a principle applicable to all inversions, also in *Dattatreya's Yogashastra*, a *Vaishnavite* text[64]. This position, that *Viparita Karani* is a principle, is also espoused here in this book. The *Viparita Karani* principle can also be extended to a handstand. The handstand, however, following the convention established by sage Gheranda, I have described under *Vajroni Mudra*.

DURATION OF VIPARITA KARANI

Brahmananda, in his commentary *Jyotsna* on *Hatha Yoga Pradipika*, states that *Viparita Karani* should be practised before

---

61 Sw. Maheshananda et al. (eds & transl.), *Jogapradipyaka of Jayatarama*, Kaivalyadhama, Lonavla, 2006, p. 116

62 Yogeshvaranand Paramahansa, *First Steps to Higher Yoga*, Yoga Niketan Trust, New Delhi, 2001, p. 382

63 Dr M.L. Gharote et al. (eds. & transl.), *Hathapradipika of Svatmarama (10 chapters)*, Lonavla Yoga Institute, Lonavla, 2006, p. 148

64 Dr M.M. Gharote (ed.), *Dattatreyayogasastram*, Lonavla Yoga Institute, Lonavla, 2015, p. 71-73

kumbhakas[65]. T. Krishnamacharya also held this view. Every avid yogi can easily ascertain that extended inversions increase the *pranic* retention rate, i.e. they make breath retentions easier to manage and their duration easier to extend. Many yogic texts emphasise the length of time that one has to spend in *Viparita Karani*. *Hatha Yoga Pradipika* holds that the time spent practising this *mudra* should be increased daily until it can be held for three hours[66]. The *Jyotsna* commentary to the same text suggests holding it only for a moment during the first day and then increase it daily[67]. Sundaradeva's *Hathatatva Kaumudi* concurs that one should start slowly and work up to three hours[68]. The *Kaumudi* promises that using such practice within six months, one will have overcome death. Shrinivasayogi's *Hatharatnavali* is supportive by suggesting that three hours per day prevents premature death[69]. The *Shiva Samhita*, in stanza IV. 46, goes even further by promising not only the conquering of death but that holding the *mudra* for three hours per day would fortify one even against *pralaya* (Armageddon)[70].

---

65 Kunjunni Raja (ed.), *The Hathayogapradipika of Svatmarama with the Commentary Jyotsna of Brahmananda*, The Adyar Library, Madras, 1972, p. 31

66 Dr. M.L. Gharote et al (eds. & transl.), *Hathapradipika of Svatmarama (10 chapters)*, Lonavla Yoga Institute, Lonavla, 2006, p. 148

67 Kunjunni Raja (ed.), *The Hathayogapradipika of Svatmarama with the Commentary Jyotsna of Brahmananda*, The Adyar Library, Madras, 1972, p. 52

68 Dr. M.L. Gharote et al (eds. & transl.), *Hathatatvakaumudi,* The Lonavla Yoga Institite, Lonavla, 2007, p. 158

69 Dr. M.L. Gharote et al (eds. & transl.), *Hatharatnavali of Shrinivasayogi*, The Lonavla Yoga Institite, Lonavla, 2009, p. 69

70 *Shiva Samhita* IV.46.

It is clearly unreasonable to expect such results, and their mentioning in yogic texts simply reflects the tendency to exaggeration (*stuti*). Authors of yogic texts were held to exaggerate the positive effects of yogic techniques to make it more likely that students would take up their practice. Unfortunately, the exaggeration also crept into the descriptions of techniques, which often one *shastrakara* (scripture author) copied from the previous text, but then exaggerated even more. To hold an inversion for such a long time is more likely to lead to glaucoma, aneurisms in the brain, draining of the kidneys or arthritis of the cervical discs than leading to immortality. I do not consider it medically sound to do such extreme practices. However, inversions held for 5 to 10 minutes or even slightly more have great benefits, especially as a support for *pranayama* and meditation, as long as the technique is executed excellently. Please remember this. If the technique is sloppy, the detriment exceeds the benefits of practising *Viparita Karani Mudra*. I cannot stress this point enough. If you are happy to believe and accept that the headstand simply means to balance on your head and place all your weight on your head, then no time spent in the posture is safe from detriment. But the headstand is no such thing!

POTENTIAL PITFALLS

Recent years saw frequent bad publicity for inversions like the shoulder stand and headstand. Most of that bad publicity circled around arthritis of the cervical discs, which can be accrued in both postures, whereas the headstand additionally is singled out for demerit incurred through increased pressure in the head. These demeritorious effects can be avoided by performing the postures to a high standard. This means that in the shoulder stand, any pressure or weight born on the cervical vertebrae must be avoided and in the headstand, pressure on the head must be minimized to the point of barely existent. I have in my various books and also in previous blog articles described how to do that in both postures. The problem seems to be persisting. I recently read an article describing the shoulder stand and headstand as balancing postures, in which only alignment matters and no exertion at all should be felt. This is dangerous advice, and too many yoga students still fall for it. To prevent demerit, it is essential to look at both postures as strength postures. Before I describe this approach, let me quickly recap why we perform inversions and preferably even hold them for longer.

VIPARITA KARANI MUDRA AS PATH TO PRATYAHARA

One of the fundamental texts on yoga is the *Goraksha Shataka*, translated as *Goraknath's One-hundred Verses*. In this slender text, the *siddha*[71] devotes 10% of the stanzas extolling the virtues of the inversions. He considers them the most straightforward way to attain *pratyahara*, the fifth limb of yoga. The purpose of *pratyahara* is to gain independence from external or sensory stimuli. As long as one depends on sensory stimulus, success in meditation practice is difficult to obtain. The relation of inversions to *pratyahara* is as follows: In the *Yoga Yajnavalkya*, we find the image of the *pranic* body (subtle body) being like an aura that during resting extends 12 *angulas* (approximately

---

71 A *siddha* is an ancient *tantric* yoga master. *Siddhas* occurred in both sexes. Juxtaposed to that is a *rishi*, a *Vedic* master. According to *Vedic* orthodoxy, *rishis* are all male.

25 cm or 10 inches) beyond the surface of the gross body[72]. Particularly during any form of agitation, *pranic* protuberances extend out much further and attach themselves to sense objects. As soon as the *prana* has attached itself to a sense object, the mind interprets it as "just wanting to have it". The *Hatha Yoga Pradipika* describes the connection between thought and *prana* thus, "Where *prana* goes there goes *vrtti* (thought) and where *vrtti* goes there goes *prana*. As milk and water once mingled are difficult to separate so mind and breath cannot be kept apart"[73]. Due to this interconnectedness of mind and breath, any sophisticated approach to spiritual growth will include mental training such as meditation and respiratory training such as *pranayama*. There is a third strata, the body, which also needs to be addressed. In yoga, this is done through *asana*.

Once the *pranic* body has made contact with a sense object, the mind may interpret that contact as "needing to have it" (or conversely "needing to avoid it"). This could be a person who, in the spur of the moment, you intensely desire, only to ask yourself after an acrimonious marriage break-up years later, "What was I thinking?" It could also be an initially promising business venture that ends disastrously or the decision to heavily invest in a particular asset class, only to see its price drop precipitously. Another common example is somebody committing a violent crime and when asked by investigators or the public prosecutor, they state they had no choice. There are, many less dramatic instances in which this mechanism is at work, but the important structural element in all of them is the seeming lack of choice. We "just needed to do it"! What if

---

72 *Yoga Yajnavalkya* IV.6-8

73 *Hatha Yoga Pradipika (four chapter edition)* IV.24

something could intercept these pranic protuberances latching on to the sense objects, seemingly taking choice away from us? In this case, the thought, "I just want it", will never occur. There may then still be an impulse, but it will never present itself comingled with a seeming lack of choice.

The good news is that such yogic techniques that restore the *pranic* support structure of choice, are actually available to us. They are called *pratyahara* techniques, i.e. techniques designed to obtain independence from sensory (or external) stimulus. They come in broadly three baskets, amongst which are *pranayama* techniques (chiefly breath retentions), *Raja Yoga* methods (*mudras* and *bandhas* applied during meditation) and *Hatha Yoga* methods (in this case, *asana-mudras*). Ideally, of course, all three approaches are combined, as there is not one better than the other. *Hatha Yoga's* approach to *pratyahara* consists of arresting *prana* in the throat *chakra* (through the shoulder stand) and in the third eye *chakra* (through the headstand). The *Hatha Yoga* approach is the easiest to implement. However, you will find relatively little beneficial influence on your mind if you hold a headstand or the shoulder stand for only one or two minutes. Longer inversions, i.e. inversions held for five to ten minutes, have a beneficial, centering effect on the mind that is surprisingly profound. This is simply due to the capacity of the two inversions to fixate *prana* in the abovementioned *chakras*. Let's look more clearly into how this works, and for that, we need to understand the yogic concept of *Amrita Siddhi*.

AMRITA SIDDHI THROUGH VIPARITA KARANI

Directly translated, *Amrita Siddhi* means deathless achievement. While some have taken this to refer to physical immortality, it means that you attain to that which is deathless, that is the pure consciousness (*purusha*) or true self (*atman*). There is confusion around the habit of yogis using different terms to describe the same thing. When the ancient treatises were written, it was considered inelegant and lacking eloquence to use the same term repeatedly, quite similar to how we look at the English language today. From our modern point of view, though, it would make life simpler if the same terms were always used to denote the same facts, as it would make yoga scriptures more akin to engineering manuals with a predictable outcome assured. For example, the terms *prana*, Shakti, Kundalini and *prakrti* describe the phenomenon of energy, power, and life force, but just from slightly different angles. In the case of inversions, the terms *bindu*, *amrita*, *soma*, and *chandra* refer to the same phenomenon. To simplify, I call this phenomenon lunar *prana*, i.e. prana that powers lunar functions. What those are will be explained in great detail.

Besides the central energy channel, the body has two main *nadi*s, called *Ida* and *Pingala*, the lunar and solar *nadi*s. The lunar *nadi*, *Ida*, directs the mind, incoming nerve signals, and the five senses (*jnanendriyas*), also called the self's five entry doors. The solar *nadi*, *Pingala*, directs outgoing nerve signals, the body and the organs of action (*karmendriyas*), which are the five exit doors of the self. Each of the two *nadi*s draw on their own energy reservoirs. The storehouse of solar *prana* – prana used for putting our stamp on the world, for being outgoing – is located adjacent to the *Manipura* (navel) *Chakra*. The lunar storehouse of *prana*, *prana* powering sensory perception and the mind, is located in the centre of the cranium, connected to the third eye *chakra*. This area above the soft palate, including the thalamus, hypothalamus, pineal and pituitary glands, centres around the larger area of the third ventricle of the brain. This is the lunar *prana* storehouse, or simply called the moon (*chandra*) in yogic scripture. Please understand that there is only one *prana*, but it has different functions depending on where it is stored or in which nadi it flows. We could compare that to electricity that can equally power your fridge, a hospital emergency ward, or an electric chair. The function depends on which conduits it is made to flow through, but the electricity is similar.

In the lunar centre (third eye or *Ajna Chakra*) is the *amrita*, the so-called nectar of immortality. In the navel area is located the solar centre of *prana*, or simply the sun (*surya*), which represents gastric fire. *Amrita* gravitates from the moon downward and is burnt by the sun in our normal upright body position. When the body is for an extended period inverted daily, *amrita* becomes stored/arrested. This can be taken to the extent of *amrita siddhi*, when the *amrita* is permanently stored and does not fall anymore into the gastric fire, which consumes it. This state is very important for developing meditation and the higher limbs, as it automatically keeps the senses focused inwardly.

Amrita, the lunar *prana*, leaves the body through the moon-doors, which are the senses. The senses notice objects we desire and drag the mind outwards. Once the mind has lost its centre, we project ourselves out into the world and 'become' the phenomena. We identify ourselves with what happens in our lives. However, as the *Maitri Upanishad* says[74], 'If the fuel of the senses is withheld, the mind is reabsorbed into the heart.' This is a metaphor for us abiding in our true nature of consciousness. Many yogic techniques prevent the reaching out of the senses. Once the senses reach out and we identify ourselves with the world, we are pulled away like a chariot

---

74 *Maitri Upanishad* VI.35

dragged away by uncontrollable horses. This reaching out of the senses is related to *amrita* (lunar *prana*) seeping out of the third eye or *Ajna Chakra*, the lunar *chakra* in the centre of the head. The most straightforward way to prevent the senses from doing this is not through meditation but by arresting this *prana* through inversions, i.e. performing *Viparita Karani Mudra*.

The headstand and shoulder stand both have a slightly different way in which they prevent the loss of lunar *prana*, that's why they need to be practised both to complete *Viparita Karani Mudra*. With the shoulder stand, the *amrita* still seeps out from the 'moon' (*Ajna Chakra*), but it is caught in the *Vishuddha Chakra* (throat *chakra*). For this purpose, it is essential to use *Jihva Bandha* (tongue lock) during the shoulder stand: the tongue is folded back on itself and inserted as much as possible into the nasopharyngeal orifice. This method is described more closely in Section 3, *Mudra 15*.

During headstands, however, the lunar *prana* is arrested in its original location, the *Ajna Chakra*. If either of these two states is achieved, one obtains a centred personality, independent of external stimuli and gratification. One's motivation is also not anymore to seek encouragement from other people or obtain their respect or friendship. Because she who has obtained *Amrita Siddhi* does not relate anymore to others from a position of need, for the first time, she is able to selflessly serve others and love them unconditionally.

TECHNIQUE

We have now understood the importance of extending one's inversions, the headstand and the shoulder stand. Let's now delve into the technical details and guidelines for extending one's time spent in inversions so that we can do so safely.

This process needs to be undertaken slowly and gradually over many years, as sudden increases in the time spent in these postures may backfire. We need to proceed cautiously and prudently. When increasing the time spent in inversions one possible avenue to pursue is to slow down your breath as much as possible. T. Krishnamacharya's idea of headstand was to take only 2 breaths per minute. This needs to be considered an extreme form of practice, which needs to be done wisely and slowly if engendered at all. However, one may breathe somewhat faster and take more breaths in total. Slow your breath down gradually over months and, if necessary, over years rather than suddenly. In inversions, the blood pressure rises initially, particularly in the head, only to again drop off after a few minutes. If you have high blood pressure, you need to reduce it before working on inversions. Blood pressure can be reduced through medication and/or dietary changes. If you do change your diet to reduce blood pressure while being on blood pressure-lowering medication, you need to be in contact with your physician to regularly adjust your medication as otherwise, it can easily drop too low.

Once you have achieved a very slow breath rate in your inversions, add breaths, perhaps one every few days (one per day is too much). Be sensitive and stop adding on before you experience adverse symptoms. If you do experience symptoms such as headache, irritability, neck pain, ear pain, ringing in your ears, pressure or a fuzzy feeling in your head, you have gone too far and need to decrease your time. Please note, headaches or other symptoms may not come on immediately. If you performed a headstand for too long in the morning and feel a headache coming on during the afternoon, the two could still be linked. Do not be ambitious and get advice from a qualified teacher.

Work simultaneously on increasing the time spent in both the shoulder stand and headstand, as both have a beneficial though different effect. With both postures, the more vertical and perfectly aligned your body is, the more effective the posture becomes. In all inversions, you need to keep the whole body active and all large muscle groups engaged to prevent blood from draining into the head. This is especially important for the leg muscles and buttocks, which could be relaxed because they carry no weight. However, they need to be kept engaged to keep intracranial blood pressure from rising. We need to look into how we can extend inversions safely to five to ten minutes, enough to have most of the beneficial effect.

SHOULDER STAND

In the shoulder stand, you must keep the cervical vertebrae off the floor. It is not a neck stand. This means you need to carry your weight on the back of the head, the shoulders and the elbows, but not on the neck. Push these three areas gently into the floor to lift the cervical vertebrae off the floor. If, even after this effort, they are still touching the floor, you have to use a blanket placed under your shoulders (not under the head). This will create additional space to prevent the jamming of the cervical vertebrae.

The other important point about the shoulder stand is that it should be performed with a short neck by pulling the head into the thoracic cavity like a turtle withdrawing its neck into its shell. While in all other postures, we try to keep the neck as long as possible (by drawing the shoulder blades down the back, engaging both the latissimus dorsi and the lower trapezius), it is the shoulder stand in which the opposite action is performed. In this regard, the shoulder stand is similar to *Jalandhara Bandha*, the chin lock, described in detail in Section 2, *Mudra* 12. This *bandha* is exercised particularly during internal breath retention (*antara kumbhaka*). Before placing the chin down on the chest, the chest is lifted upwards. This movement causes the same shortening of the neck as if you pressed the shoulders into the floor during the shoulder stand. During shoulder stand, the sternum (breastbone) needs to firmly press against the chin. This pressure is then extended by pressing the back of the head into the floor, which lifts the cervical vertebrae off the floor.

Students often wonder whether they should press the back of the head into the floor or the chin into the chest (as we would during *Jalandhara Bandha*). The answer is "both". Both actions can be performed simultaneously by withdrawing the neck as far as possible into the thoracic cavity as a turtle would do when withdrawing its head. This is akin to the movement you would perform if in an upright position, you would try to hunch your shoulders around your ears. You can also think of it as trying, during the shoulder stand, to touch the ceiling with your toes. You can think of it as sucking your entire spine upwards and away from the floor. In all of these instances, the effect is that the backs of the cervical vertebrae are lifted off the floor. If you cannot lift them off the floor, you should use a blanket or two to place your shoulders on, with your head placed on the floor. If you intend to hold the shoulder stand for longer, I suggest in all cases to use blankets as a prop. The yardstick for holding the shoulder stand should be your ability to simultaneously press the back of the head into the floor and the chin into the chest. This needs to be a continuous effort, and if at any point you are tiring of it, you need to come out of the posture.

Viparita Karani Mudra in *Sarvangasana*

HEADSTAND

This article is not a complete description of the headstand, but only how to extend it. I'm assuming you have an existing headstand and general *asana* practice. I have explained the shoulder stand and headstand in more detail, with photographic images, in *Ashtanga Yoga: Practice and Philosophy*[75].

---

75 Gregor Maehle, *Ashtanga Yoga: Practice and Philosophy*, New World

Visualize now the difference in the size of your cervical and lumbar vertebrae. The lumbar vertebrae are huge, so that many large muscles can attach to them that support your low back. The vertebrae themselves have to be incredibly strong to withstand the many opposing forces of the muscles attached, especially if you are lifting a heavy weight or are performing a rapid movement under load. Different to that are the cervical vertebrae. Compared to the lumbar vertebrae, they are minute. This is so because they are designed to only hold and carry the actual weight of your head. The head makes up, on average, between 7 – 9% of our entire body weight. If you consider that the head does rest on the floor during the headstand and does not need to be carried, the arms and shoulders should carry about 80% of the body weight so that the normal, average load on the cervical vertebrae is normal is not exceeded. This makes for a serious arm and shoulder work-out. You need to feel that these body parts carry most of your weight. Do not relax in the posture by simply balancing on your head. If at any point you cannot feel that you are carrying a huge weight in your arms, simply come out of the posture and rest in *Balasana* (child's posture). The strength to hold your weight is only gradually improved. Improvement can be sped up by emphasising the *vinyasa* movement[76] and other strength postures such as forearm balances. You will find that if you develop strength and take the weight off your head and cervical discs in both inversions, that their benefits can be enjoyed and demerit avoided.

Library, Novato, 2007, p. 117-124

76 The sequential movement connecting sitting postures, i.e. jumping back and jumping through.

The most important point to keep in mind when extending your headstand is carrying most of your weight on your arms and shoulders and not on your brain. If you allow yourself to 'dump' all weight on your head and use your arms for balancing only, intracranial pressure will rise too high. That's why it is important to be conservative with extending your time spent in the headstand. For most students, it makes sense to stay slightly longer in the shoulder stand, which is less taxing. Gradually, however, we should attempt to increase the length of the headstand to be even to the time spent in the shoulder stand.

Next, let's look at the two different arm positions we could assume for executing the headstand. To ascertain which one is the right for you, bend one of your arms and extend your flexed elbow up to the ceiling. If your elbow reaches higher than the crown of your head, then your humerus (arm bone) is longer than the distance between the crown of the head and the base of your neck. You can therefore use the long-stance or standard position for the headstand. To assume it, place the elbows down onto the mat. Check for the correct width of your elbows by wrapping your hands around them: at the correct distance, your knuckles will be on the outside of the elbows. Without changing the position of your elbows, release the grip of your hands and interlace your fingers. Place both little fingers on the floor – not on top of each other – and separate your wrists. Keep your hands and wrists upright (perpendicular to the floor) by not rolling over onto the back of your hands. This forms a strong tripod for support and balance. Keep the shoulders broad and the neck long and press the floor away with your forearms. This is the grounding action necessary in *Shirshasana*. The underneath side of the wrists is the point of balance. Stability in a headstand depends on the distance between your fingers and the centre point between your elbows. The more the elbows flare out to the sides, the shorter this distance becomes, and the headstand becomes less stable. You would now, from this position, lift up into the headstand.

If, when extending your elbow up to the ceiling, it did not reach higher than the crown of the head, then your humerus (arm bone) is shorter than the distance between the base of your neck and the crown of your head. In this case, it is not advisable to use the standard- or long-stance position, as it will compress your neck. If so, press the heels of your hands together and allow the elbows to come apart. This will position your head more centrally in the triangle and the humeri will be perpendicular to the floor. This better accommodates the length of the upper arms, but it shortens the distance from the centre point between your elbows to your fingers. This makes this arm position less stable and more challenging.

Whatever stance we are using, we are now attempting to place the highest point of the head down onto the mat with the back of the head resting against our palms. If instead, you were to balance on your forehead, you might induce excessive cervical curvature and likely compress the vertebrae of the neck. To come to the up-side-down position, straighten your legs and walk the feet in towards the head. Keep the grounding of your tripod as you walk your feet in as close as possible while extending your sit bones high towards the ceiling. The sit bones will travel backwards beyond the head so that the back is slightly in extension. Now take all of your body weight onto your arms: the head should only lightly touch the floor.

If we were new to the headstand, we would first assess our strength level rather than lifting up into the posture. This is done in the following way: being in the set-up position for the headstand described thus far, with the feet walked in as close to the elbows as possible and the legs straight, we would lift now the head off the floor for half a centimetre only or a fifth of an inch. We would then hold this position for 25 breaths. If we can hold the head off the floor for this duration with comparative ease, we are ready to go up into the headstand, otherwise not. In this so-called headstand warm-up, we are holding only the torso's weight, with the legs still resting on the floor. If you raise the legs as well, the load born by the arms would increase considerably. Hence if you are already struggling with holding only the torso off the floor, there is no point in venturing further. In this case, keep exercising this headstand warm-up daily until you can do so with ease.

If you can hold the weight of your torso for 25 breaths off the floor, we may now venture further. Inhaling, slowly raise the straight legs up toward the ceiling, extending the hip joints by engaging the gluteus maximus. Breathe slowly and keep the lower abdomen firm. Rapid breathing, especially into the abdomen, destabilises all inversions. Keep your hands relaxed to where you can still wriggle your fingers. If the fingers are squeezed together to hold the pose, what often follows is that too much weight is placed on the elbows and the elbows are positioned too widely. To balance, press the wrists down into the ground and evenly distribute your body weight between the elbows and the hands.

Set the shoulder blades wide by abducting the scapulae by engaging serratus anterior. Then draw the scapulae towards the hips by contracting the latissimus dorsi. Initially, this movement can be difficult without placing more weight on the head, as it requires a developed latissimus dorsi muscle. To open the chest, reach the armpits towards the wall in front of you. This will eliminate the hump that might exist in the upper back around T6. The entire trunk and the legs are kept active and reach to the ceiling. The feet are pointed (plantar flexed). You can hold the posture now until you feel you become incapable of holding approximately 80% of your body weight in your arms, i.e. most of it. Once this is reached, abort the posture immediately and come down.

Viparita Karani Mudra in *Shirshasana*

Your age and general condition determine the question of how fast you can extend time spent in inversions. If you are young, athletic and in pristine health, you may add on breaths quite quickly, whereas an older person or somebody with a chronic health condition might have to do it very, very slowly. Of course, you need to consider how much time you can devote to yoga in total. My general impression is that modern students spend too much time in acquiring an athletic, fancy, flexible *asana* practice. I suggest limiting such pursuits to a maximum of about 90 minutes per day and rather divert more time to the higher limbs. You would then arrive at a more holistic program for yoga methods rather than placing all your eggs in the fancy-*asana* basket.

However much energy you put into your inversions, they cannot by themselves bring about yogic states. They are similar to most other yogic techniques such as vegetarianism and general *asana* practice. It is only combined with other methods such as *pranayama*, *kriya* and yogic meditation, as a combination, that they achieve great power. If you slowly and steadily, and in an organic fashion, increase the duration of your inversions over the long term, you will find they do empower your meditation and *pranayama*, but they will teach you also to pass on the many so-called 'opportunities' in life that we would better not get involved in.

Chapter 3

VAJRONI MUDRA
(Thunderbolt Seal)

In R.B.S. Chandra Vasu's translation of the *Gheranda Samhita*, we find *Vajroni Mudra* described in verses III.45 – 48[77]. One is to place one's hands on the ground and raise the legs up in the air without letting the head touch the ground. The *mudra* is thus a form of a handstand. Gheranda suggests this *Vajroni Mudra* to awaken Shakti, another name for Kundalini, and to increase longevity. He also advises that it creates freedom, produces empowerment (*siddhi*), and preserves *bindu*, often understood as the essence of reproductive fluid. The Kaivalyadhama edition[78] and James Mallinson's translation[79] of the *Gheranda Samhita* both have this *mudra* at stanza III.39, with the technique being the same, but both editions name the *mudra Vajroli Mudra*. T. Krishnamacharya in the *Yoga Makaranda* confirms that the *Raja Yoga* version of *Vajroli Mudra* is a handstand modified through adding an internal *kumbhaka* [80]. Internal *kumbhaka* means to

77 R.B.S. Chandra Vasu (transl.), *The Gheranda Samhita*, Sri Satguru Publications, Delhi, 1984, p. 27

78 Swami Digambarji et al (eds. & transl.), *The Gheranda Samhita*, Kaivalyadhama, Lonavla, 1978, p. 84

79 James Mallinson, *The Gheranda Samhita*, YogaVidya.com, Woodstock, 2004, p. 73

80 T. Krishnamacharya, Yoga *Makaranda,* Media Garuda, Chennai, 2011, p. 108

retain the breath inside, i.e. after an inhalation. The notable yoga scholar Dr M.L. Gharote agrees in his text *Yogic Techniques* that Gheranda's *Vajroli Mudra* is a form of a handstand and that it bestows *bindu siddhi*[81]. I learned this *mudra* from BNS Iyengar, and he called it *Vajroni Mudra*. How is it then that we have two different but nevertheless similar names for this *mudra*?

The *Vajroli Mudra* in the *Hatha Yoga Pradipika* is described in such ambiguous language that it can be misunderstood as a way of practising promiscuity (and in this particular case, potentially sexual exploitation) on the way to yogic success. Some commentators believed this to be twilight language (*sandhya*), i.e. words that have a deeper meaning contrary to the surface meaning). It is likely that initially, this was the intention of the *Hatha Yoga Pradipika*, but it was understood literally by many texts coming after the *Pradipika*. To counteract this tendency towards decadence and debauchery sage Gheranda offered in his text a different method of *Vajroli Mudra*, which according to Krishnamacharya was the original *Raja Yoga* method. To keep both methods separate in the mind of the reader and practitioner, I will call the handstand technique *Vajroni Mudra* and the one involving genital manipulation *Vajroli Mudra* (discussed in section 4, *mudra* 25). That the handstand has indeed a place in yoga is confirmed in the *Yoga Rahasya*, where its capacity to purify the seven *chakras* is mentioned[82].

TECHNIQUE

Firstly, one needs to become proficient at practising a handstand. A handstand is not a beginner's posture and should be attempted

---

81 Gharote, Dr M.L., *Yogic Techniques*, Lonavla Yoga Institute, Lonavla, 2006, p. 93

82 *Nathamuni's Yoga Rahasya*, II.20

only once a student has achieved a good overall quality in their general *asana* practice. The ideal preparation for a handstand is the Downward Dog position. Important here to depress the shoulder girdle, that is to draw the shoulder blades towards the hips. The shoulders should not be hunched around the ears. One needs to also consider that the regular practice of a handstand makes your back stronger but also stiffer. A regular practice of a handstand should be taken only up once a certain progress in back-bending (*Urdhva Dhanurasana*) has been achieved. Another important precursor to a handstand is the ability to lift, at the conclusion of one's headstand, up into a forearm balance and hold this confidently for 10 breaths. This posture is significantly easier than a handstand and it is recommended that students first acquire proficiency in the forearm balance subsequent to the headstand before venturing into a handstand.

When students initially learn to jump up into a handstand, they need to either do so with a wall behind them or with a teacher/assistant to spot them. To be spotted by a teacher is the preferred option as students who regularly practice jumping up against a wall tend to not put effort into learning to brace themselves to catch their weight. They often keep hitting the wall with great impact as they know they can rely on the wall being there. There is then no incentive to learn to catch the weight.

Learning to jump up into a handstand in the middle of the room without assistance comes with a great incentive to quickly learn to brace yourself from falling over and hitting the floor. But it also comes with a great setback. Landing heavily while being in a backbend often leads to spondylolisthesis, a condition that starts with the breaking off of one or several of the small facet joints between the vertebrae, and ends with vertebrae sliding forward on each other, a condition that reduces stability and leads to more problems later down the track. Being spotted by a teacher or helper in the room is the most advantageous option.

When jumping up, always do so on an inhalation. The first obstacle will be the inability to jump high enough. Learning to continue the inhalation until one has arrived up in the handstand is of great help here. A common mistake is to inhale and then jump, while holding the breath. Students using this method will rarely make it all the way up into a handstand.

The second factor important in transiting up into the handstand, is the focal point. Form a triangle between both hands and the focal point on your mat/floor (i.e. the point to which your gaze is directed). The further you move the focal point away from the middle point between your hands, the more you will go up (but also over into a backbend). If you have difficulties transiting up, move the focal point further away from the middle point between your hands. If you hit the wall behind you hard or if your teacher/assistant feels too much weight when they catch and spot you, you need to move your gaze further towards the middle point between your hands.

When in a handstand, hold the weight close to the roots of your fingers, where they join your hands. If you hold the weight too close to your wrists, you fall out of a handstand back towards your feet. But students who practice against a wall place the weight too close towards the fingertips, hence shirking the responsibility to take their entire weight into their hands. Another important point is to breathe slowly once in a handstand and to draw the breath mainly into the chest. Rapid abdominal breathing while straining to hold up one's weight destabilizes the abdominal muscles. The abdominal muscles are the connection between the legs and the arms. Without engaging them strongly, we are likely to swing back and forth in a handstand like a pendulum, until we lose balance. A common mistake is to push the floor away from you with your hands. Imagine teaching somebody who doesn't know how to stand on their legs, how to do that. Would you tell them to push the floor away with their feet? Of course, not, as this would make them topple over backwards. Yet this is often what yoga teachers tell their students in handstands. A better instruction is to get them to stand down into the floor, that is to imagine their hands being like roots grounding down, and their centre of gravity (in a handstand, your chest and heart area) to draw down into the floor, rather than disconnecting from it.

VAJRONI MUDRA STAGE 1

When initially learning a handstand it is helpful to keep the head lifted slightly to maintain the gaze towards one's focal point on the floor. Eventually, the head is dropped more and more until it points straight down. At this point, we are relying on proprioception and interoception to hold the posture, rather than on visual clues. The disadvantage of relying on the focal point on the floor to sustain one's balance, lies in the fact that to achieve that, the head needs to be kept lifted. This leads to an increased cervical curvature which also reverberates in the low back as increased lordosis, sometimes colloquially called a banana handstand. Although easier to hold and useful for strength building, the banana handstand is useless as a *mudra*.

To turn the handstand into a *mudra* first the head must point straight down, and the entire trunk, legs and arms be kept in a straight line. For many students, this again will require an assistant to keep them in position and to encourage them to tuck in the abdominal muscles, draw in the lower ribs, and decrease excess lumbar lordosis. Essentially, we transfer the *Viparita Karani* principle of keeping the entire body in a perfect straight line to the handstand. Some authorities are including the perfectly vertical handstand under *Viparita Karani* variations.

Make sure that your breathing is slow and not laboured. The faster you breathe, the more likely you are to fall out of the posture. Maintain normal *Ujjayi* breathing (slightly contracting the glottis to create a smooth, aspirate sound as one would during whispering) and breathe mainly into your chest. Excessive abdominal breathing in any inversion destabilizes the back muscles and results in a pendulum movement of the legs, making it more likely to fall out of the posture. Inability to sustain the handstand for long enough is usually not so much a question of strength but more so of a wrong focal point and inappropriate breathing method. Once the head is dropped sufficiently, and the holding of the posture via interoception is achieved, the gaze should now be shifted to the nose (*Nasagrai Drishti*). *Nasagrai Drishti* in a handstand induces a trance-like state.

Vajroni Mudra **stage 1**

VAJRONI MUDRA STAGE 2

Once this *mudra*'s first stage is achieved and sustained with little effort, we now add internal breath retention (*antara kumbhaka*). Since this is a *mudra* and not a *pranayama* technique the length of the kumbhaka is never counted, but it is simply held to capacity. Some teachers suggest initially learning the *kumbhaka* by simply locking the throat, with the head continuing to point straight

59

down, i.e. without engaging *Jalandhara Bandha*. The rationale here is to introduce the challenging *Jalandhara Bandha* position only once one is comfortable in *kumbhaka* during a handstand. The problem with this suggestion is that it flouts the important rule that internal *kumbhaka* (holding the breath in after an inhalation) should never be done without *Jalandhara Bandha*. The first purpose of *Jalandhara Bandha* is that it protects the brain from increased blood pressure during internal *kumbhaka*. This is even more important when upside down and also when holding one's weight up with one's arms.

The exception to the rule that internal *kumbhaka* is never applied without *Jalandhara Bandha* is when the *kumbhaka* is less than 10-seconds long. In this case, it is not considered a *kumbhaka* proper, and the rule is waived. In our case here with the head pointing down I would be cautious with applying *kumbhaka* after an inhalation without *Jalandhara Bandha*. I would do so only for a short time, i.e. a few seconds, and only if no pressure in the head builds up. Another indicator would be to check whether your face gets red via a mirror, indicating excess blood building up in the head. This could also be ascertained by the person that spots you. Other indicators triggering us to exit the *kumbhaka* and the handstand would be pressure building in your ears or eyes or ringing in the ears.

However, the preferred method is to perform the internal *kumbhaka* with *Jalandhara Bandha*. This *bandha* is described in great detail in Section 2, *Mudra* 12. *Jalandhara Bandha* has to be first learned and performed in other *mudras* where the additional challenge of being upside down and holding one's weight does not occur. This makes *Vajroni Mudra* an advanced *mudra*. To be complete in my description of the *mudra*, I will sketch the *bandha* here succinctly, but it needs to be perfected before attempting it in *Vajroni Mudra*. Please note, while *Jalandhara Bandha* is essential during internal *kumbhaka*, it is ancillary during external *kumbhaka* (holding the breath after an exhale). During external *kumbhaka* *Jalandhara Bandha* adds the additional element of stretching the spinal cord and the meninges, thus adding extra stimulus to the brain. It is, however, not compulsory because during external *kumbhaka* no pressure builds up in the thoracic cavity, from which we would need to insulate the cranium. Therefore *Jalandhara Bandha* is treated completely different during internal and external *kumbhakas*.

Vajroni Mudra **stage 2**

JALANDHARA BANDHA

To perform *Jalandhara Bandha*, after a deep inhalation in a handstand, draw the sternum towards the chin and the chin towards the chest. Aim for not just simply placing the chin against the jugular notch, which results in an insufficient amount of neck flexion and contraction. Instead, firmly place the chin against the sternum, preferably a distance from the jugular notch towards the xyphoid process (lower end of the sternum). Before touching the chin to the breastbone, contract the throat muscles as if swallowing saliva. Maintain this contraction, which constitutes the actual *bandha*. Check now whether any air can pass your tracheas by trying to ex- and inhale. If this fails, then the *bandha* is properly applied. If you can still breathe, you need to repeatedly swallow and contract the throat until no air can pass the throat. It is obvious that this is not feasible in the headstand, especially not with the head tucked under. Again, this drives the point home that *Jalandhara Bandha* is to be mastered outside of this *mudra*.

Once the *bandha* is applied, hold the *kumbhaka* to capacity, i.e. no particular count and length is observed. Initially it is wise to stay in *kumbhaka* only for a few seconds, monitoring if pressure in the head, ears or eyes builds up. If so, abort the *kumbhaka* by slowly lifting your head and exhaling. It is unlikely that one can stay too long in the *kumbhaka* as it is very challenging to maintain the handstand with the tucked-under head position and being unable to breathe. Apply *Nasagrai Drishti*, i.e. gazing towards the tip of the nose. During this *drishti* (focal point) it is important not to become cross-eyed but rather look along the nose without strain. If that is impossible, gaze towards the eyebrows' center (*Bhrumadhya Drishti*).

CONTRAINDICATIONS FOR INTERNAL KUMBHAKA

Because this is the first time in this text that an internal *kumbhaka* occurs, I will list here the contraindications for such practice. They apply when an internal *kumbhaka* occurs, i.e. suspending the breath after an inhale. The practice of *kumbhaka* rarely is advised during pregnancy, menstruation or for anyone suffering from high blood pressure or heart disease. It should not be practised if hyper-acidity occurs and not for six weeks after giving birth. And it should not be done if suffering from ulcers, hernia or glaucoma. Like external *kumbhakas*, so also internal breath retentions should not be combined with psychedelic drugs. There are inhibitors in our nervous and endocrine systems that prevent tampering with our respiration and heart rate. Through years of skilful practice, the yogi learns to suspend some of these inhibitors and venture into areas not accessible to the untrained person. There are reasons these areas are inaccessible to the untrained. However, these very same inhibitors may be suspended through certain psychedelic drugs, and anything can happen if you practise *kumbhaka* under their influence.

In the Ashtanga method, a handstand (if at all) is practised after the back-bending sequence at the end of one's series of the day. The reason for this is that the handstand has a back-stiffening effect and therefore should be practiced only after sufficient back-opening. The disadvantage of this sequencing is that the handstand comes relatively late in one's practice. Therefore, it is wise to limit *Vajroni Mudra* to a maximum of three attempts or rounds. Do not force things through endlessly repeated attempts, which will only fatigue you and take energy away from *pranayama* practice, which you are hopefully conducting after your *asana* practice. The better approach is to take a long-term view of this *mudra*, i.e. integrating its practice over an extended period.

FEASIBILITY OF *VAJRONI MUDRA*

For a person struggling with a handstand, it is not feasible to embark on learning this *mudra*. In this case, a better return on invested time and energy would be attained by practising *Nauli* or *pranayama*. For somebody talented at a handstand but struggling to make sense of complex *pranayama* and meditation practices, *Vajroni Mudra* can help with arresting *prana* and creating fortitude (*sthirata*). Similarly to *Viparita Karani* and all other *mudras* in this section, *Vajroni Mudra* helps with retracting and reabsorbing *prana* that is scattered beyond the surface of the body, back under the skin. This practice also supports the withdrawing of one's psychological projections, and becoming more independent from needing constant sensory stimulus. This *mudra* helps with becoming a centred personality with an internal frame of reference.

Chapter 4

YOGA MUDRA
(Seal of Yoga)

There is scant textual evidence for Yoga Mudra, but it is in Paramahansa Yogeshvaranand's *First Steps to Higher Yoga*. Yogeshvaranand states that *Yoga Mudra* constitutes of sitting in *Baddha Padmasana* (bound full lotus posture), then folding forward on an exhalation and performing *bahya kumbhaka* (external *kumbhaka*) to one's capacity, and then repeating this cycle several times[83]. Yogeshvaranand ascribes to this *mudra* improvement of health, purification of *nadis*, an increase of *prana* and progress in meditation. Swami Niranjanananda similarly ties *Yoga Mudra* to the performance of external *kumbhaka*[84].

The second-to-last posture in the Ashtanga-Vinyasa system is *Yogamudrasana*, which translates as 'the posture in which the seal of yoga is performed'. The function of the *mudra* here is to seal a maximum amount of *prana* in the body at the very end of one's *asana* practice. *Prana* is not created through practice, but the *pranic* retention rate of the body is vastly increased through *asana* practice. Leakage of *prana* is related to the senses reaching out and attaching themselves to sense objects, a mechanism by

---

83 Yogeshvaranand Paramahansa, *First Steps to Higher Yoga*, Yoga Niketan Trust, New Delhi, 2001, p. 387

84 Swami Niranjanananda Saraswati, *Yoga Darshan*, Yoga Publications Trust, Munger, 2009, p. 391

which the mind follows and projects one's sense of self out into the phenomena. Psychologically this leads to us not seeing other people for what they really are, but instead, we are projecting our fears, desires and aversions onto them. Behaviourally, projection leads to what colloquially called 'being out there'. This term refers to a person putting on an act, of not being real, and it is opposed to resting in one's centre, or as we call it in yoga, 'living from the heart' (the terms heart (*hrt*) and centre in yoga are synonymous).

Important to understand here that the Seal of Yoga (*Yoga Mudra*) is not completed until external *kumbhaka* is added to the performance of the posture. To perform *Yoga Mudra* we first need to assume *Padmasana*, in which the spine is aligned against gravity. This alignment lifts the spine and brain upwards, producing lightness. Importantly in *Padmasana*, the soles of the feet and palms are turned upwards, receiving energy from above. Contrary to that, when sitting in a chair or when standing, there is an automatic discharge of energy out of the soles of the feet into the receptive ground. *Once it is mastered, Padmasana also facilitates a natural, effortless alignment. Shavasana* (corpse posture, i.e. lying on your back) is also effortless, but of all postures it offers the largest area for gravitational down force. It induces heaviness whereas *Padmasana* induces lightness. *Padmasana* is the only posture where the spine, through its miraculous alignment of the energy centres within it (*chakras*), automatically facilitates meditation on infinity[85] and transcendence over duality[86].

---

85 *Yoga Sutra* II.47
86 *Yoga Sutra* II.48

Padmasana is lauded in many scriptures as one of the foremost, or the foremost yoga posture. These include T. Krishnamacharya's perennial favourite, the *Yoga Rahasya*[87], but also *Goraksha Shataka*[88], *Gheranda Samhita*[89], *Yoga Chudamani Upanishad*[90], *Brhadyogi Yajnavalkya Smrti*[91], *Yoga Kundalini Upanishad*[92], *Amrita Nada Upanishad*[93], *Hatha Tatva Kaumudi*[94], *Yuktabhavadeva*[95], and Brahmananda's commentary on the *Hatha Yoga Pradipika*[96]. In some shastras, such as *Dattatreya's Yogashastra*, *Padmasana* is the only *asana* mentioned[97].

These factors assure that *Padmasana* is the pinnacle of yoga postures:

- Feet and hands are turned away from the floor so the ground cannot absorb *prana* projected out of them. This rules out sitting on chairs, where the feet face downwards.
- Legs are positioned higher than the *Muladhara* (base *chakra*) so that *prana* and blood flows are directed

---

87 *Yoga Rahasya* I.103

88 *Goraksha Shataka* stanza 41

89 *Gheranda Samhita* II.8

90 *Yoga Chudamani Upanishad* stanza 106

91 *Brhadyogi Yajnavalkya Smrti* IX.186–190

92 *Yoga Kundalini Upanishad* I.2

93 *Amrita Nada Upanishad* 18–20

94 *Hatha Tatva Kaumudi of Sundaradeva* XXXVI.6

95 *Yuktabhavadeva of Bhavadeva Mishra*, lxvi

96 *Brahmananda's commentary to the Hatha Yoga Pradipika (4-chapter edition)*, II.9

97 Dr M.M. Gharote (ed.), *Dattatreyayogasastram*, Lonavla Yoga Institute, Lonavla, 2015, p. 19-20 and p. 29

upwards. Again this rules out sitting on chairs and leaning against walls.

- The pelvis must be tilted forward (anteriorly) quite strongly so the spinal double-s curve is exaggerated, and the spine assumes the shape of a cobra ready to strike. This is a prerequisite for the serpentine power (Kundalini) to rise.

- To stimulate *Mula Bandha* the perineum must either press into the floor, which in *Padmasana* is achieved through the strong forward tilt of the pelvis, or be stimulated by the left heel, which is given in *Siddhasana*.

- Ideally, through the forward tilt of the pelvis, the heels should press into the abdomen to stimulate *Uddiyana Bandha*. The only posture where this is achievable is *Padmasana*.

- The posture must provide a firm base that can be held naturally for a long time. It must align the whole body effortlessly against gravitation, so there is no slumping or slouching. Again, of all postures, *Padmasana* reigns supreme here.

Meditation postures like *Padmasana* are usually placed towards the end of one's general *asana* practice, when the body and particularly the hip joints are warmed up. If you do not know how to rotate and move your hip joints, you might injure your knees when attempting *Padmasana* without preparation. It took me 10 years of general *asana* practice to tolerate *Padmasana* for more than just a few minutes, but 20 years of such practice, to sit in it comfortably for extended periods. I have described general *asana* practice, including *Padmasana*, in my two previous books *Ashtanga Yoga: Practice and Philosophy* and *Ashtanga Yoga: The Intermediate Series*. In the present volume I am describing postures only in a basic fashion, as this is a book on *mudras,* but also because *asana* is a complex subject that needs to be treated in separate texts. In this volume, I am assuming that you do have a general *asana* practice. You will need to have a certain foundation in *asana* to practise *mudra.*

Padmasana also is the foremost posture for *pranayama.* Goraknath, Gheranda and many other ancient authorities accept only placing the right leg first into lotus (and the left leg on top) but T. Krishnamacharya allowed the switching of sides. However, one should only alternate sides if there is a reason, such as difficulties with the right-leg-first lotus due to pelvic obliquity. Do not suddenly extend the time spent in *Padmasana.* Add only a minute, or at most a few minutes, per week. The posture is powerful and hour-long stints should be left to advanced practitioners. It is also important to not simply sit in *Padmasana,* as such sitting is not a practice in itself. *Padmasana* is a laboratory and hence it should be used for practices such as *pranayama* and *chakra*-Kundalini meditation. This has the added advantage of taking the mind away from possible discomfort in the posture. Once you are used to performing your higher limbs practice in *Padmasana,* your ability to stay in the posture will increase faster than when just sitting in it waiting for discomfort to commence.

To enter the posture safely from a straight-legged position, flex the right knee joint completely by first drawing the right heel to the right buttock. The inability to touch the buttock with your heel would indicate that your quadriceps is too short to enter *Padmasana* safely. In this case, perform *Virasana* (a posture that I have described in my previous text on *pranayama* and meditation) extensively to lengthen your quadriceps or instead sit cross-legged. Ideally, you would get used to performing functions such as eating, computer work, etc., while sitting at a low table in *Virasana* or *Ardha Siddhasana*. This provides the fastest avenue to eventually sit comfortably in *Padmasana*.

If you can touch your heel to your buttock, let the right knee fall out to the side, pointing and inverting the right foot. Another way of expressing the same is to sit in *Dandasana* position and draw the right leg up into *Marichyasana* A, before dropping it outwards into *Janushirshasana* A. Now draw the right heel into the right groin to ensure that the knee joint remains flexed in this abducted position (abduction is the action here performed at the hip joint). From here, lift the right heel in towards the navel, bringing the knee closer to the centreline. Keeping the heel in line with the navel, place the ball of the foot into the opposite groin.

Repeat these steps on the left, as if the right leg were still straight. First, flex the knee joint completely until the underside of the thigh touches the back of the leg over its entire length. Drawing the knee far out to the left, first place the left ankle under the right ankle on the floor. From here, lift the left foot over the right ankle in towards the navel, while drawing the left knee out to the side. Do not lift the left foot over the right knee, as this would mean opening the left knee joint, which would induce lateral movement into the knee during the transition. Keeping the left knee joint in the transition as flexed as possible will allow you to move the femur (thigh bone) and tibia (shin bone) as a unity with no gap between them.

Once the left leg is in position, move both heels towards each other so they touch the navel area. Bring both knees close together, so the thighbones become almost parallel (ultimately depending on ratio of length between femur and tibia). Now inwardly rotate your femurs until the front edges of the tibias point downward and the soles and heels of the feet face upward. In this way, the knee joints are completely closed and protected. Do not sit in *Padmasana* while retaining the initial lateral rotation of the femurs used to enter the posture. The key to mastering *Padmasana* is rotating your femurs internally while being in the posture. This is difficult to learn by merely sitting in *Padmasana* itself without being warmed up. An ideal tool for learning femoral internal rotation is the femur rotation pattern of the Primary Series as described in my book *Ashtanga Yoga: Practice and Philosophy*.

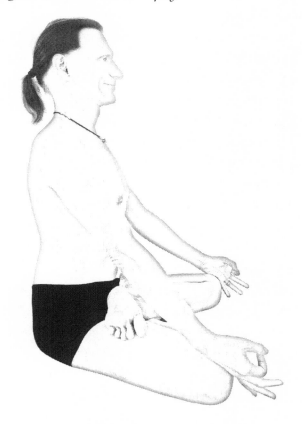

Yoga Mudra, Padmasana

Having arrived safely in *Padmasana*, the next step is now to bind the lotus to complete *Baddha Padmasana*. With your left arm, reach around your back and take the left foot's big toe with the palm facing downward. The foot on top is bound first. Now bind the right big toe with your right hand, placing the right arm on top of the left arm on your back. This is *Baddha Padmasana*. If you experience difficulty binding, cross the arms above the elbows rather than the forearms. This induces an opening of the shoulders and the chest. A tight pectoralis minor muscle is the greatest obstacle here.

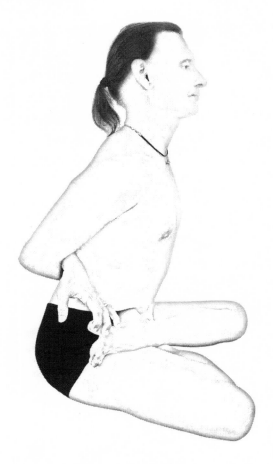

Yoga Mudra, Baddha Padmasana

Exhaling, fold forward, placing the forehead on the floor, and gaze towards the nose. Once fully exhaled, lock the throat and perform a faked or false inhalation. Because we are in a forward bend, we do not perform *Jalandhara Bandha*. Let's recall that *Jalandhara Bandha* is not a requirement in external *kumbhaka* *but* is generally treated as an optional add-on (It is, however, compulsory during internal *kumbhaka*).

A faked inhalation means that the secondary respiratory muscles act as if you were inhaling by lifting and expanding the ribcage. Because the throat is locked and contracted, no inhalation can ensue. Instead, a vacuum is created in the thoracic cavity. We are now relaxing the abdominal wall, so the abdominal contents are sucked up into the thoracic cavity and the abdominal wall is sucked backwards against the spine, which gives the abdomen the characteristic scooped-out appearance. We are now in external-*Uddiyana* (*Bahya Uddiyana*) in the state of *Yoga Mudra*. Hold it to capacity. You can either gaze towards the nose or towards the third eye, with the latter being the more advanced variation. It enables you to extend forward more and draw *prana* towards the third eye. Eventually, relax the throat and gently inhale. If you have difficulties releasing the throat, first expel the last remaining air in the lungs, which will unlock the throat. Then only commence inhalation.

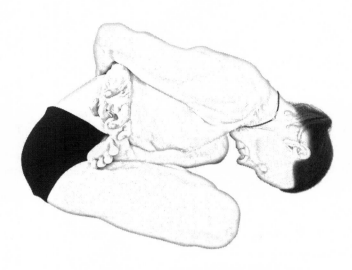

Yoga Mudra **with external** *kumbhaka*

If you already have a *pranayama* practice, a single *kumbhaka* (i.e. only a single round of *Yoga Mudra*) should be enough. If you use the *mudra* as a transitioning exercise from a mere *asana*-based yoga practice towards an *asana-pranayama* compound practice perform up to three rounds of *Yoga Mudra*. *Yoga Mudra* works well if combined with *Tadaga Mudra*, in which case the two *mudras* form the beginning and end point of one's *mudra* practice, with the two variations of *Viparita Karani Mudra* (*Sarvangasana* and *Shirshasana*) sandwiched between. Notice that ultimately the entire cool-down sequence must be made *mudric* in nature. Whereas the standing and sitting *asanas* are there for mobilizing *prana*, the purpose of the cool-down postures is *pranic* absorption.

Chapter 5
NABHO MUDRA (Sky Seal)

DISAMBIGUATION

Are *Nabho* and *Khechari Mudra* two methods or the same? The 10-chapter edition of the *Hatha Yoga Pradipika* describes *Khechari Mudra* at great length in its fifth chapter from stanza 37 to 65[98]. Until stanza 64, the technique is called *Khechari Mudra* whereas in stanza 65, the method's name is suddenly changed to *Nabho Mudra,* while only discussing the effects and without a change of method [99]. This clearly implies that the author of the *shastra* took the methods to be the same. Additionally in stanza V.11, where all *mudras* are listed, we find the name of *Nabho Mudra* instead of *Khechari,* although the text later almost exclusively refers to *Khechari Mudra* [100].

A similar case appears in the *Goraksha Shataka*[101]. Stanza 32 mentions the five *mudras* described in the text, *Maha Mudra, Nabho Mudra, Uddiyana-, Jalandhara-* and *Mula Bandhas.* However, after describing *Maha Mudra* in stanza 33, stanza 34 then calls

---

98 Dr M.L. Gharote et al (eds. & transl.), *Hathapradipika of Svatmarama (10 chapters)*, Lonavla Yoga Institute, Lonavla, 2006, p. 115-128

99 Dr M.L. Gharote et al (eds. & transl.), *Hathapradipika of Svatmarama (10 chapters)*, Lonavla Yoga Institute, Lonavla, 2006, p. 128

100 Dr M.L. Gharote et al (eds. & transl.), *Hathapradipika of Svatmarama (10 chapters)*, Lonavla Yoga Institute, Lonavla, 2006, p. 103

101 Swami Kuvalayananda (ed.), *Goraksasatakam*, Kaivalyadhama, Lonavla, 2006, p. 40

the next *mudra Khechari,* indicating that the author, Gorakhnath, took the two names to be synonymous. The view that *Nabho Mudra* is a variant name for *Khechari Mudra* is also upheld in Jayatarama's *Jogapradipyaka*[102].

However, our case is made more complicated by perusing the *Gheranda Samhita.* In stanzas III.1-3, the *Samhita* lists its 20 *mudras*[103]. *Nabho Mudra* is listed at No.2 and *Khechari Mudra* at No.8, indicating that sage Gheranda did not see them as the same. *Nabho Mudra* in stanza III.9 is then described as turning the tongue up and retaining the breath[104]. This is essentially how I learned the technique in India, and there was no association of the name *Nabho Mudra* with the need to lengthen the tongue, often associated with *Khechari Mudra.*

Gheranda then embarks on describing *Khechari Mudra* in stanzas III.25-32, emphasizing methods to first lengthen the tongue and then use it to perform *kumbhaka,* with all its associated miraculous effects [105]. So clearly two methods then, with *Nabho Mudra* simply a *Jihva Bandha* (tongue lock) combined with *kumbhaka,* and *Khechari Mudra* a complex tongue exercise which may not necessarily involve *kumbhaka.*

The view of the *Gheranda Samhita* is contradicted by Swami Niranjanananda who states in his *Yoga Darshan* that *Nabho Mudra*

---

102 Swami Maheshananda, et al. (eds & transl.), *Jogapradipyaka of Jayatarama,* Kaivalyadhama, Lonavla, 2006, p. 129

103 R.B.S. Chandra Vasu (transl.), *The Gheranda Samhita,* Sri Satguru Publications, Delhi, 1984, p. 20

104 R.B.S. Chandra Vasu (transl.), *The Gheranda Samhita,* Sri Satguru Publications, Delhi, 1984, p. 21

105 R.B.S. Chandra Vasu (transl.), *The Gheranda Samhita,* Sri Satguru Publications, Delhi, 1984, p. 25-26

is simply another name for *Khechari Mudra*[106]. He then describes cutting the tendon of the tongue without further referring to *Khechari Mudra* in name. The Swami reiterates the view that both *mudras* are the same in his publication *Prana and Pranayama*[107]. However, this evidence is weakened by the fact that the author on the next pages argues that *Shambhavi Mudra* and *Bhrumadhya Drishti* are the same, which they are not. *Shambhavi* is a very advanced continuation of *Bhrumadhya Drishti*. *Bhrumadhya Drishti* can be executed in a wide variety of yoga postures, but *Shambhavi Mudra* is only to be used when sitting in a meditation *asana*. A page further, Niranjanananda even argues that *Agochari Mudra* and *Nasagrai Drishti* are the same, which have nothing to do with each other. By extrapolation, we may question his testimony that *Nabho-*, and *Khechari Mudras* are the same.

Some readers may find my in-depth analysis excessive, but we cannot simply accept an opinion just because somebody uttered it and they appear as an authority. I have been researching, practicing, and teaching yoga for over 40 years, and the vast majority of opinions, views, and instructions I came across were questionable. A big part of our problem is that many claims pertaining to the spiritual arena are difficult to verify, if at all. An air of authority can often be projected simply by airing extreme opinions with great confidence. This is exacerbated by the audience being gullible, and regularly they are just happy to believe the first person that comes along. More than elsewhere, it is imperative to verify whether something said is correct in the spiritual arena. To do so is often

---

106 Swami Niranjanananda Saraswati, *Yoga Darshan*, Yoga Publications Trust, Munger, 2009, p. 413

107 Swami Niranjanananda Saraswati, *Prana and Pranayama*, Yoga Publications Trust, Munger, 2009, p. 319

difficult, but we must do our due diligence and simultaneously employ reason, analysis, scriptural evidence, tradition, expert testimonies and personal experience. If we do so, the likelihood that our practice is correct dramatically increases.

Acharya Bhagwan Dev in *Pranayama, Kundalini and Hatha Yoga* argues that simply turning up the tongue is called *Nabho Mudra*[108]. The lengthy descriptions of the arduous trials involving *Khechari Mudra* cannot be summarized by "simply turning up the tongue". Therefore, we must take the Acharya's comments to mean that *Nabho* and *Khechari Mudras* are not identical. The *Trishiki Brahmana Upanishad* in stanza 94-95[109] and the ancient *Brhadyogiyajnavalkyasmrti*[110] both mention that the tongue should be retroverted without referring to elaborate methods to elongate it, which are necessary for *Khechari Mudra*. The *Yoga Chudamani Upanishad* treats *Khechari Mudra* in stanzas 50-57. It does talk about placing the tongue in the cavity above the palate but not how to go about this feat. It then discusses the esoteric aspects of the *mudra* and mentions the name *Nabho Mudra,* as if both *mudras* are the same[111].

Knowing that the purpose of the advanced *Khechari Mudra* is access of *samadhi* and that the more introductory *Jihva Bandha* is an ancillary technique practiced during

---

108 Acharya Bhagwan Dev, *Pranayama, Kundalini & Hatha Yoga,* Diamond Books, New Delhi, 2008, p. 34

109 Shyam Sundar Goswami, *Laya Yoga*, Inner Traditions, Rochester, 1999, p. 51

110 Dr M.L. Gharote et al (eds. & transl.), *Brhadyogiyajnavalkyasmrti*, Kaivalyadhama, Lonavla, 1982, p. 81

111 Dr M.M. Gharote et al (eds. & transl.), *Critical Edition of Selected Yogopanisads,* Lonavla Yoga Institute, Lonavla, 2017, p. 206-209

pranayama and meditation, what is the purpose of *Nabho Mudra*, placed somewhere between *Jihva Bandha* and *Khechari Mudra*? In the *Shiva Samhita* we learn that placing the tongue against the palate during *kumbhaka* and drinking the nectar of the moon creates freedom from disease [112]. *Jihva Bandha*, like the other *bandhas*, is an ancillary technique. But by adding *kumbhakas* it becomes a stand-alone technique with a similar benefit as the inversions, headstand and the shoulder stand. "Milking the moon and drinking it's nectar" refers to directing the tongue upwards in direction of the centre of the cranium. Here is located the lunar storehouse of *prana*, or short, the moon. The lunar *prana*, or *amrita* as it is in yogic texts often called, drizzles down into the gastric fire, where it is burned. This so-called burning is a metaphorical term for losing one's vitality by projecting oneself out into the phenomena, i.e., making oneself extraverted. *Nabho Mudra* is then a stand-alone technique designed to increase *amrita* and arrest it through *kumbhaka*. Its main purpose then is fortitude (*sthirata*). It differs from *Khechari Mudra*, in its scope and difficulty. *Khechari's* main purpose is to induce *samadhi* in a person whose mind has already been made *samadhic*. *Khechari Mudra* involves a protracted period of elongating the tongue, while *Nabho Mudra* does not. It is this that is the defining difference between the two *mudras*. Passages that elaborate methods to elongate the tongue directly refer to *Khechari Mudra*. But those that address *Nabho Mudra* do not, but instead talk about *kumbhaka*. We are now ready to look at the technique of *Nabho Mudra*.

---

112 *The Shiva Samhita*, III.69- 73

TECHNIQUE

A good time to perform *Nabho Mudra* is during the sitting section at the end of one's *asana* practice and before *Utpluthi*. Perform *Jihva Bandha* (tongue lock) by turning up the underside of the tongue and pressing it against the soft palate. Draw the tongue further upwards and back with suction. Once you have, without straining, inverted the tongue as high up as possible, perform the action called "milking the "moon". This means to draw through suction secretion from the smooth area high on the soft palate. Other than during *Manduka Mudra,* where the tongue is moved left and right, here we are keeping the tongue steady. Once you taste the secretion (*amrita*), inhale, swallow the secretion and perform internal *kumbhaka* with Jalandhara *Bandha,* which includes contracting the throat. *Nabho Mudra* is sometimes taught without *Jalandhara Bandha,* but this is only valid if the breath retentions last for less than 10 seconds.

During the internal *kumbhaka* engage *Mula-* and *Uddiyana Bandhas,* too. Additionally, perform *Bhrumadhya Drishti* (gently directing the gaze towards the centre of the eyebrows), or ideally, *Shambhavi Mudra* (a more advanced version thereof) covered in Section 3, *Mudra* 16. Hold the breath retention to capacity, then lift your head, release *Jalandhara Bandha* and exhale. Repeat several times.

EFFECTS

Amrita reduces hunger and thirst and makes the body stable and healthy. The nectar of the moon has a cooling quality, which is reputed to have a life-extending quality. It also reduces extraversion and moves one towards an internal frame of reference.

Chapter 6

MATSYENDRA MUDRA
(Matsyendra's Seal)

There is scant textual evidence of this *mudra*. Shyam Sundar Goswami, a highly esteemed *tantric* practitioner and scholar, mentions it in his *Laya Yoga*[113]. Goswami doesn't actually call it a *mudra* but names it *Matsyendra*-breathing. But the place in his sequence between two well-known *mudras*, *Maha Mudra* and *Bhujangi Mudra*, identifies it clearly as a *mudra*. Goswami sees *mudras* as a preparation for *pranayama*. His *pranayama* sequence, which he suggests as a preparation for meditation has the following order:

Maha Mudra
Matsyendra Mudra
Bhujangi Mudra
Bhastrika
Ujjayi

The first three are discussed here in this book. *Bhastrika* and *Ujjayi* are *pranayama* exercises, which I have covered in the for me typical nauseating detail in my previous books. I covered *Ujjayi* in *Ashtanga Yoga Practice and Philosophy* and *Bhastrika* in *Pranayama The Breath of Yoga* (which additionally also included an *Ujjayi* section).

---

113 Shyam Sundar Goswami, *Laya Yoga*, Inner Traditions, Rochester, 1999, p. 307

TECHNIQUE

To perform *Matsyendra Mudra,* first, assume *Matsyendrasana.* There are two versions of the postures, *Ardha Matsyendrasana* and *Purna Matysendrasana,* with the latter a very advanced posture, hardly suitable for extensive breath retention, lest one should wish to twist one's sacroiliac joints. *Ardha Matsyendrasana* is then the version of choice. To enter *Ardha Matsyendrasana,* sit on the floor with both legs extended straight. Bend both legs, lifting the knees of the floor. Place the left foot outside of the right buttock and the left knee on the floor in front of you so your knee points straight ahead. Draw the right hip way back, un-squaring the hips. Attempt to bring both hip joints in line with the left knee. Point (plantar flex) your left foot and keep the toes close to your right buttock. Now place the right foot outside of your left thigh with the knee pointing up to the ceiling.

Twist to the right and place your left shoulder outside of your right knee. Take the inside of your right foot and the big toe with your left hand. Rotate your humerus (arm bone) internally so the elbow faces outwards, away from your leg. If you have the crease of the elbow facing outwards there will be a lot of pressure on your elbow, hyperextending it.

Reach around your back with your right arm and take hold of your left thigh. Draw the right sit bone down towards the floor and continue to twist as you breathe. Draw the shoulder blades down the back as you lift your heart and the back of the head up to the ceiling. Bring the back of your head in line with your spine, without letting your chin jut forward. Let your spine grow long by letting the top of the head and the sit bones reach into opposite directions.

Take a deep inhale now, utilizing *Ujjayi* to draw the breath long. Inhale only to a maximum of 90-95% of your capacity as otherwise, the pressure in your thorax would forbid to execute a breath retention. At the end of your inhale, lift your sternum high and place your chin down on the sternum into *Jalandhara Bandha* position. To complete *Jalandhara Bandha*, at the same time swallow to contract your throat and maintain the contraction during the *kumbhaka*. For a complete understanding of *Jalandhara Bandha* please study Section 3, *Mudra* 12 of this book. Hold the *kumbhaka* to capacity, i.e. the time you can do without straining. Then lift your head and gently exhale. Repeat this cycle several times and then perform *Ardha Matsyendrasana* on the left, executing the same number of *kumbhakas* there.

Matsyendra Mudra **with internal** *kumbhaka*

EFFECTS

Lays, with other *mudras*, the foundations for *pranayama*.

Chapter 7
BHUJANGI MUDRA
(Cobra Seal)

Bhujangi Mudra is well documented as it is part of *Gheranda Samhita's* list of 20 *mudras*[114]. It also occurs in Jayatarama's *Jogapradipyaka*[115] but there is refered to as *Bhujangi kumbhaka*. It is a common feature of medieval texts they sometimes refer to the same technique either as a *pranayama* or *mudra*. This shouldn't disturb us. Raghuvira's *Kumbhaka Paddhati* calls the method *Naga Kumbhaka*[116], with *naga* being a more general term for serpents. However, the method described by Raghuvira is the same as that listed by sage Gheranda as *Bhujangi Mudra*. Shrinivasayogi's *Hatharatnavali* lists the method as *Bhujangi Karana*[117], but briefly describes it. Amongst modern teachers, the *mudra* was taught by Shyam Sundar Goswami[118], Swami Satyananda[119] and T. Krishnamacharya; however, of those

---

114 *Gheranda Samhita* III.92

115 Maheshananda, Sw. et al. (eds & transl.), *Jogapradipyaka of Jayatarama,* Kaivalyadhama, Lonavla, 2006, p.103

116 Dr M.L. Gharote, *Kumbhaka Paddhati of Raghuvira*, Lonavla Yoga Institutte, Lonavla, 2010, p. 24

117 *Hatharatnavali of Shrinivasayogi* II.31

118 Shyam Sundar Goswami, *Laya Yoga*, Inner Traditions, Rochester, 1999, p. 307

119 Swami Satyananda, *Asana, Pranayama, Mudra and Bandha*, Yoga Publications Trust, Munger, 1969, p. 439

to my eye Swami Satyananda failed to understand the significance of including the cobra posture, which the other teachers rightly taught. Satyananda's omission is probably because sage Gheranda calls the technique Cobra *Mudra* but does not explicitly mention it is to be performed in Cobra Posture (*Bhujangasana*). This has to be inferred. Yogic treatises are always as terse as possible and omit a lot of vital detail for brevity. On a side note, T. Krishnamacharya included *Bhujangasana* in his so-called life-saving sequence[120], which he practised until he died at age 100, and which was taught after his death by his youngest son Shribhashyam[121].

TECHNIQUE
Lie in a prone position, face-down. Place the palms on the floor shoulder-width apart. Point the feet, engage your buttocks to extend your hip joints. Engage your quadriceps to straighten your legs. Inhaling raise the torso off the floor, like a cobra raising its head, while the feet press into the floor. Lengthen through your low back while drawing the shoulder blades down the back. Raise your head but do not hyperextend your neck backwards. Rather than that, lenghten your neck by extending out through the top of the back of the head. We are now in *Bhujangasana*.

---

120 The sequence consisted of eight *asanas* (including *Maha Mudra*, which Krishnamacharya often referred to as an *asana* rather than a *mudra*) and four *pranayamas*, followed by a meditation.
121 Jan Schmidt-Garre, *Breath of the Gods*-documentary, Pars Media

Bhujangi Mudra, **inhalation**

Inhale with the tongue sticking out, similarly as done during *Shitali Pranayama*[122], creating a serpent-like appearance. Gheranda suggests to stick the head out like a snake, but one wonders whether this detail originally referred to the tongue only and later in error extended to include the whole head. At the end of the inhalation, roll the tongue back into *Jihva Bandha*,

---

122 Maheshananda, Sw. et al. (eds & transl.), *Jogapradipyaka of Jayatarama*, Kaivalyadhama, Lonavla, 2006, p. 103

then perform *kumbhaka* with *Jalandhara Bandha*, while holding *Bhujangasana*. This means that the chin is placed against the sternum while the throat is contracted. Gaze towards the tip of the nose. Hold the *kumbhaka* to capacity, then release *Jalandhara Bandha*, lift the head and exhale employing the *Ujjayi* sound. Repeat several times.

Bhujangi Mudra **w. internal** *kumbhaka*

EFFECTS

Sage Gheranda taught that the *mudra* prevents the onset of decreptitude and alleviates digestive problems such as dyspepsia and indigestion[123]. According to T. Krishnamacharya the *mudra* has life-extending properties. B.N.S. Iyengar believed that it aids in the purification of the *Manipura Chakra* and in the raising of Kundalini. Jayatarama stated that it fills the body with nectar[124].

---

123 *Gheranda Samhita* III.93

124 *Jogapradipyaka of Jayatarama*, stanzas 486-489

Chapter 8

MANDUKA MUDRA
(Frog Seal)

Also this *mudra* is present in the *Gheranda Samhita's* list. In Chandra Vasu's translation, we find the *mudra* at stanza III.62[125], whereas James Mallinson's translation has the passage at III.51-52[126]. The respective stanzas are, however, missing in the manuscript of the Kaivalyadhama edition. Swami Rama also describes the *mudra* in his *Path of Fire and Light*[127], but combines it with *Shitali Pranayama*. We thus have scant scriptural evidence to compare. As most *mudras* in this text I learned *Manduka Mudra* from B.N.S. Iyengar who received the teachings from T. Krishnamacharya.

TECHNIQUE
Revert the tongue onto itself and place the underneath of the tip of the tongue against the soft palate, similarly as done during *Jihva Bandha* or *Nabho Mudra*. Gradually and without strain, move the tongue further back towards the naso-pharyngeal orifice. Instead of keeping the tongue steady as in *Jihva Bandha*

---

125 R.B.S. Chandra Vasu (transl.), *The Gheranda Samhita*, Sri Satguru Publications, Delhi, 1984, p. 29

126 James Mallinson, *The Gheranda Samhita*, YogaVidya.com, Woodstock, 2004, p. 77

127 Swami Rama, *Path of Fire and Light*, vol.1, Himalayan Institute Press, Honesdale, 1988, p. 42

and *Nabho Mudra*, move it left and right, thus massaging the back end of the soft palate. After a while, a sweetish tasting secretion will develop, which sage Gheranda calls the nectar of immortality (*amrita*). This secretion is then swallowed. This practice is conducted for several minutes and repeated several times with resting periods between. The nectar is thought to be the essence of lunar *prana*, that is *prana* associated with all lunar functions such as introversion, the activation of sensory neurons, anabolism, relativistic mind, parasympathetic nervous system, the intuitive-wholistic right brain hemisphere, afferent nerve currents, etc.[128].

EFFECTS
Because of its absorption of lunar *prana, Manduka Mudra* is thought to prevent symptoms of old age such as wrinkles and grey hair (Gheranda), create a longing for solitude, study and devotion (Swami Rama), and improve general health, maintain youthfulness, and freedom from hunger (B.N.S. Iyengar).

---

[128] The subject of lunar *prana* (*amrita*) is covered in detail in my book *Pranayama The Breath of Yoga*, Kaivalya Publications, Crabbes Creek, 2012, p. 44-51

Chapter 9

MATANGA MUDRA
(Elephant Seal)

Matangi Mudra is an alternative spelling of *Matanga Mudra*. Also this obscure *mudra* made Gheranda's list of 20 *mudras* (stanza III.88 of R.B. S. Chandra Vasu's translation)[129]. The *Gheranda Samhita* instructs us to be up to our neck in water and then draw water through the nostrils and expel it through the mouth, in a process similar to *Jala Neti*[130]. But then we are told to draw in water through the mouth and expel it through the nose, which is atypical of *Jala Neti*. The *mudra* is called elephant *mudra* because elephants can be observed immersed in water, taking in and expelling water through their trunks and mouths, respectively. We are told that we will acquire elephantine strength by extensively practising this mudra in a solitary place. One wonders whether practising in a solitary place is a prerequisite for acquiring such strength, or simply avoiding censorship and ridicule when displaying such obviously strange behaviour.

Among modern authors only Yogeshvaranand Paramahansa describes *Matanga Mudra*[131]. I learned the theory of this *mudra*

---

129 Chandra Vasu, R.B.S. (transl.), *The Gheranda Samhita*, Sri Satguru Publications, Delhi, 1984, p.99 – 91

130 A kriya technique described in my text *Pranayama The Breath of Yoga*, p. 195-198

131 Yogeshvaranand Paramahansa, *First Steps to Higher Yoga*, Yoga Niketan Trust, New Delhi, 2001, p. 387

from B.N.S. Iyengar, who taught that it could be executed in a lake and in the ocean with the torso submerged up to the shoulders. Practising in the ocean would increase the discomfort by taking strongly saline water repeatedly through mouth and nostrils. Iyengar said that one needs to exert care not to let water enter into the respiratory system, as this could lead to cancer. The patho-mechanism here is not clear. The practice was to be done in the early mornings on an empty stomach, and a 10-minute *Shavasana* after the *mudra* was suggested to release tension building up in the brain.

EFFECTS

Iyengar suggested that accidents caused by *karma* from previous births, and any accidental death, could be avoided through this *mudra*. But contrary to that, I almost invited accidental death by performing this *mudra*. In my juvenile exuberance, I followed the instructions and performed *Matanga Mudra* in open bodies of water in secluded locations. The most notable outcome of the *mudra* was the acquisition of amoebic dysentery. The dysentery turned out to be very difficult to get rid of and ultimately led to losing a third of my body weight. It probably didn't help a lot that I executed *Matanga Mudra* in Indian lakes, which were reasonably polluted with organic effluent, fertilizer run-off, pesticides and industrial chemicals. However, I cannot think of anywhere but the most remote mountain places where water would be clean enough to exercise this *mudra* so ingestion of pathogens can be ruled out. Any water used would first have to be run through an ultraviolet sterilizer and then through a reverse-osmosis system to eliminate any pathogens, pollutants, chemicals, excess salt or chlorine.

We can assume that in the past when environments were less degraded through human activities than they are today, the technique was safer to practice than it is today. But when reading the instructions to techniques such as *Matanga Mudra*, I sometimes wonder whether the authors of the *shastras* listing them were serious or whether they were meant tongue-in-cheek? To pull water through their trunk back and forth and squirt it around is an obvious behaviour of elephants taking a bath, readily observable anywhere in India. Did the authors make a connection between this behaviour and the strength of the elephant? Or were they wanting to test us and our readiness to accept any nonsense as serious instruction? Testing a student through giving bogus instruction is a common feature of Indian treatises and traditional teachers. In the *Chandogya Upanishad* the teacher Prajapati attempts to deceive his students Indra (a celestial) and Virochana (a demon) through bogus instruction, namely that the body is the true self[132]. Virochana falls for the teaching and spreads it among the demons. Because of the gullibility of the demon, the belief that the body is our true self has earned itself the name the demoniac teaching. Indra, however, is not so easy to deceive. He returns and admonishes Prajapati for his fraudulent instruction. Prajapati admits the intelligence of his student and promises to instruct him properly. But he makes two further attempts to fool his student before finally giving him the correct teaching (that the consciousness is the true self). I leave it to my readers to draw their own conclusions, but an obvious one would be never switching off one's critical faculties when listening to a teacher.

---

132 *Chandogya Upanishad* VIII.7.2-8.5

SECTION 2:

PRANAYAMA MUDRAS

Mula Bandha
Uddiyana Bandha
Jalandhara Bandha
Shanka Mudra
Kaki Mudra

Under this heading, you will find all *mudras*, which are essential to *pranayama* or are adjuncts to *pranayama*. The all-important sub-group under this heading consists of the *bandhas* (locks), i.e. *Mula-*, *Uddiyana-*, and *Jalandhara Bandhas*. *Jalandhara Bandha* is a *mudra*, which is essential to *pranayama*, but other than *Mula-*, and *Uddiyana Bandhas* it is not applied outside of *pranayama*. *Mula-*, and *Uddiyana Bandhas*, meanwhile have near-universal application in all yogic techniques. The fourth *bandha*, *Jivha Bandha* (tongue lock), is not exclusive to *pranayama*, and since it mainly deals with reflecting sensory *prana* (i.e. *prana* that powers a particular sensory function) back into the body, it is dealt with under *pratyahara mudras*. The other *mudras* described here in this section are *Shanka Mudra* and *Kaki Mudra*. *Shanka Mudra* is not only exclusive to *pranayama* but to a particular *pranayama* technique called *Nadi Shuddhi* or *Nadi Shodhana* (alternate nostril breathing)[133]. *Kaki Mudra*, too, is a *mudra* exclusive to a particular breathing method. Let's deal with the *bandhas* first.

The three *bandhas*, *Mula-*, *Uddiyana-*, and *Jalandhara Bandhas*, are among the most important *mudras*. They are included in both the *Hatha Yoga Pradipika's* list of 10 *mudras*[134] and the *Gheranda Samhita's* list of 20 *mudras*[135]. Serious *pranayama*, i.e. *pranayama* involving *kumbhaka*, should not be practised without prior knowledge of the *bandhas*. Modern practitioners often fail in *pranayama* and discontinue their practice because they often commence it without a proper working knowledge of the *bandhas*. *Bandhas* are neuromuscular locks that prevent the *vayu* (vital air) from going astray in *kumbhaka*. *Kumbhakas* over 10 seconds should not be practised without *bandhas* (particularly not without *Jalandhara Bandha*). This is largely because *kumbhakas* shorter than 10 seconds are not considered true *kumbhakas* in a more narrow, technical sense. Otherwise, if I were briefly holding my breath due to astonishment, this would have to be already considered a *kumbhaka*. The *Yoga Rahasya* states that *pranayama* without application of the three *bandhas* does not confer benefits[136] and that without the *bandhas*, *pranayama* is

---

133 The terms are largely synonymous and both mean energy channel purification. However, following the conventions established by the sages Vasishta and Gorakhnath, I will call the method *Nadi Shuddhi* when excluding *kumbhaka*, and *Nadi Shodhana* when involving *kumbhaka*.

134 Hatha Yoga Pradipika III.6

135 Gheranda Samhita III.1

136 *Yoga Rahasya* I.61

useless and may give rise to disease[137]. Contrarily, if done with all three *bandhas*, *pranayama* will destroy the causes of all diseases, according to its author, Nathamuni[138]. The *Hatha Ratnavali* states that applying all of the *bandhas* makes *prana* enter the central energy channel (*Sushumna*)[139], a claim also to be found in the *Hatha Yoga Pradipika*[140]. The great Shankaracharya also said that through the practice of the three *bandhas*, Kundalini arises and enters the *Sushumna*[141]. He added that through mastery of the *bandhas*, *Kevala Kumbhaka* (the culmination of *pranayama*) is achieved, particularly when one adds focus on the *Anahata* (heart) *Chakra*[142].

Shankara also states that each of the three *bandhas* leads to cleansing of the particular area of the body in which they are applied[143], i.e. throat, lower abdomen and pelvic area, and that mastery of the *bandhas* not only drives *apana vayu* (vital down current) up, hence causing Kundalini to rise, but also leads to a release of *amrita* (nectar, this is a metaphor for lunar *prana*, the prana responsible for interoception), which causes joy[144]. *Yoga Rahasya* importantly adds[145] that the *Svadhishthana-* (sacral), and *Manipura* (navel) *Chakras* can only be purified through external

---

137 *Yoga Rahasya* I.95

138 *Yoga Rahasya* II.50

139 *Hatha Ratnavali of Shrinivasayogi* II.8

140 *Hatha Yoga Pradipika* II.46

141 *Yoga Taravali of Shankaracharya* stanza 6

142 *Yoga Taravali of Shankaracharya* stanzas 8–9

143 *Yoga Taravali of Shankaracharya* stanza 5

144 *Yoga Taravali of Shankaracharya* stanza 7

145 Yoga Rahasya II.50

kumbhaka (i.e. breath retention after exhaling) with simultaneous application of all *bandhas*.

The *Yoga Kundalini Upanishad* declares that by applying *Mula Bandha* during *kumbhaka, apana vayu* rises through the *chakras* and pierces the *granthis* (*pranic* and *karmic* blockages)[146]. The same text says that the three *bandhas* should always be applied when *kumbhaka* is performed[147]. The *Shandilya Upanishad*, too, proclaims that during *kumbhaka* the *bandhas* need to be applied to draw *prana* into *Sushumna*[148]. The *Yuktabhavadeva of Bhavadeva Mishra* is supportive in declaring that all *pranayamas* are to be accompanied by the three *bandhas*[149]. The *Kumbhaka Paddhati of Raghuvira* talks of *'shat anga kumbhaka'*, meaning the six limbs of breath retention[150]. These are named as inhalation, retention, exhalation and the three *bandhas*. The *Hatha Tatva Kaumudi of Sundaradeva* also proclaims that *prana* is moved into *Sushumna* by *kumbhaka* with *bandhas* and specifies which combination of *bandhas* needs to be applied during which respiratory phase[151]. The *bandhas* are similarly treated in the *Yoga Chudamani Upanishad*[152] and the *Mandala Brahmana Upanishad*[153].

---

146 *Yoga Kundalini Upanishad* I.64–86

147 *Yoga Kundalini Upanishad* I.40

148 *Shandilya Upanishad* stanzas 26–30

149 Dr M.L. Gharote, et al, (eds & transl.), *Yuktabhavadeva of Bhavadeva Mishra*, Lonavla Yoga Institute, Lonavla, 2002, p. lxviii

150 Dr M.L. Gharote, *Kumbhaka Paddhati of Raghuvira*, Lonavla Yoga Instititute, Lonavla, 2010, p. 186–187

151 *Hatha Tatva Kaumudi of Sundaradeva* XXXIX.87

152 Dr. M.M. Gharote et al (eds. & transl.), *Critical Edition of Selected Yogopanisads,* Lonavla Yoga Institute, Lonavla, 2017, p. 202

153 Dr. M.M. Gharote et al (eds. & transl.), *Mandalabrahmanopanisad and*

Among modern authors, Swami Ramdev, too, asserts that *pranayama* without *bandha*s is incomplete and that the *bandha*s are helpful in mastering it[154]. The Kaivalyadhama researcher Shrikrishna declares that in *kumbhaka* the three *bandha*s should always be applied and, and *Mula-,* and *Uddiyana Bandha*s during inhalation and exhalation[155]. He also proclaims that detrimental results may manifest without applying the three *bandha*s during *pranayama*[156]. Theos Bernard wrote that *samadhi* is caused through success in *bandha*s, which makes *prana vayu* (vital up-current) enter *Sushumna* (the central energy channel)[157].

Swami Niranjanananda points out the importance of the *bandha*s for breaking the *granthis*[158]. The *granthis* are *pranic* blockages in the subtle body that exist because of *karma*. There are several stages of *granthi* breaking. Stage 1 is executed by applying the three *bandha*s during internal and external *kumbhaka*. Only once this is achieved can stage 2 *granthi* breaking be executed, which constitutes of *Bhastrika*, a powerful rapid-breathing *pranayama* technique. Failure to prepare for *Bhastrika* through applying the three *bandha*s during internal and external *kumbhaka* can lead to mental destabilization. There

Nadabindupanisad, Lonavla Yoga Institute, Lonavla, 2012, p. 129

154 Swami Ramdev, *Pranayama*, Divya Yog Mandir Trust, Hardwar, 2007, p. 21

155 Shrikrishna, *Essence of Pranayama*, 2nd edn, Kaivalyadhama, Lonavla, 1996, p. 81

156 Shrikrishna, *Essence of Pranayama*, 2nd edn, Kaivalyadhama, Lonavla, 1996, p. 119

157 Theos Bernard, *Heaven Lies Within Us*, Charles Scribner's Sons, New York, 1939, p. 122

158 Swami Niranjanananda Saraswati, *Yoga Darshan*, Yoga Publications Trust, Munger, 2009, p. 365

is a third stage of *granthi* breaking, consisting of the sequential application of *Maha Mudra, Maha Bandha Mudra* and *Maha Vedha Mudra*, described in Section 4, *Mudras* 21 - 23 of this text.

With many other *mudra*s the *bandha*s have in common their use during *kumbhaka* in diverting *prana* into a desired direction. To learn some of the *bandha*s properly we need to use *kumbhaka*. However, the *kumbhaka* in this training scenario does not constitute *kumbhaka* proper in the sense of *pranayama* because there is no count. When advanced *kumbhaka* is practised in *pranayama*, we may, for example, decide to perform 20 *kumbhaka*s of a length of 48 seconds each preceded by a 12-second inhalation and followed by a 24-second exhalation. To perform the *kumbhaka*s safely, we would add the *bandha*s as an ancillary technique. When learning the *bandha*s, however, or practising any other *mudra*s, we do not count the *kumbhaka*s. The instruction will always be 'hold to capacity and focus on the quality of execution of the *bandha*'. You may repeat the exercise several times, but with no predetermined number of rounds. Practise the *bandha*s, particularly *Jalandhara Bandha*, until you have mastered them, and only then insert them into counted *kumbhaka*s. Once you start counting *kumbhaka*s, you will need to have acquired competence in *bandha*s so you can focus on other aspects of your *pranayama*, such as count, *mantra*, visualization, etc.

Chapter 10

MULA BANDHA (Root Lock)

Mula Bandha means root lock, calling the pelvic floor the root of the spine and nervous system. The *Dhyana Bindu Upanishad* proclaims that the old become young again when performing *Mula Bandha*[159]. The *Gheranda Samhita* agrees that *Mula Bandha* destroys all weakness and infirmity[160], a claim supported by the *Shiva Samhita*[161]. Weakness and ageing are, according to yoga, due to losing life force, and this loss is partially due to the downward flow of life force. *Mula Bandha* preserves life force and makes it flow upwards. The *Yoga Kundalini Upanishad* calls *Mula Bandha* the forcing up of the vital downward current *apana vayu*. It states that directing *apana vayu* upwards, with igniting internal fire, will make the serpent Kundalini enter its hole, the central energy channel (*Sushumna*)[162]. The same mechanism is explained in the *Hatha Yoga Pradipika*[163]. It is to be noted that *apana* must be raised to the 'region of fire', i.e. the *Manipura* (navel) *Chakra*, where it meets *agni*, which is to be stoked by wind (*vayu*). Together they have the power to ignite Kundalini. *Mula Bandha* is also used to awaken the *Muladhara Chakra*. *Mula Bandha's* importance is attested to by a wide variety of *shastras*

---

159 Dhyana Bindu Upanishad stanzas 74–75

160 Gheranda Samhita III.12–14

161 Shiva Samhita IV.41

162 Yoga Kundalini Upanishad I.40–46

163 Hatha Yoga Pradipika III.60–64

including *Dattatreya's Yogashastra*[164] and the *Yoga Chudamani Upanishad*[165].

Among modern authors Swami Niranjanananda states[166] that *Mula Bandha* breaks the *Brahma Granthi* (you will find more on the three *pranic* blockages in the introduction to Section 4), and Shyam Sundar Goswami holds that the *bandha* rouses Kundalini if applied during *pranayama* and *dharana*[167].

TECHNIQUE

Mula Bandha initially is the pressing of the perineum with the left heel (in *Siddhasana*) and its subsequent contraction[168]. The *bandha* is ideally learned in *Siddhasana* because the left heel will apply stimulation to the pelvic floor. This can, however, be replicated in *Padmasana* by tilting the pelvis forward enough to bring the perineum in contact with the floor. *Mula Bandha* may be experienced and practised in any yoga posture, but the two mentioned above are ideal. When proficiency is gained, the *apana vayu* will turn upwards.

For beginners, *Mula Bandha* may be brought on by contracting the anus (to be covered under *Ashvini Mudra*) or the urethra (to be covered under *Vajroli Mudra*) as if one wanted

---

164 Dr M.M. Gharote (ed.), *Dattatreyayogasastram,* Lonavla Yoga Institute, Lonavla, 2015, p. 70-73

165 Dr. M.M. Gharote et al (eds. & transl.), *Critical Edition of Selected Yogopanisads,* Lonavla Yoga Institute, Lonavla, 2017, p. 203

166 Swami Niranjanananda Saraswati, *Yoga Darshan*, Yoga Publications Trust, Munger, 2009, p. 371

167 Shyam Sundar Goswami, *Laya Yoga*, Inner Traditions, Rochester, 1999, p. 90-91

168 *Goraksha Shataka* stanza 81

to stop urination. However, *Mula Bandha* is located right in the middle between the anus and genitals, at the centre of the pubococcygeus muscle. To some extent the contraction of the pubococcygeus will activate the entire pelvic floor and diaphragm. In this context, imagine the inhalation reaching to the pelvic floor, hooking into the centre of the pelvic floor and drawing it upwards. When wanting to focus on *Mula Bandha's* connection to the exhalation, feel the exhalation dropping down and, as it turns into the inhalation, feel the breath rebounding off the pelvic diaphragm as if off a trampoline. In this form, this technique is also to be practised in one's general *asana* practice. *Mula Bandha* stimulates the filum terminale and cauda equina, two anatomical structures connected to the spinal cord, anchored at the coccyx. Through that, *Mula Bandha* stimulates the entire brain and particularly the parasympathetic nervous system. It slows down the heart, lowers the blood pressure and decreases the respiratory rate. T. Krishnamacharya stated that *Mula Bandha* helped to gain his ability to slow down his heartbeat so much it appeared that it had stopped.

Mula Bandha has three aspects, layers or phases of which the first is introductory, the second intermediate, the third advanced. To learn the *bandhas,* students should first focus on the introductory aspect and then move on. The introductory aspect of the *bandha* is gross/muscular. The intermediate aspect is subtle/*pranic,* and the advanced layer is causal/mental, viz. thought-based[169]. That means that our work gets subtler as we mature, similar to the progression through the yogic limbs from *asana* via *pranayama* to meditation and *samadhi.*

---

169 This view is corroborated by Shankaracharya in his *Aparokshanubhuti* stanza 114.

So let's deal first with the gross or muscular stage of *Mula Bandha*: The pelvic floor is primarily formed by the pubococcygeus muscle (or pc muscle for short), which reaches from the pubic bone to the coccyx. It has the form of an 8, allowing for the anal orifice in the back and the urinary/reproductive orifice in the front. You may know the feeling of being at the movies and having to go to the toilet, but postponing the visit because you don't want to miss part of the movie. In this case, you might contract the entire pelvic floor or parts of it. Humans and many animals can differentiate between contracting parts of the pelvic floor. For example, you may release the front of the pc muscle to allow for urination but not the back, which would facilitate defecation. *Mula Bandha* is still considered elusive in some quarters, but that is a question of describing it properly. The fundamentals of *Mula Bandha*, i.e. differentiating parts of the pelvic floor, are already set during basic house training that we internalize during our early childhood. The same capacity is learned by many mammals and even reptiles, which use urination to mark territory. They will not defecate at the same time as they mark their territory through urination, which means they know how to control parts of the pelvic floor while releasing others.

The yogic technique called *Ashvini Mudra* deals extra with the rear part of the pubococcygeus muscle and is described in Section 4, *Mudra* 24. *Ashvini Mudra* entails the rapid contracting and releasing of the anal sphincter. There is also a technique that deals with various levels of control of the front of the pc-muscle, viz the urinary sphincter. This technique is called *Vajroli Mudra* and was sneered at by many yogis of the past (including T. Krishnamacharya) to avoid debauchery. I will mention this subject here only fleetingly but will engage with it fully in

Section 4, *Mudra* 25. *Mula Bandha* is neither identical with *Ashvini Mudra,* nor *Vajroli Mudra,* but exactly in the middle of both. However, the study and performance of both these *mudras* will improve your grip on *Mula Bandha,* simply by improving your skill levels regarding differentiation of the various areas of the pelvic floor. Bio-mechanists have measured that the pelvic floor will engage a split-second before any weight-bearing exercise, but also when shouting or singing loudly. It is something that every opera singer can confirm. Also, any top-level athletes must have a functioning *Mula Bandha.* Without it, no extraordinary performance is possible.

While peak-performers will engage *Mula Bandha* automatically without being prompted, for the majority of us, it is helpful to be instructed what exactly to do to improve our physical capacities. In the first anatomical, gross stage of the *bandha,* we need to learn to control or engage the perineum, which is the part of the pc-muscle where the two loops of the 8 meet. When you do that, you feel you can run faster, jump higher or scream louder and all simply because you become more buoyant. Any force directed out of the body whether it be speech, locomotion or grasping needs something to bounce off from. For example, when trying to push a car, your legs would push off the ground beneath you. In this vein, by engaging the perineum, the pelvic floor now acts similar to a trampoline from which any outward-directed vector can bounce off. This soon becomes very obvious when jumping through and jumping back during the *vinyasa*-movement, during arm-balances, leg-behind-head postures and drop-backs (sequential movement from standing to *Urdhva Dhanurasana* and back). These are fairly intense yogic exercises during which the outward-directed force needs to push against an internal barrier (the *bandha*), otherwise, not much of this outward-directed force reaches the environment/ exterior of the body.

What is essential for the *bandha* is that it is engaged before the vector of force that utilizes it as a base, is enacted. If not, you could actually wet your pants when attempting to scream loudly or to lift a heavy weight. If the *bandha* totally fails, we would call that incontinence. A high level of *bandha* success could be called continence. Notice how this term has a bathroom aspect, but also it means self-control or self-restraint.

Initially, let's say during the first two years of *bandha* training, focus on the above muscular or gross stage of *Mula Bandha*. The duration of this phase depends, of course, on how steep your learning curve rises. Being in this initial phase, before you load up the body with any complex *asana* (or other exercise), you always check first that the perineum is engaged. If you have difficulties locating the *bandha*, contract the anal sphincter, then the urinary sphincter, and then look for the point in the middle and release the two outer areas. Once you have established the *bandha*, try to maintain it while holding increasingly difficult *asanas* or during the performance of *pranayama* and meditation techniques.

Once you have done that for a year or two, migrate to the second tier of *Mula Bandha*, the subtle/*pranic* aspect. Let's look first at the why's and then at how's. All good things will eventually turn to poison if only you take too much of them. That you should limit the time and energy spent on pelvic floor contractions becomes most obvious when you plan to give birth soon. A super built-up pelvic floor makes it more difficult for the baby to pass through. Also, in males too much *Mula Bandha* can eventually lead to extra visits to the toilet in the night because it does limit the passage of urine. However, it is mostly the psychological changes I want to discuss here. The English language contains the beautifully descriptive term 'tight-arse'. If you get stuck at the gross, muscular aspect of *Mula Bandha,* you likely will eventually become a tight arse. The term generally denotes a miserly, un-generous person that looks at life mainly in terms of acquisition. I've seen it happen quite regularly. You may have noticed that when you say no to somebody, defend your position, or stand your ground, your stance is completed and complemented by automatically contracting your anal sphincter. Try it out if it doesn't ring a bell. Your expression will be much more congruent when doing so. Sigmund Freud noticed this tendency and called the phase during which the infant learns to say no, the anal phase. If you do not graduate to the *pranic* stage of *Mula Bandha,* its muscular layer tends to overemphasis the anal, withholding aspects of your personality. However, as yogis, we want to become appreciative, giving, caring, nurturing, loving, etc. While we must be able to say no to and reject wrong positions and actions (such as the raping and pillaging our sacred Mother Earth, genocide on indigenous people, racism, sexism, exploitation and suppression of minorities, etc.), the anal aspect of the psyche should not be allowed to take over if we are interested in managing a balanced psyche.

The second stage of Mula *Bandha* is *pranic*/energetic. During this phase, we slowly move away from the muscular contraction and use the suction of the breath to lift the perineum upwards. There are various ways of doing this. One involves imagining that you inhale through the pelvic floor. Do it and you will feel how this raises the perineum. You can also imagine how the breath lifts and expands your torso and thus creates a suction that lets the perineum billow upwards.

My favourite method, however, is to imagine the torso to be hollow and a hook to be attached to the centre of the pelvic floor. The inhalation now becomes like a hand that reaches down, hooks into the perineum, and pulls it upwards. In these and similar metaphoric descriptions, you will find the same two elements that combine to bring about an effect. The two elements are breath (*prana*) and thought (*vrtti*). It was the *Hatha Yoga Pradipika* that states these two always move together and are difficult to be kept apart[170]. In this phase of the *bandha*, we are using the imagination to direct the *pranic* force. When students master this level, one notices they become able to do things in their practice that otherwise would be difficult to do. The second phase of *Mula Bandha* adds a certain lightness and effortlessness to our practice, but if asked how this comes about, we often cannot explain how.

With this second stage of *Mula Bandha* we become able to do more while using less energy. This is exactly the effect we are trying to bring about. Yoga is not a process during which we use maximum force to bring about little effect, but it is the opposite. Stage two *Mula Bandha* takes much longer to perfect than stage one. Again, learning curves of students differ vastly but it wouldn't be wide off the mark to say that one could easily take a decade to become proficient of this second tier of the *bandha*.

Why then would we need to move on to a third stage if stage two already enables us that much? With stage three the trajectory is continued. It uses even less energy. It is described in Shankara's *Yoga Taravali* and *Aparokshanubhuti* where it is

---

170 *Hatha Yoga Pradipika* IV.24

said that eventually, *Mula Bandha* becomes pure thought[171]. No breath at all is required anymore to create the suction. This is, of course, very important when in *kumbhaka* (breath retention). When the breath does not move, the holding of *Mula Bandha* eventually has to mature to the level of pure thought.

WHEN
Ideally, *Mula Bandha* is always applied during *kumbhaka*, as it activates the parasympathetic nervous system, slowing down the heart, thus making *kumbhaka* easier. *Mula Bandha* should also be held during inhalation and exhalation. Besides that, *Mula Bandha* should also be applied when practising any *asana*, besides *Shavasana*, and during any Kundalini-raising exercise, such as yogic meditation. During *kumbhaka*, however, *Mula Bandha* is second in importance to *Jalandhara Bandha*. Divert intellectual bandwidth towards *Mula Bandha* only having assured that *Jalandhara* is turned on correctly.

WHEN NOT
The yogic scriptures recommend holding *Mula Bandha* all the time. However, this applies only to a very advanced practitioner who has completed his/her duties towards society and raises Kundalini. A person who still performs all normal functions in society and tries to hold *Mula Bandha* all the time may experience constipation. Food intake needs to be adapted if *Mula Bandha* is held all the time. Menstruation is also powered by *apana* and turning *apana* up *with Mula Bandha* may interfere with the natural menstruation process. *Apana* is also responsible for the

---

171 *Aparokshanubhuti of Shankaracharya* stanza 114

delivery of the foetus. During pregnancy, *Mula Bandha* may have to be decreased, depending on the individual's condition. For example, a female with a very advanced *asana* practice and an athletic *Mula Bandha* may benefit from releasing it towards the end of her pregnancy. But females with a generally low muscle tone and weak pelvic floor may benefit from practising *Mula Bandha* for longer.

Chapter 11

UDDIYANA BANDHA
(Flying-Up Lock)

Uddiyana means flying up. The *Dhyana Bindu Upanishad* expounds that it is so-called because it drives *prana* upwards into the central energy channel (*Sushumna*) and is flying up like a great bird therein[172]. This *bandha* is one of the most widely listed *mudras*. Among many other texts it is also listed in *Dattatreya's Yogashastra*[173] and the *Yoga Chudamani Upanishad*[174].

DEFINITION
During inhalation, only the lower abdominal wall is contracted to drive part of the inhalation up into the thorax and prevent the abdomen from distending. During internal *kumbhaka* the entire abdominal wall is isometrically[175] contracted to increase intra-abdominal pressure and drive *apana vayu* (vital down-current)

---

172 *Dhyana Bindu Upanishad* stanza 75-76

173 Dr M.M. Gharote (ed.), *Dattatreyayogasastram,* Lonavla Yoga Institute, Lonavla, 2015, p. 69

174 Dr. M.M. Gharote et al (eds. & transl.), *Critical Edition of Selected Yogopanisads,* Lonavla Yoga Institute, Lonavla, 2017, p. 204

175 During isometric contraction muscle length does not change; it is therefore static contraction.

up. During exhalation the entire abdominal wall is isotonically[176] contracted to drive air out without *apana vayu* turning down. During external *kumbhaka* the abdominal contents are sucked into the thoracic cavity to raise *apana vayu*. Technically speaking, this is not a *bandha*, as there is no muscular contraction involved, but energetically it achieves what *bandha*s do – the diversion of *prana* and *vayu* into another direction. To clarify the stark difference between this fourth method and the other three phases of *Uddiyana Bandha*, I call it external-*Uddiyana* (*Bahya Uddiyana*), following a tradition established in *shastra* in the 17th century.

Thus there are four forms of *Uddiyana Bandha*/external-*Uddiyana*, applying to the four respiratory phases: inhalation, internal *kumbhaka*, exhalation and external *kumbhaka*. At any point of the breathing cycle one or another form of *Uddiyana Bandha*/external-*Uddiyana* applies.

CONTRAINDICATIONS FOR UDDIYANA BANDHA

Do not practise *Uddiyana Bandha* on a full stomach or during pregnancy. Besides inhalation-*Uddiyana Bandha*, the other three versions are unsuitable to varying degrees for anyone suffering from peptic ulcers.

ADDITIONAL CONTRAINDICATIONS FOR BAHYA (EXTERNAL) UDDIYANA

Additionally, the more extreme form of *Bahya Uddiyana* should not be done during menstruation. However, if practised outside of menstruation, *Bahya Uddiyana* has the potency to cure menstrual disorders, especially if they have resulted from

---

176 During isotonic contraction a muscle shortens.

a prolapsed uterus. Do not practise *Bahya Uddiyana* with a weak heart, heart disease or high blood pressure.

WHY UDDIYANA BANDHA?

There are numerous references to the miraculous effects of *Uddiyana Bandha*. The *Yoga Rahasya* states it moves *prana* into *Sushumna*[177], that it cleans *chakras* and *nadis*[178] and that it helps with *apana*-related diseases such as menstrual disorders[179]. The *Hatha Ratnavali* declares that *Uddiyana Bandha* confines *prana* to *Sushumna* and makes it rise therein[180]. The *Gheranda Samhita* proclaims *Uddiyana Bandha* to be a lion against the elephant death – due to its royal status, the lion was thought to subdue even the elephant. It also claims it can confer spontaneous liberation[181]. The *Goraksha Shataka* states that *Uddiyana Bandha* conquers death[182].

INHALATION-UDDIYANA BANDHA

A complete yogic breathing cycle consists of filling the breath into the torso as if one would fill a receptacle with water, i.e. from the bottom up. The yogi inhales first into the abdomen, then into the thorax and finally into the upper lobes of the lungs, the clavicular area. Hence a yogic inhalation establishes a wave that initiates at the pubic bone and terminates at the manubrium of the sternum (upper end of the breastbone).

---

177 *Yoga Rahasya* I.65

178 *Yoga Rahasya* I.67

179 *Yoga Rahasya* I.69

180 *Hatha Ratnavali of Shrinivasayogi* II.53

181 *Gheranda Samhita* III.8–9

182 *Goraksha Shataka* stanza 77

Try the following experiment: Breathe in while keeping the abdominal wall completely relaxed. You will find that the belly expands more and more, but the breath never reaches the thorax and clavicular area. Although some spiritual schools recommend this, it is a denatured and devitalizing way of inhaling. Now keep the lower abdominal wall firm and controlled, and inhale again. You will notice that now you can draw the breath as high up as you choose. You should not contract the entire abdominal wall but only the part below the navel. Since the abdominal muscles interdigitate with the diaphragm, contracting the upper part of the abdominal wall will also lead to arresting the diaphragm. This would then make us chest-breathe exclusively – a form of breathing that is as denaturized and devitalizing as exclusive abdominal breathing. It can also lead to anxiety. Since the diaphragm is attached via a double tendon to the pericardium, a permanently contracted diaphragm can manifest as tension in the heart with may translate as fear of annihilation.

We need to fully involve the entire torso in the breathing cycle to become a complete and integrated human being. How to do so is to keep the lower abdominal wall controlled, slightly engaging the lower half of the transverse abdominis muscle with the effect of drawing the abdominal contents gently in against the spine. The diaphragm is then free to descend downwards, increasing intra-abdominal pressure and massaging and compressing the abdominal organs. This will also lead to a slight protrusion of the abdominal wall above, but not below, the navel. The slight protrusion above the navel is feedback from the body that the diaphragm is moving freely up and down. You need to watch out for this sign.

The limited expansion of the upper abdomen will now lead to the excess volume of the inhalation expanding the thorax.

It is very important for the health of the heart that the thorax is kept vibrant and pulsating. Exclusive abdominal breathing with a completely relaxed abdominal wall makes the thorax rigid, which is detrimental to *prana* supply to the heart. After the thorax is fully expanded, the controlled lower abdominal wall will drive the remainder of the inhalation into the upper lobes of the lungs. It is very important for the upper lobes of the lungs to get properly ventilated, and only a few of us draw enough air into this area. And drawing the breath into the upper lobes makes the wave of the breath reach this uppermost part of the thoracic spine. The proper function of the uppermost thoracic vertebrae will guarantee that the nerves exiting along this area can properly supply their respective areas, mainly the arms, hands, wrists and shoulders. Any problems are often related to a weak, inactive abdominal wall. Readers of my previous books will have noted that it is this form of *Uddiyana Bandha*, which I will now call inhalation-*Uddiyana Bandha*, that is used during the entire *Ujjayi* breathing cycle in Ashtanga Vinyasa Yoga.

During the classical inhalation-*Uddiyana Bandha* the lower part of the transverse abdominis is contracted and the lower abdomen tucked in slightly. The lower abdominal wall is contracted to drive part of the inhalation up into the thorax and prevent the abdomen from distending. The transverse abdominis muscle runs horizontally across the abdomen and is used to draw the abdominal contents in against the spine. It is crucial that the lower part of this muscle is isolated from its upper part. The upper half extends from the sternum to the navel. This part of the transverse abdominis interdigitates with the diaphragm and its contraction during movement would translate as tension into the diaphragm. Since the diaphragm is attached via a tendon to the pericardium, tension in the diaphragm is felt in the heart. If it reaches a certain magnitude the mind interprets it as fear of annihilation, which may then be felt as a panic attack.

To isolate the two parts of the transverse abdominis sit on the floor and place your thumbs or fingers outside of the rectus abdominis (six-pack-muscle). The rectus runs vertically in front of the spine from the sternum to the pubic bone. It's impossible to isolate the upper part of the rectus from the lower part. So, you need to place your fingers on either side of the rectus approximately 100mm or 4 inches wide. If you place your fingers 150mm or 6 inches apart on either side of the rectus you have created enough distance from the rectus to feel the transverse abdominis. Drop your fingers now to the horizontal line which would be formed by your belt if you wore one. Now experiment until you do find under your fingers the muscle that tucks in. Important is that you do not push out. Pushing out against your fingers does not activate the transverse abdominis, which can only tuck in (draw the abdominal contents in against the spine) by contracting. Once you do have the muscle that tucks in, move your fingers higher above the navel (but still outside of the rectus) and make sure that the upper part of the transverse remains relaxed so we don't tighten the diaphragm.

The importance of this is long known to biomechanical researchers. It has been shown that even when lifting a relatively light weight with your arms, the transverse abdominis will fire up about half a second beforehand. This reflex exists to protect the lumbar discs. When the transverse abdominis fires (co-contracts) it will tuck the lower abdomen in. Because the hollows in the abdominal cavity are filled with fluids (different to many in the thoracic cavity filled with air) the abdominal cavity cannot change its volume. Tucking in the lower abdomen must therefore result in shape change. Since the circumference of the abdominal cavity gets reduced by transverse abdominis contraction the height of the cavity must increase. This will lead to the lumbar vertebrae being pulled apart, increasing the lumbar intervertebral disc spaces. This means that the contraction of the transverse serves primarily the aim of protecting the vulnerable lumbar discs.

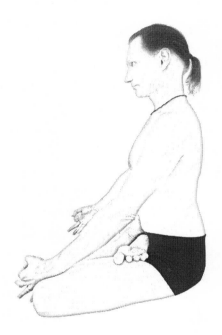

inhalation-*Uddiyana Bandha*

This is a reflex inbuilt into our bodies, however, with increasingly sedentary lifestyles, disfunction or weakness of these reflexes become more likely. However, especially when performing yogic arm balances, deep backbending or leg-behind-head postures it is essential that the transverse fires appropriately before the low-back is loaded up. *Uddiyana Bandha* should be trained to proficiency before these posture groups are tackled. One should also not wait until the *bandha* comes on "spontaneously", but one should systematically focus on it during the beginner's stage, i.e. from the first sun salutation onwards. Once one is used to doing one's *asana* practice without the *bandhas*, retraining oneself is much harder. *Bandha* instruction should be part of all beginner courses. It is much easier to focus on transverse abdominis engagement during easy beginners' postures than learning it later during more challenging postures.

If the lower abdominal wall is kept firm and the upper wall is relaxed, the diaphragm moves up and down freely. This produces a strong oscillation of intra-abdominal blood pressure, and it is exactly this mechanism that produces healthy abdominal organs. When the diaphragm moves down and the abdominal wall is held, the pressure in the abdomen rises. When the diaphragm moves up, blood is sucked out of the abdomen and blood pressure drops. This strong oscillation of abdominal blood pressure constantly massages the internal organs and leads to strong, healthy tissue. By relaxing the abdominal wall, letting the belly drop out this invigorating massage of the abdominal muscles is prevented.

INTERNAL (KUMBHAKA) UDDIYANA BANDHA

We look next at the form of *Uddiyana Bandha* applied during internal *kumbhaka*. The *Hatha Ratnavali* says *Uddiyana Bandha* should be initiated after inhalation and before (internal) *kumbhaka* begins. The *Hatha Tatva Kaumudi* proclaims that by practice of *Jalandhara Bandha* and *Uddiyana Bandha* during (internal) *kumbhaka*, *prana* can be moved into *Sushumna*. The

Kumbhaka Paddhati recommends the initiation of *Uddiyana Bandha* after inhalation and before *kumbhaka* begins, and the *Gheranda Samhita* says the same.

We encounter here a form of *Uddiyana Bandha* different to the one already discussed. The *Uddiyana Bandha* performed during internal *kumbhaka* consists of the vigorous contraction of the abdominal muscles not only below but also above the navel[183]. Its purpose is to increase the pneumatic and *pranic* pressure in the torso so much that *prana* enters *Sushumna* and rises, and *apana vayu* is forced up. For this to happen, the yogi needs to have already obtained mastery in *Jalandhara Bandha* and *Mula Bandha*; otherwise, *prana* will escape from the torso altogether. This constitutes a more advanced form of *Uddiyana Bandha*, and one should only worry about it after inhalation- and exhalation-*Uddiyana Bandha*s are learned.

One should not attempt internal *kumbhaka* of more than about 10 seconds without proficiency in *Jalandhara Bandha*. Initial sessions of internal *kumbhaka* must be devoted to checking again and again that *Jalandhara Bandha* is applied properly, so that *prana* does not force itself into the head and air into the ears and cause damage. Once *Jalandhara Bandha* is mastered, awareness in internal *kumbhaka* has to be diverted towards mastery of *Mula Bandha*, although *kumbhaka* can be performed without this *bandha* and not cause harm. But it is only after gaining mastery of both that the third *bandha*, *Uddiyana Bandha*, can be applied during internal *kumbhaka*. It will make the holding of the other two *bandha*s initially more taxing; it will also increase pressure on the lung tissue, which the novice needs to avoid. Lung tissue needs to be made resilient by slowly increasing the length and

---

183 *Hatha Ratnavali of Shrinivasayogi* II.55

intensity of *kumbhaka*. This is the same principle as applies to muscles and tendons in *asana*, and it applies to most things in life. The intensification of *kumbhaka* is the last thing a beginner should look for.

Besides aiding the entry and rising of *prana* in *Sushumna*, according to the late Dr M.L. Gharote application of *Uddiyana Bandha* during internal *kumbhaka* also slows down the heartbeat by triggering the pressoreceptors in the abdominal viscera[184]. It has this effect in common with *Jalandhara* and *Mula Bandha*. All three *bandha*s (*bandha-traya*) work together to slow down the heart, deepen meditation, reduce the oxygen consumption of the body and hence prolong *kumbhaka*.

EXHALATION-UDDIYANA BANDHA

The *Yoga Kundalini Upanishad* proclaims that *Uddiyana Bandha* should be performed at the end of internal *kumbhaka* and at the beginning of the exhalation[185]. The same is recommended in the *Yuktabhavadeva*[186], the *Hatha Tatva Kaumudi* and the *Hatha Yoga Pradipika*[187]. When these texts talk about *Uddiyana Bandha* they are referring to what I call exhalation-*Uddiyana Bandha*. This form or phase of *Uddiyana Bandha* is similar to the internal *kumbhaka Uddiyana Bandha* in it uses the entire abdominal wall, i.e. the parts above and below the navel. But it is different in its effect and level of difficulty. Pulling the entire abdominal wall back in and towards the spine enables one to exhale fully and

---

184 Dr M. L. Gharote, *Pranayama: The Science of Breath*, Lonavla Yoga Institute, Lonavla, 2003, p. 25

185 *Yoga Kundalini Upanishad* stanzas 47–48

186 *Yuktabhavadeva of Bhavadeva Mishra* lxviii

187 *Hatha Yoga Pradipika* II.45

not leave a cubic centimetre of one's respiratory volume (i.e. vital capacity) behind. This way, the maximum CO_2 is exhaled and space for the new inhalation is created. This method creates the potential for a new larger inhalation and thus a longer subsequent *kumbhaka*. But there is another important effect. The instinctive action to create a complete exhalation would be to completely collapse the ribcage, but if you do that, you will notice a distinct drop and letdown of energy (due to descending *apana vayu*) at the end of the exhalation, with the thoracic spine flexing (becoming more kyphotic) and the head drooping forward. Exhalation-*Uddiyana Bandha* enables one to keep one's spirit lifted and keeps the spine and head upright by supplying a necessary burst of energy. This way, it enables the yogi to extend the exhalation as needed.

Mastery of *pranayama* is not achieved during inhalation or *kumbhaka*. It is achieved during the exhalation. During serious *pranayama* the exhalation is to be made double the length of the inhalation and half the length of internal *kumbhaka*. The most frequently quoted *pranayama* count in the *shastras* is 16 seconds for inhalation, 64 seconds for *kumbhaka* and 32 seconds for the exhalation, although this is a very advanced count that cannot be emulated by all. Some people could hold their breath for 64 seconds if they sucked the air in within a few seconds, then held it and after that exhaled with an open mouth in a few seconds. But that is not the point of *pranayama*. The point is to be able, after a 64-second *kumbhaka*, to distribute one's exhalation gracefully over another 32 seconds, not rush at the end and not run out of exhalable air either.

This is much, much more difficult than the preceding 64-second *kumbhaka*. But here the magic of *pranayama* happens. While *prana* is extracted from the environmental air in internal *kumbhaka*, distributing *prana* to the areas of the body takes place during a smooth, long, even exhalation. And it is also generally during the exhalation that Kundalini eventually rises. But these things are possible only when exhalation-*Uddiyana Bandha* is mastered, which consists of drawing both the upper and lower abdominal walls in towards the spine. This must not be applied too rapidly, as otherwise, the air would burst out of the nostrils. A smooth, even and long exhalation is required in *pranayama*. Applying external *Uddiyana Bandha* is a fine art learned in daily practice over a significant time frame.

In the hierarchy of the three forms of *Uddiyana Bandha*, the inhalation- *Uddiyana Bandha* needs to be learned first because without it, there is no complete yogic breathing cycle. Next in line, the exhalation- *Uddiyana Bandha* needs to be learned. It provides stamina in *pranayama* but requires constant remembrance. Only after that comes the internal (*kumbhaka*) *Uddiyana Bandha*. One should tackle it only once firmly established in *pranayama*.

EXTERNAL (KUMBHAKA) UDDIYANA/BAHYA UDDIYANA

There are two very different exercises described in yogic literature with almost the same name. One is often called simply *Uddiyana* and the other *Uddiyana Bandha*. Both are used to drive the vital down- current (*apana vayu*) up. Although they are similar in name, they are very different in their application. *Uddiyana Bandha* is a muscular contraction that pushes the abdominal contents in and up. It can only have an effect when there is air in the lungs and when the abdominal muscles can push against something. Therefore it is used only during inhalation, internal *kumbhaka* and *exhalation*.

When the lungs are empty, instead of the generic *bandha* a vacuum is used to suck the abdominal contents up into the thoracic cavity. This also raises *apana vayu*, but the physiological mechanism is different. External-*Uddiyana* takes place after a complete exhalation. During external *kumbhaka* the breath is arrested, the throat locked and a faked inhalation is performed during which the diaphragm rises. The abdominal muscles are completely relaxed, and the abdominal contents are sucked into the thoracic cavity, a process supported by the latissimus dorsi and trapezius. M.V. Bhole, MD, argues in a journal article in *Yoga Mimamsa* this is not really a *bandha*[188]. Strictly speaking this is correct, as it does not involve contraction of the muscle group central to the *bandha*, here the abdominals. For example, in *Jalandhara Bandha* the throat is contracted and creates a barrier. The same applies in *Mula Bandha*, due to the controlled pelvic diaphragm. *Uddiyana Bandha* in its narrower sense is thus only a true *bandha* when the abdominal wall is controlled. Readers often mistake the significance of why the technique is sometimes named *Uddiyana Bandha* and at other times *Uddiyana*. Adding to that confusion, some rather recent schools of yoga are ignorant of the fact that, besides *Uddiyana*, there exists an *Uddiyana Bandha*, which is not only different in nature but the true *bandha*. Compounding that confusion, Theos Bernard, following his teacher's nomenclature, named *Uddiyana* the dynamic flapping of the abdominal wall, sometimes called *Agnisara* or *Vahnisara Dhauti*, a technique which I call *Nauli* stage 1. This is a different exercise, and Swami Kuvalayananda taught that *Agnisara* does not even contain *Uddiyana* (i.e. no faked inhalation).

To differentiate *Uddiyana Bandha*, which is a muscular contraction that occurs during inhalation, internal *kumbhaka* and exhalation, I have named the passive *Uddiyana*, which only

---

188 *Yoga Mimamsa* XV.2

occurs during external (*bahya*) *kumbhaka*, external-*Uddiyana* or *Bahya Uddiyana* throughout this book. In doing so I have followed a tradition that to my knowledge was initiated by Shrinivasayogi, the author of the *Hatha Ratnavali*[189]. This text was probably set down during the 17th century, and its author was well aware of the need to disambiguate *Uddiyana* from *Uddiyana Bandha*.

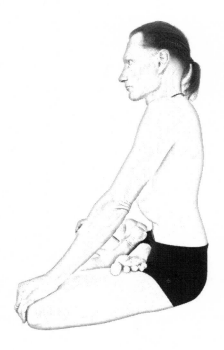

external *kumbhaka-Uddiyana*

The *Yoga Rahasya* states that, after exhalation, external (*bahya*) *kumbhaka* should be performed with a strong *Uddiyana*

189 Hatha Ratnavali of Shrinivasayogi II.56

and *Jalandhara Bandha*[190]. *Bahya Uddiyana* is said to alleviate abdominal-organ malfunctions such as diabetes and purify the *Manipura Chakra*. Besides its application during external *kumbhaka*, it is also used in *Nauli kriya* and in *mudra*s such as *Tadaga Mudra*, *Yoga Mudra* and *Maha Mudra*. It is a passive exercise in that its effect is not brought about by contracting the abdominal muscles but by creating upward suction through a faked inhalation after the throat is locked. Whereas the previous three active versions of *Uddiyana Bandha* activate the parasympathetic nervous system, slow down the heart and reduce blood pressure, this passive external-*Uddiyana* stimulates the sympathetic nervous system and speeds up the heartbeat. This it does mainly through the suction it applies to the adrenal glands. It can thus create a balance between the sympathetic and parasympathetic nervous systems, but its function also explains why external *kumbhaka* is more difficult than internal *kumbhaka*. The heart accelerates and consumes more oxygen while the lungs are completely empty. This might be another reason T. Krishnamacharya put so much emphasis on the difficult task of performing *Jalandhara Bandha* during external *kumbhaka* with *Bahya Uddiyana*. *Jalandhara* then neutralizes the sympathetic effect of external-*Uddiyana*.

While the other *bandha*s increase pressure in the abdominal organs, external-*Uddiyana* rapidly decreases intra-abdominal pressure from the normal. The organs are massaged by applying both types sequentially while going from internal to external kumbhaka and back. Old stagnant fluid is sucked and squeezed out of the organs, and then fresh blood is pumped back into

---

190 Yoga Rahasya I.62

them. Elimination of toxins is greatly enhanced, and the vitality of the organs is increased. The same is to be said for lung tissue.

In *pranayama*, external-*Uddiyana* is an advanced exercise that can only be tackled once the previous versions of *Uddiyana Bandha* have been learned. Especially if combined with *Jalandhara Bandha*, external-*Uddiyana* exerts a powerful suction on the brain and the cerebrospinal fluid. External-*Uddiyana* must be learned slowly during *Nauli*, *Tadaga Mudra* and *Yoga Mudra*, with all three offering themselves for this task because we do not have to observe count (i.e. other than in pranayama-proper, the length of each *kumbhaka* here does not have to be measured). The beginner should initially perform not over 2 or 3 repetitions per day and then slowly increase the rate over weeks and months.

Due to the intense pressure exchange, external-*Uddiyana*, like *Nauli*, should not be practised by women when they wish to conceive, during menstruation or during pregnancy. However, at all other times, it is very beneficial for the female reproductive system. Like *Nauli*, it can aid in repositioning a prolapsed uterus. The yogic tradition also holds that external-*Uddiyana* and *Nauli* can function as a form of natural contraceptive if used with certain yoga postures. It is not something that I would rely on exclusively.

Chapter 12

JALANDHARA BANDHA
(Stretching The Brain-Lock)

The late Swami Kuvalayananda explains that the term *Jalandhara* comes from *jalan* (the brain) and *dhara* (upward pull)[191]. Through the forward bending of the head, the *bandha* creates a pull on the spinal cord. Even more so than during internal *kumbhaka*, this is the case during external *kumbhaka*.

Asana practitioners must acquire an understanding of *Mula* and *Uddiyana Bandha* before venturing into *asana* practice, as it is more difficult to cultivate the *bandhas* once one is used to faulty *bandha*-less *asana* practice. The same is true for *Jalandhara Bandha* regarding *pranayama*. It is by far the most important *bandha* for *pranayama* and, while one may ignore the other two *bandhas* initially to some extent, *Jalandhara* is the essence of internal *kumbhaka*. So says the *Hatha Tatva Kaumudi* that *Jalandhara Bandha* is *kumbhaka* practice[192].

Its name comes from the stimulation it applies to the brain and spinal cord when placing the chin down on the chest in *kumbhaka*. One must first learn *Jalandhara Bandha* and only then commence internal (*antara*) *kumbhaka*. External (*bahya*) *kumbhaka*

---

191 *Yoga Mimamsa - A Quarterly Research Journal*, Kaivalyadhama, Lonavla, 1924-2004, II.3

192 Dr M.L. Gharote et al (eds. & transl.), *Hathatatvakaumudi*, The Lonavla Yoga Institite, Lonavla, 2007, p. 444

with *Jalandhara Bandha* is a more advanced form of practice, which should be learnt later on. During external *kumbhaka* additionally *Jalandhara Bandha* is not essential, whereas during internal *kumbhaka* it is.

EFFECTS

The *Hatha Yoga Pradipika* proclaims that, at the end of one's inhalation and before *kumbhaka* commences, one must apply *Jalandhara Bandha*[193], a statement repeated in the *Yuktabhavadeva*[194] and the *Hatha Tatva Kaumudi*[195], among other texts. The ancient *Brhadyogi Yajnavalkya Smrti* mentions[196] *Jalandhara Bandha* with a host of *Yoga Upanishads*, including the *Yoga Chudamani Upanishad*[197]. The *Dhyana Bindu Upanishad* expounds that when *Jalandhara Bandha* is performed, *amrita* (nectar of immortality) does not fall into the gastric fire (*agni*), where it is usually burned, and hence a long life is gained[198]. The same claim is made by the *Shiva Samhita*, which adds that through *Jalandhara Bandha* the yogi absorbs the nectar, which otherwise is destroyed[199]. The *Yoga Rahasya* proclaims that *Jalandhara* impedes the downward flow of *amrita*, hence prolonging life[200]. It also states that

---

193 *Hatha Yoga Pradipika* II.45

194 *Yuktabhavadeva of Bhavadeva Mishra* lxviii

195 *Hatha Tatva Kaumudi of Sundaradeva* XXXIX.87

196 Brhadyogi Yajnavalkya Smrti IX.186–190

197 Dr. M.M. Gharote et al (eds. & transl.), *Critical Edition of Selected Yogopanisads,* Lonavla Yoga Institute, Lonavla, 2017, p. 205

198 Dhyana Bindu Upanishad stanzas 78–79

199 Shiva Samhita IV.38–39

200 *Yoga Rahasya* I.72

Jalandhara maintains virility[201] and, by controlling the vital airs (*vayus*), overcomes many diseases[202]. The *Hatha Yoga Pradipika*[203] and the *Yoga Kundalini Upanishad*[204] both agree that *Jalandhara Bandha* moves *prana* into the central energy channel (*Sushumna*). The two outer *nadis*, *Ida* and *Pingala*, through which the life force usually dissipates, should be firmly blocked by contracting the throat.

Among modern authorities, Swami Kuvalayananda affirmed that under no circumstances should *kumbhaka* be practised without *Jalandhara Bandha*. T. Krishnamacharya taught that *Jalandhara Bandha* awakens Kundalini, but for this purpose the chin must be positioned way under the collarbones[205].

Most responsible authorities stated that, if (internal) *kumbhaka* is performed for longer than 10 seconds, *Jalandhara* is compulsory. Swami Ramdev teaches[206] that *Jalandhara Bandha* directs *prana* into the *Sushumna* (central energy channel), awakens the *Vishuddha* (throat) *Chakra* and alleviates throat ailments like thyroid malfunction and tonsillitis. The *Hatha Yoga Pradipika* informs us that *Jalandhara Bandha* prevents the air compressed in *kumbhaka* from entering the head[207], a fact that

---

201 *Yoga Rahasya* I.80

202 *Yoga Rahasya* I.81

203 *Hatha Yoga Pradipika* III.72

204 *Yoga Kundalini Upanishad* I.52

205 T. Krishnamacharya, *Yoga Makaranda*, rev. English edn, Media Garuda, Chennai, 2011, p. 105

206 Swami Ramdev, *Pranayama*, Divya Yog Mandir Trust, Hardwar, 2007, p. 21 353. *Yoga Kundalini Upanishad* stanza 51

207 Dr M.L. Gharote et al (eds. & transl.), *Hathapradipika of Svatmarama (10 chapters)*, Lonavla Yoga Institute, Lonavla, 2006, p. 142

can easily be verified by established practitioners when, upon releasing *Jalandhara* during internal *kumbhaka*, blood pressure in the head suddenly rises and one experiences ringing in the ears. *Jalandhara* also protects the ears, as the rising air during *kumbhaka* would otherwise enter the inner ear through the Eustachian tubes and cause ear pain and, in extreme cases, damage. Yogeshvaranand Paramahansa similarly opines that internal *kumbhaka* without *Jalandhara Bandha* should not be held for long, as *prana* may force itself into the brain, leading to fainting[208]. A faulty *Jalandhara Bandha* will usually announce itself first through headaches resulting from *pranayama*. This signal should be heeded before more damage results.

TECHNIQUE

Assume a yogic meditation position, such as *Padmasana*, *Virasana* or *Siddhasana*. However, only in *Padmasana* does *Jalandhara Bandha* apply the maximum stretch and thus optimum stimulation to the brain and spinal cord. Although this is also experienced in *Siddhasana* and the other meditation positions, it is only experienced to the maximum in *Padmasana*. There are two traditions in India regarding *Jalandhara Bandha*. In the somewhat more lenient tradition, the chin is simply placed into the jugular notch and, according to that teaching, *Jalandhara Bandha* and any *pranayama* sessions should be precluded by *Viparita Karani Mudra*. *Viparita Karani Mudra* is then interpreted as a somewhat watered-down version of *Sarvangasana*, in which the angle of the torso does not have to be vertical to the floor.

---

208 Yogeshvaranand Paramahansa, *First Steps to Higher Yoga*, Yoga Niketan Trust, New Delhi, 2001, p. 359

This view was shown in the section on *Viparita Karani Mudra* to be inconsistent with *shastra*.

CHIN ON CHEST

The other tradition is somewhat stricter in its requirements. T. Krishnamacharya taught in this tradition[209], which has the chin placed way down on the sternum (breastbone). According to this teaching, *Viparita Karani Mudra* does not refer to a particular body position but simply means to invert the body for a very long time until *amrita* is steadied and thus *pratyahara* achieved. The two postures used for *Viparita Karani* are *Shirshasana* and *Sarvangasana*. Paramount in both is alignment, i.e. the body has to be absolutely vertical to the floor in either of them. According to this tradition, *Sarvangasana* and *Halasana* (plow posture, which follows *Sarvangasana)* need to be practised before practising *pranayama* because these postures teach the right position for *Jalandhara Bandha*, which is not to place the chin into the jugular notch but down on the sternum at exactly the place where it is in *Sarvangasana*. Applying *Jalandhara Bandha* is defined as placing the chin on the chest also in the *Shiva Samhita*[210] and *Gheranda Samhita*[211]. As it rarely is advised to go straight into *Sarvangasana* without preparation or warm-up, the necessity for practising *Sarvangasana* before *Jalandhara Bandha* and *pranayama* requires you first to perform your general *asana* practice, then inversions such as *Sarvangasana*, followed by *pranayama* practice with *Jalandhara Bandha*.

---

209 T. Krishnamacharya, *Yoga Makaranda*, rev. English edn, Media Garuda, Chennai, 2011, p. 105

210 *Shiva Samhita* IV.38

211 *Gheranda Samhita* III.10

Having prepared the neck *with Sarvangasana for Jalandhara Bandha*, we inhale deeply and lift the chest high. The lifting of the chest will allow us to inhale more deeply as the thorax expands more, but it will also decrease the range of movement we have for bending the neck down. Lifting the chest high decreases any strain on the neck, which is especially important for novices. The powerfully expanded chest created through the lift will eventually enable us to stay in *kumbhaka* for longer.

The next important step in establishing *Jalandhara Bandha* is to lock the throat through swallowing. Understand that simply placing the chin on the chest does not constitute *Jalandhara Bandha*; it only means that now you have assumed '*Jalandhara Bandha* position'. This is perilously left out in the teaching of many modern schools, and without it *Jalandhara Bandha* remains impotent and *kumbhaka* is dangerous. *Jalandhara Bandha* is defined as contraction of the throat in the *Hatha Ratnavali*[212], *Shiva Samhita*[213], *Gheranda Samhita*[214], *Hatha Yoga Pradipika*[215] and *Yoga Kundalini Upanishad*[216]. Also, *Dattatreya's Yogashastra* teaches that *Jalandhara Bandha* is the dual action of contracting the throat and pressing the chin on the chest[217]. How anybody can teach it as simply placing the chin down is beyond my understanding, as it means that *vayu* can enter the head and cause damage.

---

212 *Hatha Ratnavali of Shrinivasayogi* II.8

213 *Shiva Samhita* IV.38

214 *Gheranda Samhita* III.10

215 *Hatha Yoga Pradipika* III.71

216 *Yoga Kundalini Upanishad* I.51

217 Dr M.M. Gharote (ed.), *Dattatreyayogasastram*, Lonavla Yoga Institute, Lonavla, 2015, p. 67

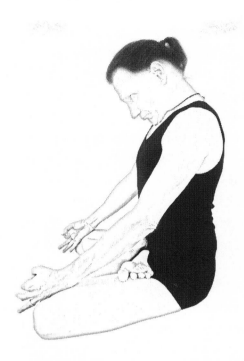

Jalandhara Bandha **during internal** *kumbhaka*

To activate *Jalandhara Bandha* means to swallow as if one is swallowing saliva and, once the throat muscles grip, to maintain that grip for the remainder of the breath retention. The test of whether *Jalandhara Bandha* is on properly is to breathe in or out. If you cannot breathe, even if trying, then and only then is *Jalandhara* correct. Apply this test the first few hundred times you perform the *bandha*.

Even if you have mastered it, re-check yourself regularly, particularly if you experience adverse symptoms such as pressure in the head, irritability or headaches. If you can breathe despite the fact that you have your chin in position, you are not applying *Jalandhara Bandha*! If need be, swallow several times until the throat is locked so that no air (*vayu*) can pass into the head. Contract the throat and place the chin low down on the sternum. The lower down you place it, the more stimulation the brain and the spinal cord will receive. However, especially initially, proceed with care and don't strain the neck, as it may lead to headaches.

Now hold *kumbhaka* to capacity and not more. That we hold *kumbhaka* only to capacity, but do not hold a *kumbhaka* of pre- determined length (i.e. *matra*), means we are not yet performing *pranayama*-proper but only exercising the *bandha* in the *mudra* stage. Once you have reached your capacity to retain the breath, lift your head, release your throat and exhale gently – but exactly in this order and no other. Never release your throat first and then lift your head, as the *prana* may still enter the head. The air should not burst out but come out in an even stream for the entire length of the exhalation. If you have to let the air out in bursts or gasp for the inhalation, you have exceeded your capacity. The bursting out and gasping constitute a loss of *prana* rather than a gain. You have created demerit instead of merit.

It is important always to accept and honour one's limitations in *pranayama*. If not, lung tissue can be damaged, which in cases of ruthless practice can lead to emphysema. Ranjit Sen Gupta believes that a proper *Jalandhara Bandha* is a safety precaution against emphysema[218]. It is important not to inhale so deeply that the lungs are overstretched. Nobody else can tell you how much you have to inhale. Be sensitive.

---

218 Ranjit Sen Gupta, *Pranayama: A Conscious Way of Breathing*, New Age Books, Delhi, 2000, p. 61

JALANDHARA BANDHA DURING EXTERNAL (BAHYA) KUMBHAKA

There is agreement that *Jalandhara Bandha* has to be applied during internal *kumbhaka* to prevent the rise of air and *prana* into the head. Opinions differ, however, where external (*bahya*) *kumbhaka* is concerned (i.e. suspending the breath after and exhalation). The *Yoga Rahasya* insists on *Jalandhara Bandha* during external *kumbhaka*[219]. Other authorities mention *Jalandhara Bandha* only in internal *kumbhaka*. The reason *Jalandhara Bandha* during external *kumbhaka* is more difficult is that you have to bend your head down much lower to reach the chest, as the chest in external *kumbhaka* is deflated and dropped.

The main reason for *Jalandhara Bandha* – protecting the brain from the pressure of the fully inflated chest – does not apply to external *kumbhaka*, as the air pressure is very low after a full exhalation. But *Jalandhara Bandha* during external *kumbhaka* is very beneficial due to the intense stimulation it applies to the brain via the spinal cord. It is a powerful Kundalini technique, but much more difficult than *Jalandhara Bandha* during internal (*antara*) *kumbhaka*.

Jalandhara Bandha during *antara kumbhaka* must be thoroughly mastered before this more advanced version of the *bandha* is tackled. When building up to *Jalandhara Bandha* during external *kumbhaka*, prepare by increasing your time spent in *Sarvangasana* and *Halasana*. Also, always practise your external *kumbhaka*s after your *asana* practice, as only in this case will your neck be adequately prepared for the additional workload. When practising *Jalandhara Bandha* during external *kumbhaka*, lift your chest as high as you can and draw your shoulders forward so

---

219 *Yoga Rahasya* I.62

the sternum and clavicles move forward and upwards to meet the chin.

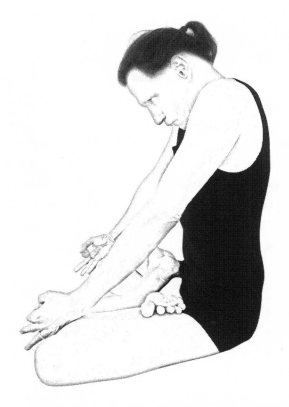

Jalandhara Bandha **during external** *kumbhaka*

This amounts to 'hunching of the shoulders around the ears', which is usually sneered at in all *asanas*. The only other posture where this is allowed is *Sarvangasana* (shoulder stand), which interestingly enough, is the posture that induces the correct *Jalandhara Bandha* position.

And extensive internal *kumbhaka*s with *Jalandhara Bandha* must be mastered before serious external *kumbhaka*s with count are tackled. Besides the Kundalini pull on the spinal cord, another strong reason teachers like T. Krishnamacharya insist on *Jalandhara Bandha* during external *kumbhaka* is its influence on the nervous system and blood circulation.

By bending the head down low and contracting the throat, pressure is exerted on the carotid sinuses. This activates the parasympathetic nervous system, lowers the blood pressure and drops the heart rate. The general purpose of the carotid sinuses is to detect rising blood pressure in the carotid arteries, which if unchecked, could damage the delicate blood vessels in the brain and eventually lead to a stroke. When the blood pressure in the carotid arteries rises, they will expand and thus put pressure on the carotid sinuses. The sinuses are now stimulated and, as a safety mechanism, they activate the parasympathetic nervous system to both drop the blood pressure back down and slow the heart rate. *Jalandhara Bandha* uses this very mechanism to improve and increase *kumbhaka*. The parasympathetic nervous system enables you to relax into the *kumbhaka*s and lowering the heart rate and dropping the blood pressure lead to a decrease in oxygen consumption of the organism. Hence, through *Jalandhara Bandha* the length of *kumbhaka* can be increased, resulting in many benefits such as deeper meditation and eventually the deletion of negative conditioning. Not only that, but success in *kumbhaka* and *pranayama* relies on success in *Jalandhara Bandha*. Its importance cannot be overemphasized.

There is some confusion as to applying *Jalandhara Bandha* outside of *kumbhaka*, i.e. placing the chin on the chest during meditation and certain asanas. The Yoga Kundalini Upanishad states that *Jalandhara Bandha* is an impediment to Kundalini rising[220]. This means that outside of *kumbhaka Jalandhara*

---

220 Sir John Woodroffe, *The Serpent Power*, Ganesh & CO, Madras, 1995, p. 211

Bandha should not be applied. It is also a misunderstanding to believe that simply resting the chin on the sternum can be called *Jalandhara Bandha*. As the *Hatharatnavali of Shrinivasayogi* confirms[221] *Jalandhara Bandha* is the contraction of the throat, and not just the position of the head. To settle the issue, the *Hatharatnavali* states[222] that *Jalandhara Bandha* is only complete when contracting the throat. This is the same definition as put forward in *Dattatreya's Yogashastra*[223].

TRIBANDHA OR BANDHATRAYA

These are terms used for the simultaneous application of all three *bandhas* in external or internal *kumbhaka* with miraculous effects. *Mula Bandha* drives *apana vayu* upwards; *Jalandhara Bandha* sends *prana vayu* downwards where it fans *agni*. The fanned *agni/apana* compound is then moved up into *Sushumna* with *Uddiyana Bandha*.

---

221 Dr M.L. Gharote et al (eds. & transl.), *Hatharatnavali of Shrinivasayogi*, The Lonavla Yoga Institite, Lonavla, 2009, p. 44

222 Dr M.L. Gharote et al (eds. & transl.), *Hatharatnavali of Shrinivasayogi*, The Lonavla Yoga Institite, Lonavla, 2009, p. 65

223 Dr M.M. Gharote (ed.), *Dattatreyayogasastram,* Lonavla Yoga Institute, Lonavla, 2015, p. 67

Chapter 13

SHANKA MUDRA
(Conch Seal)

This is a hand *mudra* (*hasta mudra*) and gets little treatment in scripture, but it is employed by almost every Indian yoga tradition. Most hand *mudras* are hardly ever mentioned in scripture. *Shanka Mudra* is so-called because in it, the fingers form the shape of a conch. The pointing and middle fingers are folded and placed on the mount of the thumb. The ring and little finger are placed together and are held opposite the thumb. *Shanka Mudra* is used to open and close the respective nostrils during alternate nostril breathing, called *Nadi Shuddhi* if done without *kumbhaka,* and *Nadi Shodhana* if done with *kumbhaka.* *Nadi Shuddhi* is to be mastered first.

In Vedanta the symbolism of the fingers is:

Thumb	Brahman (infinite consciousness)
Pointing finger	*atman* (individual self)
Middle finger	*buddhi* (intellect)
Ring finger	*manas* (mind)
Little finger	*kaya* (body)

In the Brahmanical tradition only the right hand is used for performing this *mudra.* The left hand in India is used for cleaning one's *derriere.* It is considered unclean and therefore not used while eating or touching one's face. Even touching others with one's left hand can be considered an insult. But Tantrics and particularly left-hand Tantrics will often use the left hand to perform this *mudra*, and part of the reasoning here is to defy the order given by Brahmanical tradition. The Tantrics themselves would argue more along the line it was to restore a philosophical sense of balance, i.e. because the Divine is everywhere it must also be in the left hand. If you do have a shoulder imbalance caused by excess use of the right arm, you may find it beneficial to alternate.

Shanka Mudra is used during an active purification process. The individual self and intellect are already in synchronicity with infinite consciousness and, in a gesture of obedience, are bowing to Brahman. The body and mind, however, need to be purified so Brahman may be attained. Hence, they are used here in interaction with the thumb, representing Brahman. Some schools teach an alternative version in which the first and second fingers are resting on the third eye. This is the version of the *mudra* I myself am applying.

When using *Shanka Mudra*, touch the nostril only to the extent that the nostril closes, not more. The septum should not be squeezed to the extent that it warps into one direction. The touch should be gentle. During alternate nostril breathing and when using *Shanka Mudra*, no *Ujjayi* sound is produced, and the throat is kept completely unrestricted. The principle applied here is that restriction is only applied once, i.e. either at the nostril or at the throat but not in both places at the same time. Keep spine and head upright. Do not turn the head to the left when your right thumb applies pressure to the right nostril. Also, do not lift your right shoulder (assuming that you are using your right hand to manipulate your nostrils). Sometimes practise in front of a mirror (not too often, mirrors draw *prana* to the surface, the opposite of what you want to happen) or film yourself to ensure that head, shoulder and spine positions are correct. And see that both collarbones are on the same level and do not lift the collarbone on the right. Rather than lifting the arm out to the side, which could cause shoulder imbalance and eventually impingement, let the arm hang down so your elbow touches the ribcage; otherwise, you may tire quickly and build up tension. The version in which the arm is held out to the side is not sustainable and anatomically unsound.

When using *Shanka Mudra*, as in all other *pranayamas*, we want to sit in a traditional meditation *asana*, which fulfils these requirements:

- Head, neck and spine in a straight line
- Knees firmly on the floor and not hovering above it
- Both soles of the feet and palms of the hand turned upwards in a receptive position.

There are variant names for this *mudra* such as *Vishnu Mudra* or *Mrgu Mudra* (Deer Seal), but the purpose and technique are the same. The variant names indicate the use of the *mudra* by different schools. The name *Shanka Mudra* is generally used by Shaivite schools since Shankar (conch blower) is one of Lord Shiva's epithets.

TECHNIQUE

Shanka Mudra is exclusively used during alternate nostril breathing (*Nadi Shuddhi* or *Nadi Shodhana*), the most important pranayama method with multiple layers of technique. I have described the method and all its attached layers in great detail in *Pranayama The Breath of Yoga* and it is beyond the scope of this book. To be complete, however, I will describe here the direct action performed during application of the *mudra* only. Depending on which hand is used the respective fingers of that hand are used to close the right nostril and one inhales through the left nostril. At the conclusion of the inhalation the left nostril is then closed, and exhalation is performed through the right nostril. This is followed by an inhalation through the right nostril. The right nostril is then again closed and exhalation through the left nostril is performed. This constitutes one round of alternate nostril breathing followed immediately by the second inhalation through the left nostril. After a predetermined number of rounds or time period the practice is always concluded by an exhalation through the left nostril. A beginners practice may involve 5 minutes of such breathing. An advanced practice may last up to 30 minutes with internal and external *kumbhakas* included, preceded by rapid breathing pranayamas such as *Kapalabhati* and *Bhastrika*.

Shanka Mudra is additionally used when only a half-cycle of alternate nostril breathing is practiced. The first half-cycle of alternate nostril breathing consists of inhaling through the left and exhaling through the right nostril. This half-cycle is exclusively practised when the intention is to increase only lunar *prana*, which powers introversion, relativistic mind, the right wholistic-intuitive brain hemisphere, afferent (incoming) nerve currents, sensory neurons, anabolism and the parasympathetic nervous system. Because of its association with lunar prana, this method of breathing is called *Chandra Bhedana* (Lunar-Piercing). When practising *Chandra Bhedana*, we would then perform a pre-determined number of rounds during which all inhalations are taken through the left nostril and all exhalations are performed through the right nostril.

The second half-cycle of alternate nostril breathing consists of inhaling through the right and exhaling through the left nostril. This half-cycle is exclusively practised when the intention is to increase only solar *prana*, which powers extraversion, fundamentalist mind, the left analytical-rationalistic brain hemisphere, efferent (outgoing) nerve currents, motor neurons, catabolism and the sympathetic nervous system. Because of its association with solar *prana* this method of breathing is called *Surya Bhedana* (Sun-Piercing). When practising *Surya Bhedana*, we perform a pre-determined number of rounds during which all inhalations are taken through the right nostril and all exhalations are performed through the left nostril.

Chandra or *Surya Bhedana* should be practiced only to bring back to balance an existing solar or lunar aggravation. This means that our psyche leans excessively to either the solar or lunar side with the associated manifestations and tendencies listed above. For more details, please consult my text *Pranayama The Breath of Yoga*.

Shanka Mudra

143

Chapter 14

KAKI MUDRA (Crow Seal)

Kaki and *Kaka Mudra* are alternative spellings of the same *mudra*. *Gheranda Samhita* in stanza III.66 states that the *Kaki Mudra* consists of forming a crow beak with one's mouth and slowly drinking the air through this thus-formed aperture [224]. This practice is thought to lead to freedom from disease and long life. The technique is more extensively described in the *Shiva Samhita* but here in the pranayama section. In the *Shiva Samhita* an entire ten stanzas are dedicated to *Kaki Mudra* and its effects[225]. Again we find the connection with drinking air with the crow beak, additionally combined with turning the tongue up (*Jihva Bandha*) and *kumbhaka*[226]. Stanza 74 suggests doing this in the morning and the evening and stanza 75 suggests to even do it day and night. The remaining stanzas are devoted to repeatedly pressing the importance of the upturned tongue and to exaggerated results we may derive from the technique.

The important 10-chapter edition of the *Hatha Yoga Pradipika* also teaches the method[227]. Also, here we find the connection

---

224 This stanza appears on p. 95 of the Kaivalyadhama Edition. R.B.S. Chandra Vasu's edition has this stanza at III.86-87, which is p. 33-34.

225 R.B.S. Chandra Vasu (transl.), *The Shiva Samhita*, Sri Satguru Publications, Delhi, 1986, p. 35-37

226 *Shiva Samhita* stanza III.73

227 Dr M.L. Gharote et al (eds. & transl.), *Hathapradipika of Svatmarama (10 chapters)*, Lonavla Yoga Institute, Lonavla, 2006, p. 124

between the crow beak, the upturned tongue, and the drinking-like quality of the inhalation. The translator points out that the technique here is called *Kaka Cancuka* but that it is the same as the *Kaki Mudra* in the *Gheranda Samhita*. The monumental 800-page *Hathatatva Kaumudi of Sundaradeva* describes the method at XII.1-11[228]. Again here, the combination of inhalation through the crow beak, *kumbhaka* involving *Jihva Bandha*, or if possible *Khechari Mudra* (a more advanced version of *Jihva Bandha*, described in Section 5, *Mudra* 31), and then exhaling through both nostrils. The *Hatha Tatva Kaumudi* argues that *Kaka Mudra* frees from premature death[229] and that combined with *Shanmukhi Mudra* (described in Section 5, *Mudra* 29) it raises Kundalini, if performed daily to capacity[230]. Both the 10-chapter edition of the *Hatha Yoga Pradipika* and the *Hathatatva Kaumudi* mention that during *Kaki Mudra,* the tongue is rolled as is done during *Shitali Pranayama,* and that the air is drawn in through the rolled tongue. *Shitali* is a *pranayama* technique that I have described in *Pranayama The Breath of Yoga*. Some scriptures and commentators consider both techniques to be the same. When observing crows, you can notice they often have their beaks half-open and their tongues sticking out. When I was instructed in *Kaki Mudra*, the detail of inhaling through the rolled tongue was omitted. For years I struggled with manifesting the supposed benefits of the *mudra*. Without inhaling through the rolled tongue, simply by

---

228 Dr M.L. Gharote et al (eds. & transl.), *Hathatatvakaumudi,* The Lonavla Yoga Institite, Lonavla, 2007, p. 147-149

229 Dr M.L. Gharote et al (eds. & transl.), *Hathatatvakaumudi,* The Lonavla Yoga Institite, Lonavla, 2007, p. 147

230 Dr. M.L. Gharote et al (eds. & transl.), *Hathatatvakaumudi,* The Lonavla Yoga Institite, Lonavla, 2007, p. 684

forming with one's mouth a crow beak, the *mudra* soon becomes very unpleasant as it dries out the mouth and the throat. It is only through scriptural study I noticed that a vital part of the instruction was omitted. Once I added the rolled tongue the *mudra* quickly lived up to its promises as listed in *shastra* (most, anyway).

What is then the difference between *Kaki Mudra* and *Shitali*? In reality, there is little difference. The method is called *Shitali* when we look at its positioning within a *pranayama* sequence. The term *Shitali* is often used when referring to the ratio between inhalation and exhalation, the exact number of repetitions, and its function to reduce excess *pitta*[231] created by other techniques. The term *Kaki Mudra* more often is used when the actual position of the mouth is high-lighted. We could state that the pranayama technique *Shitali* occurs in *Kaki Mudra*. Are there any perceived differences between *Shitali* and *Kaki Mudra*? Descriptions of *Shitali* rarely include the instruction to

---

231 *Vata, pitta* and *kapha,* according to *Ayurveda,* are the three humors of the body. Similar to the other two, translating this complex term into English does *pitta* little justice. Orientalists translated it as 'bile' but this belies the complexity of the term. *Pitta* is vitiated *agni*, which is pure, elemental fire. *Pitta* is also derived from *sattva*, intelligence, but being the energy system of the body, it easily overheats and causes inflamation and other health problems. In *Ayurveda* our main goal would be to balance *pitta* with the other two humors to guarantee a long life. In yoga our main focus is to convert a maximum of *pitta* back into elemental fire and intelligence. Such conversion supports the understanding of the order of the cosmos and enables us to align ourselves with the Divine, which is cosmic intelligence. In order to comprehend the differences in outlook between yoga and Ayurveda we need to appreciate that Ayurveda is an *upaveda* (ancillary *Veda*) that deals with life extension. Yoga on the other hand is a *darshana* (system of philosophy) that deals with spiritual liberation.

form a crow beak. However, it is difficult the stick out the rolled tongue without performing some sort of crow beak. I found that the method, however we call it, becomes more efficient the more we stick out the lips and the tongue, as both together form a larger cavity used to moisten the incoming air. On a side note, *Kaki Mudra* usually also forms part of *Shanmukhi Mudra,* described in Section 5, *Mudra* 29. Especially when extensively practising this important *mudra,* it quickly becomes important that the crow beak alone is not enough but must involve the rolled tongue. Otherwise, the mouth dries out very quickly and the *mudra* becomes not only unpleasant but also scant beneficial effects manifest.

TECHNIQUE

Form a crow beak with your lips, letting the lips protrude as much as possible. Then roll your tongue and stick it out beyond the lips. Moisten the tongue as much as needed with saliva so it doesn't dry during inhalation. This is done to add moisture to the respiratory system, which increases *kapha* and reduces excess *pitta*. Upon inhaling, imagine that you suck in the air as if it was water. At the conclusion of the inhalation, place the tongue into *Jihva Bandha* and exhale through the nose, producing the *Ujjayi* sound.

Kaki Mudra **with** *Shitali*

Make the inhalation as long as the exhalation, i.e. the ratio is 1:1. Make each breath as long as possible, ideally coming close to a cycle length of one minute[232]. The official demarcation line between *Kaka Mudra* and *Shitali* is that during *Shitali* count is

---

232 The cycle length of a breath is the entire length of all it's components added up. In this case this is the length of the inhalation plus the length of the exhalation. In complex *pranayamas* the cycle length also includes the length of internal and possibly external *kumbhakas*.

used. This means that if you are using a *mantra* to count the length of each breath (and hopefully a metronome to determine that each interval is accurate), you are practising *Shitali*. An ideal time to do so in your practice is at the conclusion of your *pranayama* practice and before *Shavasana* (corpse posture). The practice can then equalize *pitta* and *kapha*. Especially when practising *Shakti Chalana Mudra* (Power Conduction Seal) it is easy to aggravate *pitta*. Many practices used for *Shakti Chalana*, especially *Nauli, Kapalabhati* and *Surya Bhedana*, increase *pitta*. Any left-over and un-accounted for *pitta* can, at the end of one's practice, be neutralized using *Kaki Mudra/ Shitali*. The longer each breath is and the more the tongue is moistened, the more *pitta* can be neutralized. The other important factor is the number of rounds/ breaths. *Kaki Mudra* breaths are traditionally performed in odd numbers. The lowest number used generally is three, said to represent the three *gunas*[233]. Another popular number is seven, the number of the main *chakras*. The maximum number is usually 21, i.e. three by seven, but this constitutes an extreme practice. As long as each breath is drawn out to its maximum length, most levels of *pitta* aggravation can be kept under control by doing fewer repetitions[234]. I should mention this method cannot be practised in polluted air as we find it in many of today's metropolises. Since we are by-passing the nose,

---

233 The three *gunas* are the qualities or elementary particles of *prakriti* (nature). They are *tamas, rajas* and *sattva*, handily translatable as mass-particle, energy-particle and intelligence-particle.

234 This statement is based on a cycle length of 1 minute, i.e. inhalation and exhalation are each approximately 30 second long. If shorter breaths are used, more repetitions are to be done to achieve a similar effect.

we also cannot utilize the nose's capacity of air filtration, which it is capable of with the many fine hairs it contains.

A variation of *Kaki Mudra* includes internal *kumbhaka*. After inhaling, perform *kumbhaka* to capacity by initiating *Jalandhara Bandha*. Then lift your head and exhale. If this practice is performed then *Jihva Bandha* is engaged at the beginning of the *kumbhaka*, rather than at the beginning of the exhalation. From my personal experience, I prefer to practice my internal and external *kumbhakas* during *Nadi Shodhana/ Chandra Bhedana* and additional external *kumbhakas* during *Nauli*. After that, I consider it unnecessary to practice additional *kumbhakas* during *Kaki Mudra/ Shitali*, making my total practice too long. I regularly practice more than 10 – 15 minutes of *Kaki Mudra/ Shitali* to neutralize excess *pitta*. *Kumbhakas* would extend this practice to 20 or more minutes, which is unreasonable, considering the durations already spent practising other techniques.

During *Bhujangi-*, and *Kaki Mudras* but also during *Shitali-*, and *Sitkari Pranayamas,* all inhalations are taken through the mouth, but exhalations are always performed through the nose. It is rarely, if ever, that yogis exhale through the mouth, which is thought to lead to losing *prana*.

EFFECTS

This *mudra* is said to extend longevity due to increase of *kapha* and the storing of liquified *prana*. It neutralizes *pitta*, cools the body, and according to the *shastras* destroys diseases and decrepitude.

SECTION 3:

PRATYAHARA MUDRAS

In this section, you will find all *mudras*, which are essential to *pratyahara*, the fifth limb of yoga, defined as independence from sensory stimulus. The common feature amongst this group of *mudras* is that they are closing the lunar gates and are projecting lunar *prana* back into the body, thus aiding *pratyahara*. *Pratyahara* in the system of yoga is positioned after *pranayama* (breathing exercises), but before the various stages of mental exercises, *dharana* (concentration), *dhyana* (meditation) and *samadhi* (revelation). The term *pratyahara* is often translated as sense withdrawal, a phrase that tells us little about what it actually is. The deeper meaning of *pratyahara* is independence (or freedom) from sensory (or external) stimulus. The lunar gates are the sensory gates of the body. Lunar *prana* reaches out through the lunar gates, attaches itself to the sense objects and pulls the mind with it. This process is referred to in the *Yoga Sutra* and in sage Vyasa's commentary on it (*Yoga Bhashya*) [235].

Lunar *prana* is *prana* associated with experiencing the world and creating an image of it. In a person who is not centred, this

---

235 *Yoga Sutra* II.54-55

process will destabilize the mind, similarly to a stone dropped into a still lake will ruffle the surface so that whatever is reflected in it, will appear distorted. That is why Patanjali, the author of the *Yoga Sutra*, defines yoga as the stilling of the mind waves[236].

There are varying approaches to *pratyahara*, an *asana*-based approach, a *pranayama*-focussed approach, and a mind-centred approach. The three approaches are not exclusive but are ideally practised side-by-side. The physical tier of *pratyahara* was taught by the *siddha* Gorakhnath, and the *mudras* in Section 1, chiefly *Viparita Karani* reflect this approach[237]. The *pranayama* aspect of *pratyahara* was handed down in the tradition of the sages Yajnavalkya and Vasishta[238]. The *mudras* taught in Section 2 represent this approach. The current group of *mudras* deals with the third approach, called the mental or *Raja Yoga* approach to *pratyahara*. In *Raja Yoga pratyahara* means the reflecting of lunar *prana*, which leaks out through the sensory gates, back into the body via seals. This means we are using *mudras* to project *prana* associated with the audio, visual, kinaesthetic/tactile, olfactory and gustatory functions back into the body. This is one of the main factors contributing to success in meditation. These group of *mudras* could also be called meditation *mudras*, but the term for meditation used in yoga, *dhyana*, primarily implies success

---

236 *Yoga Sutra* I.2

237 Gorakhnath was the founder of the *Hatha* tradition. He authored several *shastras* but his first and most influential is the *Goraksha Shataka*.

238 Yajnavalkya and Vasishta are two *Vedic rishis* of prime importance. Yajnavalkya is the main focus of the ancient *Brhad Aranyaka Upanishad*. Vasishta looms large in the *Vedas* and also has a important role in the *Ramayana*. For our context, the two *rishis* are the authors of the important *yoga shastras Vasishta Samhita* and *Yoga Yajnavalkya*, which describe *Vedic* yoga.

in, and deepening of, *pratyahara* and *dharana*, without being a separate technique of its own.

To understand the content of this chapter, we need to look briefly into yoga's concept of mind. Yoga calls the mind *manas*, and from this Sanskrit term, the English *man, woman* and *human* are derived. We could thus define the human being as the thinking animal, with the dangers and advantages this may bring (In biology, humanoids do not represent a kingdom of their own but are taxonomically filed under the animal kingdom. Other kingdoms are plants, fungi, and three kingdoms of microbes). Yoga puts a lot of emphasis on differentiating mind (*manas*) from intelligence or intellect (*buddhi*). *Manas* and *buddhi* are like computer applications that can work on similar problems, but which one we choose depends on whether our preference to perform a particular task is speed or quality. In most circumstances it is enough to opt for speed and in this case, we choose *manas*. *Manas* is the application we choose when survival, or any quick decision to which we allocate only a few seconds, is at stake. The choice 'mind/*manas*' was enough in most situations that we encountered during the first few million years of planetary evolution and is sufficient in many situations that we confront during daily life today. The mind uses about 1 second for an average analysis, whereas the yogic definition of intelligence/ *buddhi* is to sustain a focus on the very same object for at least three hours. That means yoga thinks that intelligence only comes into play when we attempt to understand a complex object. But yoga sees the mind (*manas*) simply as an organizer of sensory data, akin to a master sense. If we define perception as the intake of raw sensory data derived through the senses, then the *manas*/ mind is the cognizer of that data.

Cognition processes raw sensory data so a quick decision can be made and the object at hand can be identified swiftly, often just for survival. If we perceive a certain sound or visual image, we do not sit down and meditate deeply over what the meaning of that sensory input might be and what it could mean regarding the origin of the universe – which would be a typical inquiry undertaken by *buddhi*, the intelligence. Contrary to that, within a split second our *manas*/ mind would compare the signal with all sensory data perceived in the past and would spit out whether this signal could mean the approach of danger or something harmless, such as a supply of food. If this cognition took more than about 1 to 1.5 seconds, we wouldn't be able to survive.

The mind is thus an incredible survival tool, but this benefit comes at the expense of precision. To achieve the feat of cognising quickly, the mind does not deeply analyse data but simply superimposes all data collected onto the present object until a reasonably close match is achieved. But this match is not close enough for most of the complex tasks that occur in today's human society. For example, the credit given to witness testimonies in criminal court proceedings has been more and more eroded. This is because what people believe to have seen and what actually took place are often two different things. The mind/ *manas* becomes an obstacle particularly when we want to obtain deep knowledge about the world as it truly is (in yoga called *vijnana, prajna* or *rta*) or knowledge of the true self (*jnana*). Because the mind identifies simply by superimposing the past onto the present, it will only ever show us what was a reasonably close match in the past. It will use past conditioning to produce the best shot at the truth it can provide in the shortest time possible. This shouldn't instil us with a lot of trust in the mind.

Manifold problems in human life occur due to that mechanism. For example, we tend to relate to others, even select our life partners, according to their ability to fulfil our subconscious needs, dictated to us by our past hurts, rather than relating to them according to who they truly are. That sounds already scary enough. But it is particularly the process of meditation impeded by this structure of the mind (*manas*). The tendency of the mind to superimpose past conditioning (*vasana*) and subconscious imprint (*samskara*) onto the present, stops us from arriving in the present. Patanjali said, 'Yoga is the suspension of the fluctuations of the mind'[239]. In the following *sutra* he stated this suspension of the mind is the precursor to the mystical state[240].

However, suspension of mind is impossible in one step: it is a multi-step process. At the outset of the third chapter of the *Yoga Sutra*, Patanjali defines concentration (*dharana*, the sixth limb, the binding of the mind to a place) as one important step in this process[241]. Due to its task as an organizer and interpreter of sensory data, the mind is orientated outwards. Outward orientation is not helpful in meditation. By suspending the mind, inward focus, and thus meditation, become possible.

We now turn to what is one of the essential keys to meditation – the secret to *pratyahara*, Patanjali's fifth limb of yoga. The mind organizes and compares data from five senses: the eyes, ears, nose, taste buds and the tactile organ, the skin. Because of this, the mind has five components or aspects, which are the audio,

239 Yoga Sutra I.2
240 Yoga Sutra I.3
241 Yoga Sutra III.1

visual, kinaesthetic/tactile, olfactory and gustatory aspects of mind. While it is sufficient initially to bind the combined mind to a single place, such as the visualization of the *chakras* or a *mantra*, to practise concentration effectively, the five components of the mind need to be bound to their respective places. This means, for example, that the visual aspect of the mind needs to be bound to a visual signal. If you use only an auditory signal, you will leave the visual cortex to go about its (subconscious) activities unrestrained. Because each sensory component of the mind, if unattended to, still runs rampant, all components need to be engaged by *mudras*. This is a great skill, and to acquire it we need to learn how to bind them one after the other. As we add more components, meditation will deepen.

If you sit in meditation and simply focus on a sound or visual image, this will engage only your conscious mind. The conscious mind, however, utilizes only a few per cent of the total computing power of your mind. A much larger part is taken up by the subconscious mind. To harness the power of the subconscious mind for meditation we need to practice *pratyahara*. For, even if we are not conscious of it, our senses still reach into the future and subconsciously create fear or desire. Or the mind turns to the past and processes past trauma, often involving shame and guilt. This escaping of the subconscious mind into the past or future takes place until we become proficient in *pratyahara* and bind all senses through appropriate yogic techniques, i.e. *pratyahara mudras*. *Mudras* covered in this section are:

Jihva Bandha	- to bind gustatory *prana*
Shambhavi Mudra	- to bind visual *prana*
Jnana Mudra	- to bind tactile *prana*

Akasha Mudra	- to bind tactile *prana*
Agochari Mudra	- to bind auditory *prana*
Dhyana Mudra	- to bind kinaesthetic *prana*

A brief note on the olfactory function. The *mudra* used to reflect olfactory *prana* back into the body is *Mula Bandha*. The olfactory sense is related to the *Muladhara Chakra* and the element earth. *Mula Bandha* is the *mudra* used to stimulate and harness the *Muladhara Chakra*. This *bandha* was covered in Section 2, Mudra 10, and it is essential for success in meditation.

Chapter 15

JIHVA BANDHA
(Tongue lock)

DISAMBIGUATION

Disambiguation of *Jihva Bandha* from *Nabho Mudra* and *Khechari Mudra*. The demarcation of the three techniques is not always clear and sometimes *shastras* use some terms synonymously or simply as graduations of the same technique with increasing achievement and difficulty. After much research I came to define the three terms as separate techniques all involving the tongue. I use the term *Jihva Bandha* as the simple folding backward to the tongue to arrest it against the soft palate. *Jihva Bandha* is never a stand-alone technique but always an ancillary of a *pranayama* or meditation technique. This technique is covered here. *Nabho Mudra*, covered in Section 1, *Mudra* 5, involves an effort to suck the tongue higher up to release secretions and it generally also involves *kumbhaka*. It is, therefore, always a stand-alone technique. *Khechari Mudra* is the highest level of achievement, involving the inserting of the tongue into the cavity above the soft palate. It is often accommodated by complex and sometimes dubious procedures to elongate the tongue. It does not involve wilful *kumbhaka*, but usually does involve the absorption of secretion with the tongue and is commonly used as an entry point to *samadhi*. It is covered in Section 5, *Mudra* 31.

Jihva Bandha means tongue lock. It is the folding of the tongue backwards, placing its underneath side up against the hard and soft palate and pushing it as far back as possible towards the naso- pharyngeal cavity. The *Hatha Tatva Kaumudi* promulgates that when the tongue is fixed against the palate behind the uvula, *prana* will enter *Sushumna,* and one hears *nada*[242]. *Nada* means inner sound, and it is regarded as the most straightforward method to enter *samadhi.* However, the stanza in the *Hatha Tatva Kaumudi* does not pertain to *Jihva Bandha.* The technique mentioned by the *Kaumudi,* is really *Khechari Mudra.* The term *Khechari Mudra* should not be used to refer to *Jihva Bandha.* Be able to recognize descriptions referring to one or the other even if they have been wrongly labelled, i.e. if the wrong name is used. We have seen a similar problem when disambiguating *Uddiyana Bandha* from *Bahya* (external) *Uddiyana.* If the two methods are mixed, or if instruction pertaining to one is used where the other applies, confusion, if not detriment, will ensue.

Jihva Bandha is the basic ingredient of *Nabho Mudra,* which refers to the milking of the uvula with the tongue, releasing *amrita. Khechari Mudra* is an advanced version of *Nabho Mudra. Khechari Mudra* is reputed to greatly reduce respiratory speed, thus enabling much longer *kumbhakas.* It makes *prana* steady and thus steadies the mind. These effects are also provided by *Jihva Bandha,* albeit to a lesser extent. One mechanism through which the subconscious (*vasana*) can express and manifest itself is through subtle movements of the tongue and eyes. If the yogi arrests these movements, the subconscious loses its grip and *kumbhaka* and meditation can deepen. One of the main reasons for applying *Jihva Bandha* is that it steadies the subconscious by removing one of its expressions. In that way *Jihva Bandha*

---

242 Dr M.L. Gharote et al (eds. & transl.), *Hathatatvakaumudi,* The Lonavla Yoga Institite, Lonavla, 2007, p. 382

performs for the tongue and the gustatory sense what *drishti* (focal point) and its advanced form, *Shambhavi Mudra*, do for the eyes and the visual sense.

Jihva Bandha is thus an important adjunct for *pranayama* and all forms of meditation. Some yogic schools claim it can be used in internal *kumbhaka* to replace *Jalandhara Bandha*. This is not the case in my experience, and I consider it unsafe advice. It is better to add it to *Jalandhara Bandha* and to perform both *bandhas* simultaneously. This view is also supported by the *Jyotsna* commentary on the *Hatha Yoga Pradipika*[243]. Following this suggestion, one first applies *Jihva Bandha* and then, while maintaining it, enters *Jalandhara Bandha*. *Jihva Bandha* may be applied during the entire breathing cycle. Be aware of tension building up in your head. If you contract a headache release *Jihva Bandha*. Phase it into your practice slowly and keep your teeth slightly separate to avoid the building up of tension from clenching your jaws.

Swami Sadhananda Giri explains that *Jihva Bandha* retains speech and taste[244]. Speech is obvious because we cannot talk with the tongue curled back, but taste is important. Taste is powered by gustatory *prana*. The component of mind that deals with taste is bound by using *Jihva Bandha*. Taste is the sense associated with the *Svadhishthana Chakra*, in the vicinity of the sacrum. The element of this *chakra* is water. Sensations are conveyed to tastebuds through a watery medium – for

243 Kunjunni Raja (ed.), *The Hathayogapradipika of Svatmarama with the Commentary Jyotsna of Brahmananda*, The Adyar Library, Madras, 1972, p. 30

244 Swami Sadhananda Giri, *Kriya Yoga*, Jujersa Yogashram, Howrah, 2005, p. 169

example a gustatory stimulus may be experienced as 'mouth-watering'. The gustatory component of mind and its associated subconscious express themselves through subconscious tongue movement. If tongue movement is arrested, the subconscious aspect of the gustatory mind is more likely to be stilled. As with all other mental capacities, its activity may be transferred to other mental domains and we endeavour to still them all one by one.

The mechanisms through which the subconscious can express and manifest itself are often subtle movements, such as the one's of the tongue and eyes. If the yogi arrests these movements, the subconscious loses its grip and meditation deepens. One of the main reasons for applying *Jihva Bandha* is that it steadies the subconscious by removing one of its expressions. The *Hatha Tatva Kaumudi* states that performing *Jihva Bandha* arrests *prana* (which still the mind)[245]. *Jihva Bandha* has also a mystical component, which is linked to the lunar storehouse of *prana*, the *Ajna Chakra* (or more precisely one of its subdivisions, the *Soma Chakra*). This lunar storehouse is sometimes simply called 'the moon', and the *prana* contained in it is sometimes referred to as *soma* or *amrita*, the nectar of immortality. By force of gravitation, this nectar oozes out of the lunar *chakra* and, once it reaches the sun in the navel (i.e. the *Manipura Chakra*), it is burnt by the gastric fire (*pitta*). This burning of *amrita* equates to losing lunar life force, which is life-giving, nurturing and anabolic. Besides weakening the body and inviting death and disease, its loss also weakens the mind. The weaker the mind, the more liable it becomes to lose its equilibrium through external stimuli, such as food, sex, drugs, acquisition, money, power and

---

245 *Hatha Tatva Kaumudi* of Sundaradeva XXXVIII.32

entertainment. A strong and vital mind relies on its equilibrium solely by realizing the Divine within and then the cosmic Divine with- out. Losing lunar *prana* leads to the mind losing its inner magnetism, and if it does, the senses will settle on their objects of desire. Like a boat without rudder and helmsman, the mind is then at the whim of the senses and follows them outwards for sensory satisfaction, losing its internal frame of reference and sense of self.

The Rishi Vyasa says in his commentary on the *Yoga Sutra* that the senses can be likened to a population of bees with the mind as the queen bee[246]. If the queen bee settles, all the other bees will settle too. If she flies out, all the other bees will follow. If, however, the mind loses its lunar *prana*, the *amrita*, it becomes weak and will follow the senses outwards. If the mind is weak, *pratyahara*, the fifth limb of yoga, cannot happen. *Pratyahara* means exactly that: The mind is in equilibrium and is strong. When it settles (on a sacred meditation object), the senses will simply follow their master (the mind) and this process is called *pratyahara*. Without *pratyahara* the higher limbs cannot be undertaken. Lunar *prana* has to be arrested and restored.

There are two physical methods of arresting lunar *prana* to keep it from being lost, and ideally both of these methods are combined. One method is to practise inversions such as the shoulder stand and headstand for an extended period. This practice has been described in Section1, under *Viparita Karani Mudra*. The second method is to use *Jihva Bandha* and its more advanced forms, *Nabho-*, and *Khechari Mudras*, to reabsorb the *amrita* (lunar *prana*). As with most yogic techniques, their combination increases the probability of success. *Khechari Mudra*

246 *Vyasa Bhashya* on the *Yoga Sutra* II.54

(elongation of the tongue until it's used to perform breath retention) is reputed to prevent the loss of *amrita* altogether. To use *Jihva Bandha* to reabsorb *amrita*, you need to fade it in slowly – slowly extend the time you keep the tongue rolled back. All yogic techniques need to be faded in slowly and responsibly. There cannot be sudden bursts in yoga.

Jihva Bandha may lead to tension in the brain and the soft palate and sometimes to headaches. If this happens, release the tongue and press it against the root of the upper teeth. This technique is called *Rajadanta*. It's not quite as effective as *Jihva Bandha*, but it is better than creating too much tension. *Rajadanta* will still arrest the movement of the tongue and help suspend the associated subconscious mind. However, it will not contribute to the absorption of *amrita*. Once the tension in the soft palate has subsided, go back to *Jihva Bandha* and slowly increase the time you apply it every day. On a side note, I think that *Jihva Bandha* is less efficient during *asana* practice. The main problem with such application is that the entire body is in motion during one's general *asana* practice. If one then applies *Jihva Bandha* intensely (i.e. use suction to draw the tongue far back) it will often result in tension along the soft palate, which is to be avoided. If one doesn't use suction, lunar *prana* will still be dissipated. While there is nothing wrong with using a mild form of *Jihva Bandha* during one's general *asana* practice, *Jihva Bandha* calls for a seated higher limbs practice, i.e. *pranayama* and *chakra*-Kundalini meditation. Only then can it really come into its own.

Note: The water element and the gustatory sense are related to the *Svadhishthana Chakra*. Another *bandha* that is related to this *chakra* is *Uddiyana Bandha*. To quote one scriptural example, the *Siddha Siddhanta Paddhati*, a treatise of the Natha order, says that *Uddiyana Bandha* opens *Svadhishthana Chakra*, which is the seat of the gustatory sense[247]. This is particularly the case for *Bahya* (external) *Uddiyana*, which I described in this volume in Section 2, *Mudra* 11. During this *bandha* the breath is suspended outside (i.e. after an exhalation) and the abdominal content is sucked into the thoracic cavity. Some authorities, including T. Krishnamacharya, say this external breath retention (*bahya kumbhaka*) with *Bahya* (external) *Uddiyana* is the only way of purifying the *Svadhishthana* and *Manipura chakras*. The best way of learning both external *kumbhaka* and external *Uddiyana* is during *Nauli*. *Nauli* is described in Section 4, *Mudra* 27, but additionally in greater detail in *Pranayama The Breath of Yoga*[248].

---

247 *Siddha Siddhanta Paddhati* II.2

248 Gregor Maehle, *Pranayama: The Breath of Yoga*, Kaivalya Publications, 20212, p. 176.

Chapter 16

SHAMBHAVI MUDRA
(Parvati's Seal)

Shambhu is a name of Lord Shiva. Shambhavi is Shiva's spouse. Hence *Shambhavi Mudra* is Parvati's *Mudra,* and it is a complex subject. The *Gheranda Samhita* lists it under the six ways of accessing *samadhi.* I could have easily treated it under *samadhi mudras.* However, because it is such an important adjunct practice for *pranayama* and meditation, I have treated it here already. This view is no clearer expressed than in the *Kumbhaka Paddhati of Raghuvira,* which says that success in *pranayama* comes when practised with *Shambhavi Mudra*[249]. The same is, of course, true of meditation.

Both in the four-chapter edition[250], and the 10-chapter edition of the *Hatha Yoga Pradipika*[251] this *mudra* is described as concentrating on an internal object (such as *chakras,* flow of *prana,* etc.) while the gaze is devoid of blinking and the pupils motionless. What is implied here is that the raising of eyes by itself is not enough, but only the added internal object

249 Dr M.L. Gharote, *Kumbhaka Paddhati of Raghuvira,* Lonavla Yoga Institute, Lonavla, 2010, p. 95

250 Kunjunni Raja (ed.), *The Hathayogapradipika of Svatmarama with the Commentary Jyotsna of Brahmananda,* The Adyar Library, Madras, 1972, p. 68

251 Dr M.L. Gharote et al (eds. & transl.), *Hathapradipika of Svatmarama (10 chapters),* Lonavla Yoga Institute, Lonavla, 2006, p. 218

completes the *mudra*. The *Hathatatva Kaumudi of Sundaradeva* adds[252] that fixing the gaze at the third eye helps controlling the vital down current [which holds Kundalini down] and that the true *Shambhavi Mudra* is gazing outwards yet seeing nothing[253]. *The Mandala Brahmana Upanishad* in stanza I.iii.6 confirms that *Shambhavi Mudra* means to open one's spiritual vision internally while the physical eyes appear half open but see nothing and also do not blink[254]. The *Gheranda Samhita* agrees that *Shambhavi Mudra* means fixing the gaze between the eyebrows to behold the self-existent and calls this the secret of all the *tantras*[255]. It then repeats a sentence already found in *Hatha Yoga Pradipika* IV.34, which we would consider sexist today, that *Shambhavi* alone is like a respectable lady whereas the *Vedas* and *shastras* are like prostitutes [because knowledge of them can easily be obtained by everybody]. Although the *Hatha Yoga Pradipika* contains an entire chapter on *mudras* (chapter III), it treats *Shambhavi Mudra* separately in chapter IV, the chapter on *samadhi* (revelation). In stanzas IV.35 – 36 the *Hatha Yoga Pradipika* defines *Shambhavi Mudra* as inwardly focussing on consciousness, while keeping the eyes half-open without blinking, appearing to see the outer world while in reality seeing externally nothing. This definition is similar to the one in the *Yoga Amanaska*, stanza II.10, which

---

252 Dr M.L. Gharote et al (eds. & transl.), *Hathatatvakaumudi,* The Lonavla Yoga Institite, Lonavla, 2007, p. 91

253 Dr M.L. Gharote et al (eds. & transl.), *Hathatatvakaumudi,* The Lonavla Yoga Institite, Lonavla, 2007, p. 615

254 Dr. M.M. Gharote et al (eds. & transl.), *Mandalabrahmanopanisad and Nadabindupanisad,* Lonavla Yoga Institute, Lonavla, 2012, p. 64

255 *Gheranda Samhita* III.64

says that fixation of the mind on an internal object while keeping the eyes open without blinking is known as *Shambhavi Mudra*[256].

The *Mandalabrahmana Upanishad* in stanza II.i..9 states that *Shambhavi Mudra* stabilizes both mind (*manas*) and intellect (*buddhi*)[257]. Many shastras describe the effect and inner attitude of this *mudra*, but what are we exactly to do with the eyes? The *Hatha Tatva Kaumudi* explains that fixing the gaze at the third eye helps controlling *apana* (the vital down current, which holds Kundalini down)[258] and that fixing the eyes at the eyebrow centre brings *prana* (the life force) to rest[259], which is usually skittish and makes the mind unstable. I was instructed that fixing the eyes between the eyebrows was an essential aspect of *Shambhavi Mudra*. This is also confirmed by Theos Bernard, who learned that *Shambhavi Mudra* was the rolling back of the eyes, while keeping the eyelids half open (so that the white is seen), and the focussing on the light in the head or on the third eye[260]. Also, Shyam Sunder Goswami calls *Shambhavi* internal gazing while concentrating the mind internally on the third eye centre[261].

---

256 Dr M.M. Gharote et al (eds. & transl.) *Amanaska Yogah- A Treatise On Laya Yoga*, Lonavla Yoga Institute, Lonavla, 2019, p. 63

257 Dr. M.M. Gharote et al (eds. & transl.), *Mandalabrahmanopanisad and Nadabindupanisad*, Lonavla Yoga Institute, Lonavla, 2012, p. 92

258 Dr M.L. Gharote et al (eds. & transl.), *Hathatatvakaumudi*, The Lonavla Yoga Institite, Lonavla, 2007, p. 91

259 Dr M.L. Gharote et al (eds. & transl.), *Hathatatvakaumudi*, The Lonavla Yoga Institite, Lonavla, 2007, p. 382

260 Theos Bernard, *Hatha Yoga*, Rider, London, 1950, p. 89

261 Shyam Sundar Goswami, *Laya Yoga*, Inner Traditions, Rochester, 1999, p. 74

From a *pratyahara* perspective, *Shambhavi Mudra* deals with projecting visual *prana* back into the body, *prana* which powers the visual component of the subconscious mind. In the human, this is the most developed component of mind, and hence yogis give it great attention. Due to its prevalence in the human mind and brain, one's *pranayama* or meditation technique is unlikely to succeed unless it has a strong visual component. For this reason the most important application of *Shambhavi Mudra* is not as a stand-alone technique (which it would be when using it to access *samadhi*) but as an ancillary technique during *pranayama* and meditation. For example, when employing yogic *chakra*-Kundalini meditation, the visualization of *Sushumna* and the related *chakras*/lotuses is designed to harness the power of the visual cortex for meditation. As we manage to slow down the breath, we gradually gain more time in each *chakra* and will utilize it to make our visualization more vivid. This will empower our meditation in its task of influencing and creating reality, i.e. producing lasting change in the quality of our minds. Another very important area of practice where this *mudra* serves as an ancillary technique is *Nadi Shodhana* and all other slow-breathing *pranayama* techniques. Also here the method assists the already existing sun/moon visualization. *Shambhavi Mudra* is not applied, however, during rapid-breathing *pranayama* techniques (such as *Kapalabhati* and *Bhastrika*), nor during one's general *asana* practice. These practices require too much attention to divert enough awareness to such ancillary techniques. *Shambhavi Mudra* as a rule of thumb is only done when sitting in a meditation posture.

The *Manipura Chakra*, in the spinal cord at the level of the navel, is also called the fire *chakra*, since it represents the fire element. Patanjali and others call it the navel *chakra*[262]. It is this fire *chakra* that we are targeting with *Shambhavi Mudra* because both are related to the visual sense. This *chakra* is important: on the physical level, fire in the body represents gastric and metabolic fire, but on the mental level it powers intelligence. Both gastric fire and the fire of intelligence are representations of the same cosmic force that powers the ongoing nuclear reaction in the sun, providing us with heat and light. The faculty associated with the fire *chakra* is the visual sense. It is only due to the light coming from the sun that the visual sense can function. Humans have learned to harness fire to see at night, initially just through campfires, but later with more refined forms of controlled fire such as gas and electric lamps. The same fire pierces and cuts through ignorance with inquiry and analysis and empowers us for scientific inquiry.

The relationship between fire in higher intelligence and the visual sense is still apparent in most languages. Even in today's English a seer is a person who is through mystical insight able to see things invisible to others. The term is also used for forecasters in the economic and political arenas, areas that remain opaque due to their apparent complexities.

As a preparation for *Shambhavi Mudra* we may first employ *Bhrumadhya Drishti*, described already in my previous books, particularly in *Ashtanga Yoga: Practice and Philosophy*[263]. *Bhrumadhya Drishti* means to gaze towards the centre of the eyebrows. What is meant here is a soft gaze, not an eye-crossing strain. Gazing between the eyebrows arrests unconscious eye

---

262 *Yoga Sutra* III.29

263 Gregor Maehle, *Ashtanga Yoga: Practice and Philosophy,* New World Library, Novato, 2007, p. 7

movement. The term REM (rapid eye movement) is used to describe the unconscious darting around of the eyes during dreaming, denoting activity of the subconscious mind. The mechanism powering REM happens not only during dreams, but also in the waking state when we do not focus our eyes on a particular object. Preventing the subconscious movement of the eyes during meditation is a powerful tool for stilling the subconscious mind and directing it towards purposeful activities. The art of performing *Bhrumadhya Drishti*, as with *Jihva Bandha*, is to fade it in slowly, as it can otherwise lead to tension in the forehead and brain.

A holistic way of doing this is to first raise the eyes to a horizontal level and fix them to an imagined object or focal point at eye level about a metre or 40 inches in front of you. Keep the eyelids relaxed, so the eyes are half-closed. Once your eyes are used to being in this position, bring this imagined object closer while lifting it higher. Initially if the eyes become tired it may be necessary to lower the gaze or even let the eyes close for a while. However, notice this is a function of *apana* (vital down current), and it means that the *apanic* force has overwhelmed your eyes.

Over weeks, months and sometimes years, bring the eyes higher and higher until their gaze finally meets in the middle of the forehead. This is the blossoming of *Shambhavi* Mudra; it is extremely powerful. It has this power because it reverses *apana* up and arrests the life force in the *Ajna Chakra* (third eye *chakra*). It is extremely important that you fade in this powerful technique over a long time, as forcing things may strain your optic nerves.

TECHNIQUE
To begin with, focus your eyes on a spot about half a metre away at eye level. The eyes have an automatic tendency to drop

down, at which point the subconscious mind will take over their control. Even just lifting the closed or half-closed eyes to the horizontal level will take them out of reach of the subconscious mind. But you will need to concentrate to keep them there.

Shambhavi Mudra

Once you get used to this level, lift the eyes about 10 degrees higher. Do not right from the beginning turn them up all the way: eyestrain would likely be the result. Stay at this new level until you are completely accustomed to it. This may take days, weeks

175

or months. In this way, over a sufficiently long-time frame, you raise the eyes until you have turned them up all the way.

Once you have achieved this, bring the focus closer and closer until it is in the centre of the forehead. If you develop headaches or pain in the eyes, ease off. Initially the eyes should be locked in this position only for a minute at a time before they are again lowered somewhat. Only gradually increase the time you spend with eyes raised. It does not matter whether your eyes are half-closed or fully closed: since they are turned up, even if they are only half-closed you will see little to nothing.

Chapter 17

JNANA MUDRA
(Knowledge Seal)

The kinaesthetic-tactile component of the mind is bound by sitting in a stable *asana*, such as *Padmasana* or *Siddhasana*. I have described these postures in great detail in four of my previous books. Kinesthesis is tactilation distributed over the entire body, not only its surface but also its structures and core. Important aspects of meditation in *asana* are:

- If seen from the side, the ears, shoulder joints and hip joints need to be in a straight vertical line. The head should not be forward of this line.
- The pelvis should be tilted anteriorly to emphasize lumbar curvature. This creates dynamic equilibrium by negating gravitational force (this is, of course, only the case during sitting; this instruction does not apply for a standing posture). If sitting in *Padmasana* (lotus posture), tilting the pelvis forward will stimulate *Mula Bandha*, as the perineum will come in contact with the floor.
- Sit as tall as possible. Imagine a hook attached to the highest point of your head that pulls you upwards and elongates the spine.
- In whatever position you sit, make sure that both palms of the hands and soles of the feet are turned away from

the ground and upwards to the ceiling. This rules out sitting in a chair.

- Keep drawing the shoulder blades down the back; if they slump forward, then draw them towards each other. These actions keep the heart area open and the region of the heart *chakra* floating.

The kinaesthetic/tactile component of mind computes data associated with the sense of touch and proprioception. The sense of touch represents the element air, and it is located and encrypted in the heart *chakra* (*Anahata*). The movement of air is felt by the skin as touch. We convey a sentiment of heart by touching somebody or by hugging, an embrace of the heart. Due the fact that kinesthesis is distributed throughout the body, whole-body *mudras* (*kaya mudras*) in yoga are given pre-eminence over hand *mudras* (hasta *mudras*). There are, however, a few hand *mudras* that yoga uses to prevent the projection of tactile *prana* out of the hands. The utilisation of these *mudras* instead makes this *prana* rebound back into the body. We could therefore say that *hasta mudras* primarily fulfil the function of *bandhas* for the hands. Typically these *mudras* are used for any activity involving *dharana* (concentration), *dhyana* (meditation) or *samadhi* (revelation). *Hasta mudras* are always ancillary techniques and never the primary method. The most important *hasta mudras* are:

- *Jnana Mudra* (seal of knowledge), which consists of the joining of the thumb and pointing finger with the other three fingers extended, palms facing up. This *hasta mudra* is covered here.
- *Akasha Mudra* (space seal), which consists of placing the right hand on top of the left hand with the thumbs

touching and palms facing up. This *hasta mudra* is covered under the next heading.

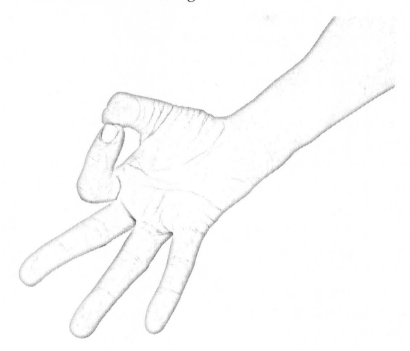

Jnana Mudra

Place the hands into *Jnana Mudra* (seal of knowledge) by joining the thumb and pointing finger and extending the other fingers. The significance of the fingers is:

> Thumb represents Brahman (infinite consciousness).
> Pointing finder represents *atman* (true nature).
> Middle finger represents *buddhi* (intellect).
> Ring finger represents *manas* (mind).
> Little finger represents *kaya* (body).

While there is a certain neatness in attributing these meanings to particular fingers, let's keep in mind these meanings are humanly created. In reality, the little finger is as close to Brahman as the thumb, because according to the *Upanishads* everything comes from the Brahman, is supported by the Brahman, and returns into the Brahman. We should regularly remind ourselves of these truths so we don't fall for fundamentalism.

Placing your thumb and pointing finger together seals the intention of realising that your true nature (*atman*) is nothing but infinite consciousness (Brahman). These two terms are of *Vedantic* origin, and for the success of the *mudra*, it is not essential we use them. What is essential, however, is that with this *mudra* we are professing our recognition of a higher power capable of instructing us. We need not be religious to do that. A scientist may profess their realization that the cosmos is inherently lawful and intelligent. Anthropomorphisation (i.e. projecting human characteristics) of cosmic intelligence can actually be an obstacle in yoga.

The palms of the hands are turned up in a receptive position acknowledging that knowledge is not something we create but something that it revealed to us, something we receive from a power greater than us, whatever we want to call this power. The arms are generally kept straight in this position but without the elbows being locked. Especially in a long meditation session, insisting on keeping the arms artificially straight would signal the inability to go beyond the body.

Chapter 18

AKASHA MUDRA
(Space Seal)

This *hasta mudra* is an alternative to *Jnana Mudra*. One may also alternate between both. Sit in the *asana* of your choice, placing your hands *Akasha Mudra*. Brahmanical schools will always place the left hand first and the right hand on top of it. The left hand is often called the earth hand and the right hand as the sky hand. However, this labelling should have us suspicious of sky religion, which replaced earth-based, indigenous spirituality. Sky religion placed the sacred into heaven, nirvana or emptiness and far away in time. In earth-based, animistic spirituality the sacred exists in nature and in the body. *Tantrics* often turn the Brahmanical order around and place the left hand on top of the right hand.

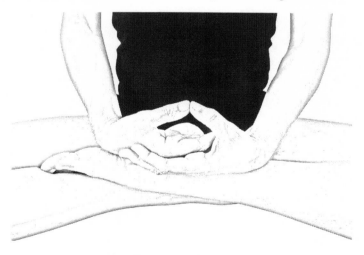

Akasha Mudra

When using a *hasta mudra,* if possible, give up the desire to move or sway and resist the urge to move your hands. But do not make this a process forced upon you from the outside; rather let it come from the inside. The desire to move around can be given up when, through focusing on breath, *chakras, mantra* and binding the other components of mind, one realizes that the entire creation is already in a state of balance and dynamic equilibrium. Silence and stillness of posture and hands is a way of listening to the message of the Divine in your heart that tells you this moment now and this place here are perfect: nothing needs to be changed.

Chapter 19

AGOCHARI MUDRA
(Imperceptible Seal)

There are different opinions as to the nature and purpose of this *mudra*. Some schools simply treat it as an alternate name for *Nasagrai Drishti*, i.e. gazing towards the tip of the nose. However, *agochari* means 'imperceptible to the senses. There are five senses, and the first four senses are different to the fifth. The first four are the olfactory, gustatory, visual and tactile senses. They are making perceptible the elements of earth (*prithvi*), water (*ap*), fire (*agni*) and air (*vayu*), respectively. We have dealt with *mudras* recovering *prana* lost through their sensory processes, i.e. *Mula Bandha* (olfactory), *Jihva Bandha* (gustatory), *Shambhavi Mudra* (visual), and *hasta mudras* (tactile). *Agochari* refers to the fifth element (ether, space) is imperceptible and more subtle than the others. The sense associated with ether is the auditory sense and it reveals sound (*shabda*). However, in yoga *shabda* is not limited to soundwaves that travel in air. The concept of *shabda* includes all vibratory patterns, including light, photons, quarks, gravitational waves, thought waves (*vrtti*) and the wave function of all particle states. These varied forms of vibratory patterns are divided into four categories, which are called *para* (beyond), *pashyanti* (manifest), *madhyama* (subtle) and *vaikhari* (audible). I have described these four phases of sound in my

2009 text *Ashtanga Yoga The Intermediate Series*[264]. Only the last category, *vaikhari*, travels in air and is perceptible to the ear.

Some yogic schools see *Agochari Mudra* as listening to the inner sound, sometimes called *anahata nada* or *nadanusandhana*[265]. Others see it as focussing on the inaudible or audible recitation of *mantra*. This is certainly an important aspect of it and ideally *mantra* is not only used as a stand-alone practice but also as the auditory aspect of yogic *pranayama* and meditation. For many yogic *pranayama-*, and meditation techniques there are certain root syllables (*bija askharas*) that need to be uttered while performing various phases of the technique.

Another important aspect of focussing on the imperceptible is to close the ears. This can be done through the thumbs as would be done during *Bhramari-*, and *Shanmukhi Mudras*, which are both described in Section 5, *Mudras* 28 and 29. However, especially during extensive sessions, holding up the arms, as done in these *mudras*, can be tedious and may prevent us from going beyond the body. Going beyond the body here means perceiving a deeper level of universal reality that temporarily demands of us to let go of our surface self, which includes identification with the body. To make this easier, yogis often used to close the ears with a mixture of bees wax and cotton. So says S.K. Das in *Divine Light* that *Agochari Mudra* is closing the ears with wax or cotton to listen to *Anahata Nada*[266]. This use of the *mudra* works excellently as an ancillary meditation

---

264 Gregor Maehle, *Ashtanga Yoga The Intermediate Series*, New World Library, Novato, 2009, p. 21-24

265 This discipline is the focus of the 4th chapter of the *Hatha Yoga Pradipika (4-chapter edition)*.

266 S.K. Das, *Divine Light*, New Age Books, New Delhi, 2002, p. 119

technique, especially when practising yogic *chakra*-Kundalini meditation in a noisy, urban environment. From my experience, such meditation works particularly well in nature against the backdrop of the sounds of wind in the trees, chirping of birds and humming of insects. This is because all nature expresses the same cosmic intelligence that gradually reveals itself to us through yogic *chakra*-Kundalini meditation and other forms of meditation. However, practising such subtle and powerful methods in an artificial, denaturated, noisy, urban environment is an altogether different task. It often is an uphill struggle. Therefore the plugging of the ears can be of great help. Yogis may employ this method to improve sensitivity to *mantric* soundwaves. This blocks out environmental sound and helps to focus more on *mantras*.

Agochari Mudra can also be combined with *Bhramari Mudra*. During this *mudra* the sound of a humming bee is produced. The throat is contracted and then the air is rapidly inhaled. Other than during *Ujjayi*, the vocal cords here are engaged by producing the 'ng' sound (*anushvara*). This is done by pronouncing the end of a word like gong or king and then continuing the sound by sustaining the breath and by humming. The same is done during the exhalation, but here much less air is needed, so one can draw out the sound much more. Usually, during this *mudra*, the ears are closed with the thumbs. However, this is tiring when performing the *mudra* for extensive periods. The thumbs can easily be replaced with ear plugs.

Chapter 20

DHYANA MUDRA
(Meditation Seal)

DISAMBIGUATION

Some schools use the name *Dhyana Mudra* to refer to the *hasta mudra* in this text labelled *Akasha Mudra*. I have, however, described *Dhyana Mudra* here as it is taught in *shastra*.

Although the name of this *mudra* offers itself as a prime label for an important practice, it is even in *shastra* not a very prominent *mudra*. It is mainly listed as an attitude of turning the attention inwards, hence its function is predominantly of *pratyahara* nature. *Dhyana Mudra* is mentioned in the *Hathatatva Kaumudi of Sundaradeva* in stanzas XLIX.31-33, and described as focussing the eyes on an external object and turning the mind inside while keeping the body steady and upright[267]. In stanza 33 of the same passage, *Bhrumadhya Drishti* is advised, i.e. looking towards centre of the eyebrows. The *Hatha Yoga Pradipika* similarly teaches *Dhyana Mudra* as the keeping of the body motionless, with gaze fixed and mind focussed inside[268]. Only the *Jogapradipyaka of Jayatarama* goes a bit more into

---

267 Dr M.L. Gharote et al (eds. & transl.), *Hathatatvakaumudi,* The Lonavla Yoga Institite, Lonavla, 2007, p. 617

268 Dr M.L. Gharote et al (eds. & transl.), *Hathapradipika of Svatmarama (10 chapters)*, Lonavla Yoga Institute, Lonavla, 2006, p. 188

detail[269]. Here *Dhyana Mudra* is defined as meditating on the six *chakras* and finally taking attention up into *Sahasrara Chakra* (thousand-petalled lotus), where, we are told, the object of meditation disappears from perception. Jayatarama is correct because *prana* held in the *Sahasrara Chakra* leads to *samadhi* on the formless Absolute, which in the language of the *Yoga Sutra* is objectless *samadhi*. The *Jogapradipyaka* then sees in this *mudra* a more advanced practice than the other two texts, or at least it describes a more advanced outcome of the same method.

Amanaska Yogah in stanza 14 says that a true yogi is a person whose vision is fixed, although no object is cognized, with movement of *prana* effortlessly suspended, and with mind stable beyond requiring an object to rest on[270]. Elsewhere this *mudra* is called *Vaishnavi Mudra*. We find an instance of that in *Nadabindu Upanishad* stanza 29, which states that a yogi adopts *Siddhasana*, while maintaining *Vaishnavi Mudra*, i.e. keeping the eyes open while gazing inside, until one hears *nada* (inner sound)[271]. We noticed this tendency already with *Shanka Mudra*, where a *mudra* initially used in the Shaivite tradition was adopted by Vaishnavism, and its name changed to remove the reference to a competing school of thought.

---

269 Swami Maheshananda et al (eds & transl.), *Jogapradipyaka of Jayatarama*, Kaivalyadhama, Lonavla, 2006, p. 133

270 Dr M.M. Gharote et al (eds. & transl.), *Amanaska Yogah- A Treatise On Laya Yoga*, Lonavla Yoga Institute, Lonavla, 2019, p. 15

271 Dr. M.M. Gharote et al (eds. & transl.), *Mandalabrahmanopanisad and Nadabindupanisad*, Lonavla Yoga Institute, Lonavla, 2012, p. 239

SECTION 4: DHARANA MUDRAS

This is arguably the most important and quintessential group of *mudras*. Discussed under this heading are *mudras* to facilitate *dharana* (the 6th limb of yoga, generally translated as concentration). *Dharana* is an archaic term and in more modern terms, it means raising Kundalini. In the days of the composition of the *Yoga Sutra* emphasis on Kundalini was not yet necessary because the entropic process (entropy is a term related to the second law of thermodynamics and it implies an increase of disorder) that caused Kundalini to drop was not yet fully formed. I have described this entropic process in *Ashtanga Yoga Practice and Philosophy*, Part 3[272]. It also supports the Four *Yuga* doctrine taught in the *Puranas* and the *Mahabharata*. Sir John Woodroffe in the *The Serpent Power* confirms that rousing of Kundalini is *dharana*[273]. The same fact was also corroborated by Om Prakash Tiwari, director of the Kaivalyadhama Institute[274]. Especially

---

272 Gregor Maehle, *Ashtanga Yoga Practice and Philosophy,* New World Library, Novato, 2007, p. 133ff

273 Sir John Woodroffe, *The Serpent Power*, Ganesh & CO, Madras, 1995, p. 223

274 O.P. Tiwari, *The Concept of Kundalini*, Kaivalyadhama Lecture Series on DVD, Lonavla,

to modern practitioners of *asana*-based yoga forms such as Ashtanga Vinyasa Yoga it is often lost that T. Krishnamacharya placed a lot of emphasis on Kundalini[275]. For modern practitioners who are far removed from the ancient source of spirituality, spiritual revelation without Kundalini raising techniques is often an uphill task. All *mudras* covered in this section are ones that deal with Kundalini raising.

Mudras covered here:

> *Maha Mudra*
> *Maha Bandha Mudra*
> *Maha Vedha Mudra*
> *Ashvini Mudra*
> *Vajroli Mudra*
> *Pashini Mudra*
> *Shakti Chalana Mudra*

Here a different approach to *mudra* emerges. The *mudras* in the first section, *asana mudras*, are methods practised during one's *asana* practice or added to it. The second section, *pranayama mudras*, involves ancillary, but essential seals, without which *pranayama* practice would not be possible. The third section, *pratyahara mudras*, consisted of seals added to our meditation practice, which complements it and makes it more potent. But similar to the *pranayama mudras*, they do not constitute stand-alone practices and hence do not require a separate time commitment. The current, fourth section of this text breaks this pattern since

---

275 T. Krishnamacharya, *Yoga Makaranda*, Media Garuda, Chennai, 2011, p. 170

it contains *mudras* that constitute practices in themselves. They are dedicated stand-alone practices designed to bring about Kundalini-raising. Raising Kundalini can be utilized for creativity, increase of intellect and memory, achievements in the fields of art and science, and mystical states and revelation. As Gopi Krishna has shown with the example of the evil genius, Kundalini can also be abused for the satisfaction of one's egotism[276]. The person doing so will inevitably meet their own downfall, but in doing so, they can beforehand do much damage. Yogis need to adhere to ethics (*yamas* and *niyamas*) and particularly place themselves into the service of the Divine (*ishvara pranidhana*). The term *ishvara pranidhana* is of such import it occurs in the *Yoga Sutra* four times[277]. I have described a hands-on approach to surrendering to the Divine in *How To Find Your Life's Divine Purpose – Brain Software For a New Civilization*.

In the current section are covered all *mudras* supporting the process of *dharana*. According to yogic mythology *dharana* was a process readily mastered when during the *Treta Yuga*[278] the Kundalini (divine creative force), previously located in the third eye *chakra*, dropped down to the lowest two *chakras*. This took place due to enculturation (humanity developing the erroneous belief we would progress by competing against each other and other organisms, and subdueing and controling nature, ultimately leading us to the yawning abbyss of ecocide and environmental holocaust), entropy, (the breakdown of order caused

---

276 Gopi Krishna, *Kundalini The Evolutionary Energy in Man*, Shambala, Boston, 1997

277 *Yoga Sutra* I.31, II.1, II.32 and II.45

278 The *Treta Yuga* is the second of the four *Puranic* world ages. The four are *Satya-, Treta-, Dvapara* and *Kali Yugas*.

by time, similar to oxidation and rusting) and collective *karma* and trauma (comparable to the biblical myth of eating from the Tree of Knowledge of Good and Evil and our subsequent expulsion from the Garden of Eden). I have described this complex process in my previous books *Ashtanga Yoga Practice and Philosophy*[279] and in more detail in *How To Find Your Life's Divine Purpose*[280]. Reiterating it here would be beyond the scope of a book on *mudras*. Ever since this entropic process took place, humans found the process of *dharana* challenging. Therefore gradually, an entire science developed around raising Kundalini back up to where it rightfully belongs. With Kundalini raised, *dharana* becomes readily available and *dhyana* (meditation) and *samadhi* (revelation) will fall like domino stones.

In the last section, we discussed *pratyahara mudras*, which deal predominantly with projecting lunar *prana*, i.e. *prana* associated with the sense organs (*jnanendriyas*), back into the body. These include *mudras* that withdraw *prana* powering gustatory, olfactory, visual, audio and tactile/kinaesthetic perception. In this current section we predominantly look at solar *prana*, *prana* associated with the *karmendriyas*, the organs of action, which perform locomotion, grasping, speech, urination/ sexual intercourse and defecation.

WHAT IS KUNDALINI?

The *Purusha Sukta* of the *Rig Veda* states that in the beginning there was the Brahman only. The Brahman is the deep reality

---

279 Gregor Maehle, *Ashtanga Yoga Practice and Philosophy,* New World Library, Novato, 2007, p. 133ff

280 Gregor Maehle, *How To Find Your Life's Divine Purpose,* Kaivalya Publications, Crabbes Creek, 2020

or the infinite consciousness. Physicists call it the unified field or the state before the Big Bang. To create the world and bring about its quality of reflectiveness/awareness the Brahman became polar. The two poles are in India often called Shiva (pure consciousness) and Shakti (divine creative force). In the language of modern Western philosophy, we would call them the God transcendent and the God immanent. While Shiva remains unchanged (mythologically anthropomorphized as the deity sitting immovably on Mount Kailash in *samadhi*), Shakti crystallizes from divine creative force through intelligence, space, air, fire and water into the earth element, in the process manifesting the world. Earth, this final and most dense element in the human body manifests as the base *chakra* (*Muladhara*), within which the divine creative force now lies coiled and dormant. In this coiled dormant state, the divine creative force is called Kundalini. Kundalini means coiled. The Kundalini is our potential for spiritual, natural, intellectual and artistic evolution.

There is a general cosmic law that says for the general equilibrium of the universe to be maintained, each manifestation must contain its own undoing, counterforce or annulling. For example, the first law of thermodynamics says that energy is never lost but only ever transformed into other forms of energy. For example, kinetic energy may be transformed into potential, electric, magnetic energy, or heat, but the energy as such is never lost. This is another way of saying that the sum total of all energies in a system remains always the same. The same is expressed in Newton's laws of gravitation. You can also see in the life of our greatest teachers such as Krishna, Jesus Christ, Gautama Buddha or Socrates, that towards the end of their lives, they orchestrated their own undoing. They did so in order the restore the equilibrium of the world that was briefly imbalanced through the evolutionary impetus they provided.

How does this impact Kundalini? Creating the world, the Shakti set in motion a massive down-force that reached from cosmic intelligence down to the element earth, and with it to the base *chakra*. To fulfil the above-mentioned cosmic law, a strong downward force has to bring with it a balancing upward force, often right in its middle. This annuls and neutralizes the upward force, so the sum total is again zero. Shakti's act of creating the universe produced an inner upward force, an upward wave we can ride up the spine to get back up to the experience of infinite consciousness, the God transcendent (Shiva).

This inner upward force in the body is called Kundalini. It is an invitation of the Divine Feminine (Shakti) to return to our spiritual origin. Shakti and Kundalini are really one and the same thing, or better, two sides of the same coin. The reason I write both in upper case and not italic is that they are names of the Divine Feminine, the divine creative force. Shakti is the Great Goddess as downward action, whereas Kundalini is the same as upward movement. When thinking of Kundalini, don't mistakenly relegate it to a physical force or physical sensation. What it really is, is the force that powered the manifestation of the entire cosmos, and the spiritual and natural evolution of life in it.

WHAT ARE GRANTHIS?
Before discussing the *mudras* in this section, we need to first clarify the concept of *granthis*. *Granthi* means knot or blockage and *granthis* refer to pranic obstacles in the course of the central *pranic* channel, *Sushumna*, that prevent Kundalini from rising beyond a certain level. Due to this, insights and revelations

beyond that level cannot be gained. *Granthis* are manifesting through the power of one's previous actions (*karma*). They need to be broken or dissolved, a process in *shastra* usually called 'piercing', so that spiritual evolution can take place unimpeded and swiftly.

What makes the subject of *granthis* hard to grasp is that they are awkwardly named after the three main Hindu deities, Brahma, Vishnu and Shiva (the third *granthi* carries the *Vedic* name of Shiva, i.e. Rudra). This conjures up the image of an anthropomorphic God who haphazardly throws obstacle into your path. However, understand that the names of the three deities are metaphors for the three realms of human existence, for societal realms. The three realms appear in all creation myths. In the Nordic mythology, for example, they have been called Utgard, Midgard and Asgard, or the netherworld, middle earth and the celestial realm, or heaven. These terms are all metaphors, too. They imply realms of human development, evolution and experience. Let's look into them more closely:

This first *granthi* is the Brahma *Granthi*, the blockage of the force of the creation. The knot is so called because Brahma is the Hindu god of creation. This *granthi* blocks the most basic and elemental aspects of our life. It can block either of the two lowest *chakras* or both, so the blocked *chakra* is ill-supplied with *prana*. With blocking the base *chakra* (*Muladhara*) one's survival is at risk, and one may display either risky or destructive behaviour with no apparent understanding of the dangers, or suicidal tendencies may play out.

Brahma *Granthi* can also block the sacral *chakra*, the *Svadhishthana*. In this case, one can either suffer from extremely low libido, i.e. incapacity of owning one's sexuality, or the *granthi* can cause the inability to mature beyond one's sexual identity, which is the case in the perennial gigolo or seductress. Males, for example, who excessively use pubescent, penile vocabulary are also inhibited by this *granthi*. The *granthi* can also cause the inability to conceive offspring, to adequately care for one's progeny, and also to own and express one's emotionality. This *granthi* inhibits proper limbic brain function.

The second *granthi* is the Vishnu *Granthi*, which can again block either of two, or both, of the navel-, and the heart *chakra*. The *Hathatatva Kaumudi of Sundaradeva* confirms that the blockage of the navel *chakra* (*Manipura*) is brought about by the Vishnu *Granthi* [281]. The term knot indicates that the life force (*prana*) cannot flow into or beyond this *chakra*. The blockage is so named because Vishnu in Hindu mythology is the maintainer of society. All aspects of our life that deal with how we interact with the larger society around us, with the role we play in society, are directed by the navel-, and heart *chakras*. The Vishnu *Granthi* may stop you from becoming a fully integrated individual operating within society, i.e. asserting yourself from a position of power (navel *chakra*) if necessary and coming from a position of unconditional love (heart *chakra*) if possible.

The Vishnu *Granthi* can block the navel *chakra* in two ways. First, it can prevent life force (*prana*) from entering the *chakra* at hand, so the evolutionary brain circuitry associated with this *chakra* is not available to you. This is the typical scenario of a powerless person who may get victimized and cannot take the mantle of the leader, even if needed. Let me clarify that I am not indicating that victimization is the fault of the victim. A perpetrator will skilfully scan for a suitable victim, but the *karmic*

---

281 Dr M.L. Gharote et al (eds. & transl.), *Hathatatvakaumudi*, The Lonavla Yoga Institite, Lonavla, 2007, p. 690

responsibility is still with the perpetrator and the civil code of law must protect any victims. It is, however, a blocked power *chakra* that lets a predator skilfully select a suitable victim over another person, whose defence code would be more difficult to crack. For a predator, this is a necessary skill they usually can perform to great accuracy.

The other way the Vishnu *Granthi* may operate, is that it prevents us to go beyond the navel *chakra*, thus activating the heart *chakra* (*Anahata*). This is the present dilemma of our human society. Although increasing attempts are being made, our society still creates toxic hierarchies like wealth, power and status. With the heart *chakra* activated, we will see each individual as a manifestation of the Divine, we see them for their essence, even if they themselves cannot yet see this. The heart *chakra* powered the life of visionaries like Gandhi, Martin Luther King, Nelson Mandela, and, of course, Jesus Christ.

If the Vishnu *Granthi* is powerful, it may block the navel and heart *chakra* simultaneously. If so, higher spiritual exercises (such as meditation on awareness or on the higher *chakras*) may provide mentally destabilizing. Instead of that, the focus should be on activating these middle *chakras* first. This is done through *pranayama*, *chakra*-meditation, and particularly exercises such as *Bhastrika* or *Nauli*. If through an accident, the higher *chakras* open, while Vishnu *Granthi* blocks the two middle *chakras*, schizophrenia may ensue. A typical scenario in which this can occur is through psychedelics such as LSD, DMT, psilocybin or ayahuasca. I have described spiritual problems associated with psychedelic use in *Chakras, Drugs and Evolution – A Map of Transformative States*[282]. Schizophrenia here means that one

---

282 Gregor Maehle, *Chakras, Drugs and Evolution – A Map of*

cognises such powerful knowledge that one cannot integrate it into one's life. With the navel- and heart *chakras* opened, most of life's challenges can be handled, but without them we may find ourselves in a deep crisis. Especially the heart *chakra* fosters submission to a higher intelligence and power, which is the key to overcoming crises. Another dangerous constellation is if the heart *chakra* remains closed and *chakras* above it, such as the throat-, or third eye *chakra*, open. Such a case could lead to the formation of a cult-leader, somebody who may place higher spiritual insights into the service of their power *chakra*, fulfilling their need for self-aggrandisement and adoration through recruiting gullible followers.

The third and last *granthi* is the Rudra *Granthi*. Also, this *granthi* can block either, or both, of the throat-, and third eye *chakra*. The throat *chakra* (*Vishuddha*) enables us to see that the entire cosmos is a crystallization of sacred law and that everything, including all matter, is crystallized spirit. With an activated third eye *chakra* we can see that plants, animals, microbes, rocks, mountains, rivers, lakes, and forests are forms of intelligence that can teach us, if only we can understand their language. It is this *chakra* that opens to us the world of indigenous experience, the world of animism and shamanism. It would not be wrong to say that modern industrial society's ignorant beliefs that the cosmos is an insentient world machine consisting of dumb and dead matter, that animals may be tortured with impunity in laboratories or bred in captivity to be eaten, that forests are at our disposal to be cut down for woodchips, that lakes and oceans are little more than latrines and chemical waste dumps, that indigenous people are primitives and savages, are

---

Transformative States, Kaivalya Publications, Crabbes Creek, 2021

proof that our modern materialistic culture collectively suffers from a dormant throat *chakra,* blocked by Rudra *Granthi.* An active throat *chakra* would enable us to feel the pain of all the life forms and entities listed above and would therefore render us incapable of metering out to the magnificent natural world the level of primitive brutality we still exert to coerce and bully it into submission.

The Rudra *Granthi* can also block the third eye *chakra* (*Ajna*), as confirmed by *Hathatatva Kaumudi of Sundaradeva*[283]. Different to the throat *chakra,* the *Ajna* empowers us to have a direct experience of cosmic intelligence, the intelligence that crystallizes itself as the sum total of all universes. In the yogic tradition, this intelligence is usually called the Divine, but the term does not imply an anthropomorphic god. The belief in an anthropomorphic god, a god in the likeness of a human, results from projecting into the sky our need for a father figure in form of a giant tribal chieftain. Michelangelo's image of the Father giving life to Adam is clearly a copy of the pagan god Zeus rather than an approximation of the Biblical Yahweh.

Rudra *Granthi* blocking the third eye *chakra* expresses itself as the incapacity to personally experience divine revelation. This can either lead to materialistic reductionism and empiricism (the belief that only matter exists and sensory perception is the only valid means to obtain knowledge) or the belief that the Divine cannot be personally experienced at all. We are made to believe that the Divine has authored a certain book, which now represents the only means of understanding the Divine, and any other books dealing with the same subject are false, and

---

283 Dr M.L. Gharote et al (eds. & transl.), *Hathatatvakaumudi,* The Lonavla Yoga Institite, Lonavla, 2007, p. 690

their adherents infidels or pagans. Again, it is easy to see that most of modern humanity suffers from a collective blockage of the third eye *chakra* through Rudra *Granthi*.

Rudra *Granthi* is blocking both *chakras* in the majority of modern humans. Under the influence of this *granthi* we manoeuvred ourselves into a situation where we are now gazing into the yawning abyss of ecocide, environmental holocaust and omnicide (the murder of all life). The *granthis* are caused by *karma*, in this case, the collective *karma* of humanity. They are caused by all the suffering we have caused each other, to nature, to all species, and to the supposedly inanimate world. Imagine what could happen if Rudra *Granthi* was broken in most humans? Our children, grandchildren and their progeny would certainly thank us for it!

The *granthis* need to be broken in the right order with Brahma *Granthi* first, then Vishnu *Granthi*, then Rudra *Granthi*. This is corroborated by *Yoga Kundalini Upanishad* I.63-65, which also confirms the location of the *granthis* as stated in the present text [284]. The *Upanishad* again confirms in stanzas I.80-81[285]. The same is also stated in the *Hatha Yoga Pradipika*[286] and in *Hathatatva Kaumudi*, stanzas XLIII.9-10[287]. If Rudra *Granthi* is broken without previous activation the heart *chakra*, psychotic or schizo-

---

284 Dr. M.M. Gharote et al (eds. & transl.), *Critical Edition of Selected Yogopanisads*, Lonavla Yoga Institute, Lonavla, 2017, p. 126-7 stanzas 66-69, and again stanzas 85-86

285 Dr. M.M. Gharote et al (eds. & transl.), *Critical Edition of Selected Yogopanisads*, Lonavla Yoga Institute, Lonavla, 2017, p. 137

286 *Hatha Yoga Pradipika (10-chapter edition)*, V.50

287 Dr M.L. Gharote et al (eds. & transl.), *Hathatatvakaumudi*, The Lonavla Yoga Institite, Lonavla, 2007, p. 505-506

phrenic tendencies can develop. Fortunately, this is unlikely unless one takes psychedelics or engages in extreme practices. This then is a warning not to engage in extreme practices but to act responsibly. An extreme practice would be to engage in the practices described in this chapter without suitable preparation through *asana, pranayama* and *kriyas,* such as, for example, *Nauli.* The *mudras* listed in the *dharana* section must be seen as Stage 3 *granthi*-breaker. *Hathatatva Kaumudi of Sundaradeva* states that prolonged practice of *Shakti Chalana Mudra* pierces the knots[288]. To prepare for Stage 3 *granthi*-breaking, we must first prepare the body through *asana*. Then we enter into the process known as Stage 1 *granthi*-breaking. Stage 1 means to apply all three *bandhas* in both internal and external *kumbhaka* (breath retention), while practising the *pranayama* method *Nadi Shodhana* (or, depending on individual tendency, *Chandra* or *Surya Bhedana*). Only when established in Stage 1 *granthi*-breaking, do we go on to Stage 2 *granthi*-breaking, which is *Bhastrika*. This is confirmed in *Yoga-Kundalini Upanishad* stanza 39. If you are not properly prepared for *Bhastrika*, you can have a similar disorienting effect as when taking a hallucinogen. Some teachers advise going straight to *Bhastrika* and there are dubious versions of it on the internet. No surprise then that people have Kundalini-accidents.

The process briefly listed so far is described in great detail in my textbook *Pranayama The Breath of Yoga*. Once this process of *granthi-* breaking (or piercing as it is sometimes called) is completed, we can then engage in Stage 3, comprising of the *mudras* described in the following section. Do not practice these *dharana mudras*, i.e. *mudras* designed to raise Kundalini, unless you have

---

288 Dr M.L. Gharote et al (eds. & transl.), *Hathatatvakaumudi,* The Lonavla Yoga Institite, Lonavla, 2007, p. 72

largely attained the state of hemisync (brain hemisphere syn-chronization) *with Nadi Shodhana pranayama.*

ETHICAL CONSIDERATIONS OF KUNDALINI RAISING

The *dharana mudras* aid or bring about the raising of Kundalini. The *mudras* in the other section are only influencing your own life, that is they make your *asana, pranayama,* meditation or *samadhi,* respectively, more efficient. The Kundalini raising *mudras* are different. Depending on the proficiency developed by the individual, powers can be harnessed that influence the life of the community around us. Kundalini is the divine creative force. While it is usually associated with enhanced creativity, love for one's fellow beings, and spiritual revelation all the way to cosmic consciousness, it can also be harnessed for the dark arts. So pointed out Gopi Krishna that also the phenomenon of the evil genius was powered by Kundalini. The reason characters like Hitler and Stalin could cause the damage they did was that they achieved access to extraordinary energy resources. They only used them for the wrong purpose. Even if we initially have no intention to attain such far-flung goals like world dominance, it is not a safe approach to simply try out these Kundalini *mudras* and then deal with the energy once we have it. By then, it might be too late to control them. With Goethe's *The Sorcerer's Apprentice* we may then say, "The spirits I summoned, I can't get rid of them". This could express itself in trivial abuses of powers, such as using one's charisma to manipulate people to supply sexual favours, something that has frequently occurred in yoga. But it also could lead to much worse. To prevent this, we need to first firmly establish ourselves in ethics and an attitude of service.

The first form of ethical practice we need to consider is *shaucha*, often translated as cleanliness, but more comprehensively defined as physical, emotional and mental purity, or abstaining from physical, emotional and mental toxins. *Shaucha* is one of the yogic *niyamas* (observances) listed in the *Yoga Sutra*[289]. Any desire to manipulate others or to self-aggrandize is based on fear and not realizing that all beings share the same *atman* (self, consciousness). We need to abstain from negative thoughts and emotions of ambition, competition, greed and anger. Our life needs to be devoted to the good of all and not just spent acting for our own advantage. This always starts on the emotional and thought level. A regular forgiveness practice also is helpful. If approaching Kundalini while harbouring toxic thoughts and emotions against others, we will experience shipwreck. Physical purity and abstaining from physical toxins also imply that we abstain from animal products and adhere to a plant-based diet. Sugar and salt also need to be reduced to a minimum. And psychedelics, marijuana, alcohol and coffee must be shunned when attempting to raise Kundalini, lest we intend to undermine our mental sanity. While stimulants such as these may be seen as fun, once approaching Kundalini, kindergarten time is over. If we abuse Kundalini for means of personal aggrandisement or for the satisfaction of our egotism we may fly high for some time, and for that time, we may even convince ourselves of our own greatness and entitlement. However, the *karmic* boomerang always comes back. We need to place ourselves right from the beginning into the service of the Divine, or fulfil our life's divine purpose. This practice in yoga is called *ishvara pranidhana*. This phrase is listed in the *Yoga Sutra* four times, and I have described

---

289 *Yoga Sutra* I.32

it in great detail in my previous textbook, *How To Find Your Life's Divine Purpose*. It is an important and life-changing step to consecrate oneself to a higher intelligence.

PREREQUISITES FOR KUNDALINI RAISING

Rising Kundalini may unleash significant energy sensations. We need to prepare the vessel, our body, for power conduction (*shakti chalana*). The first step to this is to establish ourselves in a daily *asana* practice. A minimum would be to practice *asanas* for 60 minutes 5 days per week, but more is better, and needed for somebody in their 20s or 30s. I consider the Ashtanga Vinyasa method ideal for preparing the body for power conduction. However, I know this form of yoga is not suitable for everybody. The system that I am offering here can, of course, also be supported by a different form of *asana* practice. However, energetic forms of yoga will generally show effects more quickly, and in the long term, are more efficient. For more info on Ashtanga Vinyasa please refer to my two previous volumes, *Ashtanga Yoga Practice and Philosophy* and *Ashtanga Yoga The Intermediate Series*.

The manifold purposes of posture practice are
- Removing the physical strata of conditioning from the body
- Increasing longevity to prepare for a long practice life
- Creating an adamantine body that withstands disease better and can conduct energy surges
- Improving the *pranic* retention rate during *kumbhakas*
- Enabling the body to perform sufficiently long inversions to arrest *prana* in the *Vishuddha-*, and *Ajna Chakras*

- Enabling the body to sit in the cardinal meditation *asanas* to practice *pranayama*, meditation and *samadhi*

Once we are to a certain level established in *asana*, we then add *pranayama* practice. Before engaging in pranayama, we should not wait until we have reached some mythic proficiency level in *asana*. *Pranayama* is a significant undertaking that takes time to master, therefore, it is better after an initial period where only *asana* is performed, to learn and study *asana* and *pranayama* side-by-side. There are multiple layers, practices and stages to *pranayama* practice, and it would be reasonable to practice *pranayama* daily for 30 minutes before approaching Kundalini. During Kundalini raising more may be required, depending on which avenue one exactly choses. The main goals of *pranayama* are:

- Slowing down the breath as much as possible which leads to a slowing and concentrating of the mind.
- Drawing *prana*, which is scattered beyond the boundaries of the physical body, back into the core. In psychological terms this equates to a withdrawing of projection, an end to "being out there", and to independence from sensory stimulus.
- Through alternate nostril breathing we attain brain hemisphere synchronization, and a balance of the sympathetic and parasympathetic nervous systems, afferent and efferent nerve currents, introversion and extraversion, catabolism and anabolism, fundamentalist and relativistic mind, and lunar and solar *prana* respectively.

- Through breath retentions (*kumbhakas*) the mind eventually is arrested, and *prana* is inducted into the central energy channel (*Sushumna*).

After being established in *pranayama*, the next step is to introduce ourselves to *chakra*-Kundalini meditation or yogic meditation as I have called it in my 2013 text *Yoga Meditation – Through Mantra, Chakras and Kundalini to Spiritual Freedom*. This is a demanding practice that is on its own capable of raising Kundalini, without resorting to the practices described in this present volume. However, if Kundalini raising is intended through *chakra*-Kundalini meditation, this method needs to be practised for extensive periods and such practice requires a reasonably focussed mind and a somewhat cerebral orientation. I have repeatedly seen the cerebral type of student take to this meditation with little preparation and have great success. Some students, though, struggle with this method. Those who struggle may be the more kinaesthetic, tactile and feeling types, and possibly also those with very busy lives. They may find in the present volume a more suitable approach.

If *chakra*-Kundalini meditation is a stand-alone method for Kundalini raising, it would need to get practised 90 (or sometimes more) minutes per day. If used simply as a preparation and support for the Kundalini *mudras* described in this book, a much shorter time frame, possibly as little as 10 minutes per day, is enough. The reason we cannot do without it altogether is because this meditation teaches us how to conduct *prana* from *chakra* to *chakra*, and that skill is irreplaceable once Kundalini rises. For when this takes place, we need to skilfully place Kundalini in the *chakra* needed to achieve a particular outcome. For more information on this subject and for a detailed insight into the function of the chakras, please consult my 2021 text *Chakras, Drugs and Evolution – A Map of Transformative States*.

Chakra-Kundalini meditation, even if practised only for a short time daily, eventually enables us to conduct *prana* up and down the *chakras* similar to playing a xylophone, or any similar instrument. The type of spiritual experience we encounter depends on where *prana* is at the time, i.e. into which *chakra prana* has entered. This depends simply on which *chakra* we focus on. This mechanism has been explained in the *Hatha Yoga Pradipika*, which says, 'where thought goes there goes prana and where prana goes there goes thought'[290]. In *Chakras, Drugs and Evolution – A Map of Transformative States*, I have outlined a nomenclature and topography of mystical states/ spiritual experiences. Such peak experiences, as Abraham Maslow called them, are classifiable depending on the *chakra* that powers them. Types of practitioners have certain *karmic* preponderances to attain particular states, and inertia often blocks them from experiencing others. With *chakra*-Kundalini meditation, we have a reliable tool to make all categories of mystical states attainable to all. The likelihood for that to occur depends, of course, on the intensity and sophistication with which we are conducting our *sadhana* (spiritual practice). Everything in life comes with a price and mystical states follow this cause-and-effect rule closely. Mystical states do not come about spontaneously but are directly proportional to the *karma* we are producing through our *sadhana*.

Besides the major yogic techniques of *asana, pranayama* and meditation, ancillary elements such as *kriya, bhavana* and *sankalpa*, and *bhakti* are also necessary. *Kriyas* are purification

---

290 *Hatha Yoga Pradipika* IV.24

exercises such as *Nauli* and *Kapalabhati*, described in *Pranayama The Breath of Yoga*. Information on *bhavana*, cultivation of thought processes in alignment with the Divine and *sankalpa*, the process of resolution and affirmation, you will find in *How To Find Your Life's Divine Purpose*. *Bhakti*, yoga of love, was also introduced in this book, but I hope to cover it in more detail in an upcoming volume.

The question when we find the time to perform all these practices I have answered in *Yoga Meditation*[291]. Succinctly answered, not all at once! The *Vedic* teaching of the four stages of live, *ashramas*, calls for the integration of yogic practices across all stages of life. This ideally means that we start with *asana* sometime after puberty, we add *pranayama* when starting our profession or family, we add yogic meditation once our main duties towards society are completed and enter *samadhi* practice around the time of retirement. Those with a great urge, or those who feel the calling to be spiritual teachers, can, of course, accelerate this process. What we should not start yoga with is the attitude this is a sprint that can be completed in few years. Yoga is more like the process of life. It is ongoing if we are alive. Rightly the Indian sage Sri Aurobindo in said in *A Synthesis of Yoga*, "All life is yoga". We need to be in it for the long haul!

EFFECTS OF KUNDALINI RAISING

In human evolution to date, Kundalini is powering the three lower *chakras*, which are supplying functions in line with the so-called triune brain theory. MacMillan's triune brain theory

---

291 Gregor Maehle, *Yoga Meditation: Through Mantra, Chakras and Kundalini to Spiritual Freedom*, Kaivalya Publications, Crabbes Creek, 2013, p. 173-175

divides the brain into three primary structures, the reptilian brainstem (according to yogic thought powered by the base *chakra*), the mammalian limbic brain (powered by the sacral *chakra*), and the primate neocortex (powered by the navel *chakra*). Since these structures are well understood I will outline the functions of the three lower *chakras* here only briefly, before turning to the higher *chakras*. The base *chakra*, which represents reptilian brain circuitry, is responsible for survival and thus directs the fight, flight and freeze reflex. In the evolutionary *chakra* model, the second level is the mammalian *chakra*, which determines our family life, interaction with our spouse, children, parents, and our emotional life, such as secure attachment. It is also responsible for our sense of belonging to small groups, such as clans, tribal bands and the need for territory. This *chakra* powers the limbic brain and its non-verbal communication and the ability to be seen, accepted, supported, and feel loved. The navel or power *chakra* is the evolutionary blueprint that helped to create the primate brain, the neocortex. It regulates our status and position in complex societies, including economic and civic affairs and membership in religious communities. For somebody whose highest operational level is the navel *chakra*, this *chakra* empowers their ability to lead, coerce, manipulate and dominate others.

Kundalini, in our current stage of evolution, is powering these three functions. When using the phrase Kundalini raising, we refer to raising it beyond the third *chakra*, to the heart *chakra* or beyond. On a psychological level, the heart *chakra*, when activated, reveals to us the unconditional love that the Divine experiences for us, and that the Divine, due to Her lack of an ego, cannot withhold grace from us and only ever sees us in the divine perfection in which She has created us. This recognition of the Divine in oneself also extends to all other beings and therefore heralds the end of conflict.

The 5th evolutionary *chakra* level, the throat *chakra*, enables us to see the whole cosmos as lawful and as the crystallized body of a higher intelligence. Animism, shamanism, science and art are all expressions of this *chakra*. This *chakra*, when activated, shows us that our purpose in life is to extend service to the community of life around us (including non-human life). Through such service, our life becomes meaningful, and we maintain the incredible beauty and balance of the natural world around us. On a skills level, the activating of the throat *chakra* then lets us download skills directly from the intellect of the Divine. Such skills can be assessed and validated through external observers and will give us the esteem and recognition from the community around us, and resulting from that, self-esteem.

The 6th *chakra*, the third eye *chakra*, opens us to a realization of cosmic intelligence. For the yogic mystic, this does not simply end in passively adoring this immanent aspect of the Divine. Rather than that, the yogic mystic learns from the Divine via vision practice. She learns information pertaining to how the Divine wants to embody Itself through the natural world and us. This is based on the realization that the Divine must individuate through us to become active on an embodied level. It cannot do so by Itself because lacking an ego (the term meaning limiter in space and time). The Divine can only be the cosmic, the universal, and not the individual.

The 7th *chakra*, the crown *chakra*, powers revelation of the transcendental aspect of the Divine, the infinite consciousness. Ultimately this leads to ego-transcendence, finding an expanded sense of self beyond one's limiting ego, and absorption in the

God transcendent via the mystical state at the completion of one's incarnations (*Mahaparinirvana*).

If we do not develop *chakra* awareness through *chakra*-Kundalini meditation, the activated Kundalini might jump ahead and activate higher *chakras*, while ignoring the upcoming ones. This will often lead to suffering and pathology. Activating for example, the throat-, third eye-, or crown *chakra* through psychedelic drugs, without prior attending to the navel-, and heart *chakras*, will with great regularity lead to psychotic and schizophrenic tendencies. A similar constellation, with additional blocking of the sacral *chakra* (i.e. blockage of empathy), could lead to becoming a psychopath. If only the heart *chakra* is blocked, but all other *chakras* are activated, we would be met with the case of a cult-leader personality, who uses insights from the higher *chakras* to place them into the service of the power *chakra*, i.e. to manipulate followers for the gain of the cult leader.

Raising Kundalini leads to spiritual experiences falling into one of the four above listed categories, i.e. seeing others as emanations of the Divine (heart *chakra*), seeing the entire material cosmos as a crystallization of divine law (throat *chakra*), directly realizing cosmic intelligence (third eye *chakra*), or infinite consciousness (crown *chakra*). A Kundalini expert or somebody who has become proficient in *chakra*-Kundalini meditation can consciously travel from one experience to another, without being married to either of them and without reducing the manifoldness of these experiences to a single layer.

These are the important and significant results of Kundalini raising. There is a public perception that Kundalini activity is present if we experience weird body sensations, or a feeling of burning or tickling going up and down the spine. Such sensations may present themselves initially, but they are neither proof nor guarantee we are presented with a case of Kundalini rising. The only proof is if somebody can bring about reliably, predictably and repeatedly experiences of revelation, spiritual realization and expansive ecstasy, and particularly if these experiences change one's personality towards being more genuine, loving, supportive and kind to other beings, including non-human life forms.

KUNDALINI ACCIDENTS AND SPONTANEOUS AWAKENING

Today reports have become common of strange, intense body sensations, sometimes involving loss of consciousness, intense surges of energy, burning sensations accompanied by emotional highs, and emotional discharges and catharses. Some of these experiences are described as ecstatic or epiphanic, others as frightening and threatening. A hallmark common to them is that they are described as beyond control. Sometimes these experiences seem related to experimenting with *Mula Bandha* and breathing, but often, they seem completely spontaneous. Those with these experiences after initial euphoria often struggle to make sense of them, and to integrate them meaningfully into their lives.

When inquiring into such sensations we first must out rule any underlying medical condition. If you have repeated episodes involving loss of consciousness, uncontrolled catharses and spasms, etc., the first port of call should be a medical doctor. We would need to rule out any underlying medical condition that could impinge on safely operating machinery, such as driving a car. The next compound to rule out would be psychiatric/ psychological disorders such as bipolar, multi-personality disorder, schizophrenia, anxiety/depression or borderline disorder. If any of the above-mentioned physical sensations cause disfunction, it might be worth being assessed by a psychologist. Having ruled out a medical or psychiatric condition, let's look next at the origins that such intense physical sensations are linked to Kundalini. The father of this notion is the late Indian yogi, writer and civil servant Gopi Krishna, who in his 1967 book *Kundalini The Evolutionary Energy in Man*, described how a seemingly innocent meditation technique plunged him into a 12-year-long abyss of madness, pain and burning sensations, described by him as a state between life and death. Once he had transited through that period, his experience stabilized and morphed into genuine spiritual awakening and ecstatic, mystical experience. By looking at Gopi Krishna's life and work we can shed light on these strange, physical and energetic experiences related to Kundalini.

According to his own account, Gopi Krishna's awakening was not spontaneous, but caused by 17 years of daily, hour-long meditation on the crown *chakra* (*Sahasrara*), while sitting in lotus posture (*Padmasana*). As many critics have pointed out, Gopi Krishna had no instruction on yoga stemming from within the yoga tradition. He did not prepare himself in any meaningful way[292], besides reading on the subject whatever he could find. Yogic adepts would never start their practice by meditating on the crown *chakra* for any significant length of time, especially not while sitting in *Padmasana* for extended periods. Judging from the many sincere books Gopi Krishna wrote, in which he describes not only his own mystical states, but also researched

292 Gopi Krishna, *Kundalini The Evolutionary Energy in Man*, Shambala, Boston & London, 1997, p. 137

and evaluated those of others, his attainment is genuine. He himself ascribes his success to a. the fact that he became expert in concentration and b. heredity, that both of his parents were Hindu saints. If you add to both these preconditions that Gopi Krishna meditated 17 years daily in *Padmasana* on the crown *chakra*[293], and spent another 12 years in a Dark-Night-of-the-Soul-type spiritual crisis, the whole process took him 30 years. We need to then let go of the notion that anything in G. Krishna's account amounted to 'spontaneous' awakening. He makes no claims to have found any form of shortcut. If we are investing many decades of our life into spiritual pursuit, we should use technology that makes progress to some extent smooth, traceable and reliable. Yet Gopi Krishna's first book created a whole new genre of Kundalini accidents and spontaneous awakening and spawned a flood of reports of people seeking spiritual causes and explanations for weird physical symptoms they experienced. The difference between G. Krishna's account and most of these new reports was that Krishna's experiences were caused by decades of spiritual practice, but the new reports were about spontaneously occurring symptoms, not preceded by prolonged practice.

During his 12-year ordeal, G. Krishna realized that the physical symptoms of his state arose because Kundalini ascended through the solar *nadi* (*Pingala*), instead of through the central nadi (*Sushumna*). He briefly rectified this by meditation on the silver, lunar *nadi* (*Ida*), but later, he failed to revisit this important issue. Had he balanced the three *nadis* from the outset, he would not have experienced little if any physical

---

293 Gopi Krishna, *Kundalini The Evolutionary Energy in Man*, Shambala, Boston & London, 1997, p. 34

symptoms! By practising *pranayama*, precisely *Nadi Shodana* and its two cousins *Surya* and *Chandra Bhedana*, including *mantra*, sun/moon visualization, and internal and external *kumbhaka*, we can, through skill, conduct Kundalini safely. Of course, we wouldn't do this all at once, but we would gradually start with simple alternate nostril breathing. Yogis harped about this point for thousands of years and only as recent as a few decades ago T. Krishnamacharya said, '*Pranayama* is instrumental for attaining *samadhi'*.

For whatever reason G. Krishna's first book introduced into the public sphere the notion that rising Kundalini is spontaneous and chaotic. Rather than something that G. Krishna intended to communicate, this was a narrative that our culture at this point wished to hear. 1967, the year when G. Krishna's book was first published, was the year in which both the psychedelic revolution and the sexual revolution converged into the 'Summer of Love'. However, Kundalini raising is not a chaotic and spontaneous occurrence. If approached through a systematic long-term practice of *asana, kriya, pranayama,* Kundalini meditation and *samadhi,* based on the yogic *shastras* (scriptures), Kundalini-rousing has lawful, predictable, and repeatable outcomes. G. Krishna himself stated that we need to prepare for Kundalini awakening by mastering beforehand *asana, kriya* and *pranayama*[294]. After his initial bestseller, Gopi Krishna published another 10 books in which he tried to clarify that his readers had misunderstood him when believing that the Kundalini was a physical force. He stated that Kundalini truly is the divine creative force, even identically with the Divine. But

---

294 Gopi Krishna, *Kundalini The Evolutionary Energy in Man*, Shambala, Boston & London, 1997, p. 130

by then, the horse of public perception had bolted. The public wanted to believe that weird body sensations were a sign and proof of a spontaneously, unpredictably rising, spiritual force.

Weird physical symptoms accompanying spiritual experiences indicate that the solar *nadi* is overcharged in which case *pranayama* needs to be practiced. Since today everybody has an overcharged solar *nadi*, Kundalini-raising should not be attempted without a serious daily *Nadi Shodana* practice. After one has gained a foothold in *pranayama*, *chakra*-Kundalini meditation needs to be practiced in a daily, consistent form to bring about repeatable effects. Both meditation and *pranayama* need to be supported by a daily *asana* and *kriya* practice. If all of these are practiced as an integrated whole, progress will be steady, and no adverse symptoms will be encountered.

A final word on the spontaneity with which some of these states are supposed to occur. The whole world is an endless chain of cause and effect. Like all other aspects of life and the world, also spiritual experiences fall under the laws of causation. That genuine spiritual experiences come about spontaneously and uncaused is about as unlikely as somebody awarding you a PhD in quantum physics (or any other difficult academic discipline) uncaused. Genuine spiritual awakenings are brought about by long periods of *sadhana* (spiritual practice). All traditional spiritual teachings, whether indigenous shamanism and animism, Daoism, Sufism, Qabalah, Zen, Tibetan Buddhism, or Yoga, have in common that breakthrough experiences come through, and after, long periods of practice. That these things just happen spontaneously is a product of Western neo-colonialism. Neo-colonialism here is the belief that us modern people can get whatever we want without giving in return (in this case, a period of our life for practise), doing away with so-called primitive and long-held beliefs of traditional and indigenous societies. These beliefs are not primitive; they are accurate.

The other driving force of so-called spontaneous spiritual experiences is consumerism. Consumerism in this context is that we are entitled to immediate gratification without putting in any work. If we are seriously interested in spiritual awakening and spiritual evolution, we need to first let go of ideas according to which we are entitled to something without giving something else in return. Spiritual awakening is powered by the law of *karma*. We may have short-term experiences, caused, for example, by psychedelics, but none of that is sustainable or can be integrated without time spent on *sadhana*, spiritual practices such as *asana, pranayama, kriyas, mudras* and meditation. The following practices are extremely powerful and can lead to fast progress. However, it is necessary to integrate them into a supporting network of long-term yogic practices.

Chapter 21

MAHA MUDRA (Great Seal)

Maha Mudra is one of the most important *mudras*. It features in all common compilations of *mudras,* including *Goraksha Shataka*[295], *Hatha Yoga Pradipika*[296], *Gheranda Samhita*[297], and *Shiva Samhita*[298]. Besides that the method is also recommended in the *Hathatatva Kaumudi of Sundaradeva*[299], the *Kapala Kurantaka Yoga*[300], the *Hathayoga Manjari of Sahajananda*[301], the *Jogapradipyaka of Jayatarama* [302], the 10-chapter edition of the *Hatha Yoga Pradipika*[303], the *Dhyanabindu Upanishad*[304], the *Yoga*

---

295 *Goraksha Shataka* stanzas 59-63

296 *Hatha Yoga Pradipika* III.10-18

297 *Gheranda Samhita* III.6 – 8

298 *Shiva Samhita* III.6 – 8

299 Dr M.L. Gharote et al (eds. & transl.), *Hathatatvakaumudi,* The Lonavla Yoga Institite, Lonavla, 2007, p. 178

300 Swami Maheshananda et al (eds. & transl.), *Kapalakurantaka's Hathabhyasa-Paddhati,* Kaivalyadhama, Lonavla, 2015, p. 91

301 O.P. Tiwari (publ.), *Hathayoga Manjari of Sahajananda,* Kaivalyadhama, Lonavla, 2006, p. 41

302 Swami Maheshananda et al. (eds & transl.), *Jogapradipyaka of Jayatarama,* Kaivalyadhama, Lonavla, 2006, p. 121

303 Dr M.L. Gharote et al (eds. & transl.), *Hathapradipika of Svatmarama (10 chapters),* Lonavla Yoga Institute, Lonavla, 2006, p. 105

304 *Dhyanabindu Upanishad* stanzas 90-93

Chudamani Upanishad[305], the *Hatharatnavali of Shrinivasayogi*[306], *Dattatreya's Yogashastra*[307] and the *Yoga-Tattva Upanishad*[308]. *Yoga Rahasya* interestingly calls *Maha Mudra* an *asana* and suggests it for *brahmacharis*, which means it is to be learned before *pranayama*, a *grhasta* practice[309]. The student *ashrama*[310] (*brahmachary*), making up the first 25 years of life (the exact timeframe depends on several factors), is the period during which we are engaged in education and learning skills for our later life. Because the *Yoga Rahasya* identifies *Maha Mudra* as an *asana*, it suggests introducing it early in life and this defines it as a technique preparing for *pranayama*. The householder *ashrama* (*grhastha*) takes up the next 25 years of life and now the focus shifts to forming a family and attending to one's professional duty, both together forming one's duties towards society. The practice ideally suited for the householder *ashrama* is *pranayama* and, of course, during that time, *asana* practice is to be maintained. It is peculiar that the

---

305 Swami Satyadharma, *Yoga Chudamani Upanishad*, Yoga Publications Trust, Munger, 2003, p. 156-170, same stanzas appear in the Lonavla edition, pp. 212-214

306 Dr M.L. Gharote et al (eds. & transl.), *Hatharatnavali of Shrinivasayogi*, The Lonavla Yoga Institite, Lonavla, 2009, p. 55-57

307 Dr M.M. Gharote (ed.), *Dattatreyayogasastram,* Lonavla Yoga Institute, Lonavla, 2015, p. 63-63

308 *Yoga-Tattva Upanishad* stanza 112

309 T.K.V. Desikachar (transl.), *Nathamuni's Yoga Rahasya*, Krishnamacharya Yoga Mandiram, Chennai, 1998, p. 102-107

310 The term *ashrama* means stage of life. According to Vedic philosophy there are four stages of life, student (*brahmachary*), householder (*grhastha*), forest dweller (*vanaprashta*) and sage (*sannyasi*). Each of these stages has yoga practices appropriate for it. These are, however, only rough guidelines.

Yoga Rahasya considers *Maha Mudra* a much more basic yoga technique as other *shastras* do. Most other *shastras* believe that *Maha Mudra* is only practised once proficient in both *asana* and *pranayama,* and they teach it somewhere between *pranayama* and *samadhi*. I consider the majority view here to be the more helpful one, but it is interesting to notice that some *yoga shastras* disagree on an important and obvious point.

EFFECTS
The *Hatharatnavali of Shrinivasayogi* ascribes to *Maha Mudra* the effect of blocking the lunar and solar *nadi* (*Ida* and *Pingala*) and instead opening the central *nadi* (*Sushumna*). The *Hatha Yoga Pradipka with Jyotsna* argues that *Maha Mudra* is called the Great Seal because it vanquishes the five forms of suffering[311], *kleshas,* mentioned by Patanjali, the author of the *Yoga Sutra*[312]. The *Yoga Chudamani Upanishad* enthusiastically declares this *mudra* destroys all diseases, a tired claim that various yoga texts ascribe to almost any yoga method. The *Gheranda Samhita* states that *Maha Mudra* cures consumption, constipation, wrinkles, grey hair, old age, the enlargement of the spleen, indigestion and fever – it cures all diseases, and, so Gheranda, even destroys death itself. *Shiva Samhita* opines that vitality is increased and its decay is checked, and that all sins are destroyed. And so the *Samhita,* all diseases are healed, and the gastric fire is increased. B.N.S. Iyengar additionally told me that *Maha Mudra* purifies the *chakras,* is helpful with respiratory diseases, prepares for extreme hip-rotation *asanas,* raises Kundalini, improves

311 Kunjunni Raja (ed.), *The Hathayogapradipika of Svatmarama with the Commentary Jyotsna of Brahmananda,* The Adyar Library, Madras, 1972, p. 39
312 Yoga Sutra II.3

memory and tunes the brain. One does wonder how such a simple technique can fulfil all these claims. I advise the reader to not simply accept them simply because they are written in *shastra*, but to rather take them with a pinch of salt.

The much-esteemed Dr M.L. Gharote, founder of the Lonavla Yoga Institute and translator of many essential yoga texts, gives in both the *Hatharatnavali of Shrinivasayogi*[313] and the 10-chapter edition of the *Hatha Yoga Pradipika*[314] a summary of the various versions of *Maha Mudra* in different texts. He points out, for example, that the *Hatha Yoga Pradipika* omits *Uddiyana Bandha* from *Maha Mudra's* description, whereas Brahmananda's *Jyotsna* commentary talks only about *Jihva Bandha* instead of the three main *bandhas*. The *Gheranda Samhita* only mentions *Jalandhara Bandha* and *Bhrumadhya Drishti*, but not the other *bandhas*. The *Shiva Samhita* follows the same pattern but omits *Bhrumadhya Drishti*. In the *Madhaviya* tradition, *Ujjayi* is emphasized whereas the other texts are silent about it. Dr Gharote infers from such omissions a sliding scale of difficulty or detail in which *Maha Mudra* was taught in various traditions. However, I argue that we cannot from such omissions infer that some traditions taught a *Maha Mudra*-light, or a *Maha Mudra* with less detail. Traditional yoga texts were never meant to give an exhaustive and complete description of a technique. Remember that the *Gheranda Samhita* describes a handstand as, "place your hands on the floor and throw your

---

313 Dr M.L. Gharote et al (eds. & transl.), *Hatharatnavali of Shrinivasayogi*, The Lonavla Yoga Institite, Lonavla, 2009, p. 55

314 Dr M.L. Gharote et al (eds. & transl.), *Hathatatvakaumudi*, The Lonavla Yoga Institite, Lonavla, 2007, p. 105

legs into the air". Most translators did not even recognize this description refers to a handstand. You recognize the handstand in this description only if you already know this is what the description refers to. No, yogic texts list stanzas only as a memory aid so techniques would not be forgotten. The entire technique had to still be personally learned from a teacher and none of the texts endeavours to give a complete description. Often, confusing details are purposely included to lead readers, who are not part of the oral tradition, astray. This is because in days of yore, yogic schools were extremely private and secretive about their techniques. Techniques were only written down in such a way that the text alone was not enough to understand and reconstruct the method. You had to be personally selected and found worthy to receive a teaching. Many texts, such as the *Shiva Samhita*, instil into the practitioner that the methods are to be practiced in secrecy, and never to be given to the uninitiated[315]. If this is repeated in *shastra* ad nauseam, why would we expect descriptions to be complete enough so they could be practised from the text? No, what we are expecting to see is that the descriptions are purposely worded in a way to confuse us, and to make the seeking of an exponent of a particular tradition necessary. And this is exactly what we find when studying *shastra*. This needs to be considered when taking gleans in regard to proper technique. When analysing *shastra* we can never expect a description to be complete. To the contrary, we need to expect that descriptions purposely omit vital details, only to be gained through oral, personal instruction. But *shastra*

---

315 Chandra Vasu, R.B.S. (transl.), *The Shiva Samhita*, Sri Satguru Publications, Delhi, 1986, p. 20

study, side-by-side with personal instruction, is vital, a fact admitted even by Gopi Krishna, who stated that yoga in the last few centuries has gone through a serious process of deterioration[316].

Dattatreya's Yogashastra teaches that the left leg has to be bent first[317], and that *Maha Mudra* is performed with an internal *kumbhaka*[318]. The *Hatha Yoga Pradipika* emphasises that the perineum be pressed with the heel of the bent leg, and the foot of the straight leg be grasped with the thumb and index finger. One then inhales and performs internal *kumbhaka* with *Jalandhara Bandha*. The *prana* now leaves the lunar and solar *nadis* and enters *Sushumna*[319]. Like the *Pradipika*, the *Gheranda Samhita* says that first the right leg needs to be straightened and the left leg bent[320]. The throat is then contracted via *Jalandhara Bandha* and the gaze fixed between the eyebrows. The *Shiva Samhita* agrees regarding the order of the legs and the action of the hands but adds the closing of the nine sensory gates of the body [321]. The nine sensory gates are the eyes, ears, nostrils, mouth, genital and anus. These are generally closed through *Shanmukhi-, Vajroli-, and Ashvini Mudras* respectively, which are to be covered later in this text. However, *Shanmukhi Mudra* requires the hands to close

---

316 Gopi Krishna, *Kundalini The Evolutionary Energy in Man*, Shambala, Boston & London, 1997, p. 119

317 Dr M.M. Gharote (ed.), *Dattatreyayogasastram*, Lonavla Yoga Institute, Lonavla, 2015, p. 62

318 Dr M.M. Gharote (ed.), *Dattatreyayogasastram*, Lonavla Yoga Institute, Lonavla, 2015, p. 63 and again p. 108

319 *Hatha Yoga Pradipika* III.11-12.

320 *Gheranda Samhita* III.6 – 8

321 *Shiva Samhita* IV. 16.

the eyes, nostrils, ears and mouth. Since we are using the hands to grasp the foot of the outstretched leg, we must discard this suggestion as an outlier view.

TECHNIQUE

Maha Mudra is ideally performed towards the end of one's *asana* practice, once appropriately warmed up. This is due to the following facts: The position of the heel of the bent leg against the perineum is crucial. This position leads to considerable obliquity of the pelvis with resulting torsional forces on the sacroiliac joints. This would not be a problem if only held briefly, but we need to hold the position during the length of potentially several internal *kumbhakas*. This can lead to a twisting of the sacroiliac joints, especially when not warmed up through previous *asana* practice.

Sitting in *Dandasana*, bend your left leg and press the left heel against the perineum, thus stimulating *Muladhara chakra*, while keeping the right leg straight. The position of the left leg needs to resemble something between *Janushirsasana* A and B[322] with the right thigh grounded on the floor. In *Janushirsasana* A, the knee is further back, i.e. the angle between both thighbones is greater, and the heel of the bent leg is in the groin of that same leg. In *Janushirsasana* B, the knee is more forward; hence the angle between both thighbones is considerably smaller. But the entire foot in this position is placed under the sit bones, hence we are sitting on the foot. In *Maha Mudra* the position of the heel is somewhat

322 For detailed instruction on these two postures please see Gregor Maehle, *Ashtanga Yoga Practice and Philosophy*, New World Library, Novato, 2007, p. 79-82

between that of both *asanas*, with the back of the heel touching the perineum. The difference to both *Janushirshasanas* is, of course, that in these *asanas* we would first perform them with the right leg bent before going on to the left side. In *Maha Mudra*, however, it is the left leg bent first. Another point of difference is, of course, that we would not perform *kumbhaka* during the *Janushirshasanas*.

Engage your right quadriceps to keep the right foot upright in a neutral position. Take the right big toe with two fingers of the right hand and left hand and square your torso and shoulders to the right leg. If the hand position is too demanding due to stiff hamstrings, one may hold the toe with the right hand only and clasp the wrist of the right hand with the left hand. A more demanding hand position would be to clasp the foot with both hands. Inhale *with Ujjayi pranayama*[323] and lift your chest high, particularly the sternum. Most people will have to pull up the shoulders, too, to achieve that. This also elongates and straightens the spine. At completing the inhalation, initiate *Jalandhara Bandha* by swallowing and locking the throat, while placing your chin down on your sternum. Keep lifting the sternum up towards the chin as you do so. Those already proficient in *Jalandhara Bandha*, can perform *Jihva Bandha*, too, i.e. rolling the tongue back and pressing it against the soft palate.

Contract your perineum, stimulated by the left heel, and engage *Mula Bandha*. Those proficient in the technique so far

---

323 Described in detail in the above *Ashtanga Yoga Practice and Philosophy*, p. 9-11. One creates during in- and exhalation a whispering/ hissing sound by slightly closing the glottis for the purpose of stretching the breath long.

can engage *Uddiyana Bandha*, too. The order of importance of *bandhas* during internal *kumbhaka* is first *Jalandhara-*, then *Mula-*, then *Uddiyana Bandha*. Established practitioners may engage all three simultaneously, but only after *Jalandhara-* and *Mula Bandha* have been perfected. The gaze is now fixed between the eyebrows, constituting *Bhrumadhya Drishti*, or its more advanced cousin, *Shambhavi Mudra* (Section 3, *Mudra* 16), and mentally we focus on the *Ajna Chakra* (third eye *chakra*).

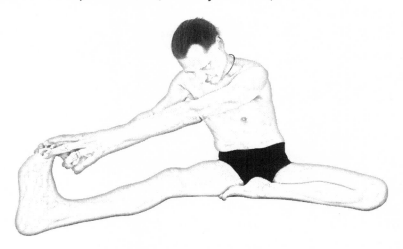

Maha Mudra **with internal** *kumbhaka*

Practice internal *kumbhaka* to your individual capacity without observing count, which would be observed if this was not a *mudra* but a *pranayama*-proper technique. Feel how the pull on the spine and stimulus of the perineum strongly forces *prana* up. Eventually, exhale very slowly, again using the *Ujjayi* sound. Perform initially three rounds with the left leg bent, then the same number with the right leg bent. Increase the length of *kumbhakas* und number of rounds as proficiency increases. A maximum of 21 rounds on each side can be practised, but this would constitute an extreme practice. Some *shastras* recommend repeating sets of *Maha Mudra* throughout the day every 8 or even 3 hours, but a more wholistic approach would be to combine the *mudra* with other methods. This potent combination will be explored under the heading of *Shakti Chalana Mudra*, Section 4, *Mudra* 27.

Chapter 22

MAHA BANDHA MUDRA
(Great Lock Seal)

Maha Bandha Mudra, too, is one of the most common and celebrated *mudras*, being described in the *Hathatatva Kaumudi of Sundaradeva*[324], the *Kapala Kurantaka Yoga*[325], the *Yoga Makaranda*[326], the *Jogapradipyaka of Jayatarama*[327], the *Hatharatnavali of Shrinivasayogi*[328], the *Hatha Yoga Pradipika*[329], the 10-chapter edition of the *Hatha Yoga Pradipika*[330], the *Gheranda Samhita*[331], *Dattatreya's Yogashastra*[332], and the *Shiva Samhita*[333].

---

324 Dr M.L. Gharote et al (eds. & transl.), *Hathatatvakaumudi*, The Lonavla Yoga Institite, Lonavla, 2007, p. 181

325 Swami Maheshananda et al (eds. & transl.), *Kapalakurantaka's Hathabhyasa-Paddhati*, Kaivalyadhama, Lonavla, 2015, p. 92

326 T. Krishnamacharya, *Yoga Makaranda*, Media Garuda, Chennai, 2011, p. 106

327 Swami Maheshananda et al (eds. & transl.), *Jogapradipyaka of Jayatarama*, Kaivalyadhama, Lonavla, 2006, p. 121

328 Dr M.L. Gharote et al (eds. & transl.), *Hatharatnavali of Shrinivasayogi*, The Lonavla Yoga Institite, Lonavla, 2009, p. 58

329 *Hatha Yoga Pradipika* III.19-22

330 Dr M.L. Gharote et al (eds. & transl.), *Hathapradipika of Svatmarama (10 chapters)*, Lonavla Yoga Institute, Lonavla, 2006, p. 110

331 *Gheranda Samhita* stanzas III.18-20 in the Chandra Vasu translation, and III.14-16 in the James Mallinson translation

332 Dr M.M. Gharote (ed.), *Dattatreyayogasastram*, Lonavla Yoga Institute, Lonavla, 2015, p. 64 and again p. 109

333 *Shiva Samhita* IV. 21-22

Maha Bandha Mudra could be described as a *Maha Mudra* without the outstretched leg; however, there is no universal agreement which posture exactly is used. T. Krishnamacharya's *Yoga Makaranda* states that *Maha Bandha Mudra* is to be performed in *Siddhasana* and with an internal *kumbhaka* (i.e. holding the breath after an inhalation). The *Hatha Yoga Pradipika* in III.19-22 holds that the left heel should press against the perineum and the right foot is to be placed on the left thigh. An internal *kumbhaka* is then performed with *Jalandhara Bandha* and *Bhrumadhya Drishti*. After a slow exhalation, which implies the use of *Ujjayi*, one then reverses sides and practices the *mudra* with reversed leg position. This is corroborated by the *Shiva Samhita*, which says that the *mudra* should be practiced alternately with first the left heel, then the right.

That an internal breath suspension is used is also confirmed in *Jayatarama's Jogapradipyaka*, which additionally points out the importance of *Uddiyana Bandha*, a point omitted by other texts[334]. Both Jayatarama and the 10-chapter edition of the *Hatha Yoga Pradipika* agree on *Bhrumadhya Drishti/ Shambhavi Mudra* on one hand and *Jihva Bandha/ Khechari Mudra* on the other, the latter of each pair representing a more advanced version of the earlier.

The *Gheranda Samhita* introduces a new element[335]: The left heel is placed against the perineum and the right foot placed on the left foot. This description tallies with T. Krishnamacharya's statement that *Siddhasana* should be used (in which the left heel is always placed first and the right leg on top). In most traditional text both *Siddhasana* and *Padmasana* are direction-

---

334 Swami Maheshananda et al. (eds & transl.), *Jogapradipyaka of Jayatarama,* Kaivalyadhama, Lonavla, 2006, p. 63 and again p. 121

335 *Gheranda Samhita* III.14-16 (in the James Mallinson edition)

sensitive postures[336]. For *Siddhasana* the left leg is usually placed first and the right leg on top, whereas the order is reversed in *Padmasana*. *Gheranda Samhita* now states that the left heel is to be gently moved to stimulate the contraction of the perineum, i.e. *Mula Bandha*, while an internal *kumbhaka* is performed with *Jalandhara Bandha*.

Among contemporary authorities, Paramahamsa Yogeswaranand confirms that only the left heel is used to stimulate the perineum and the right foot is placed on top[337]. An inhalation is then performed, followed by an internal breath retention with *Jalandhara Bandha*. *Vasishta Samhita* also uses *Siddhasana* combined with internal *kumbhaka*[338].

EFFECTS
Jayatarama's *Jogapradipyaka* argues this *mudra* leads to effortless *samadhi* and that nothing remains hidden to the practitioner due to the accumulative effect of *Maha Mudra, Maha Bandha Mudra* and *Maha Vedha Mudra*, which is described next. Sage Gheranda states that by this *mudra* anything can be achieved. The *Shiva Samhita* holds this practice makes *prana* enter the central energy channel, *Sushumna*, invigorates the body, accomplishes all desires and awakens Kundalini.

---

336 Please note that apart from the fact that the order of the legs are reversed, there are additional points in which both postures differ. For in depth descriptions of both please consult Gregor Maehle, *Pranayama The Breath of Yoga*, Kaivalya Publications, Crabbes Creek, 2012, p.134-138

337 Yogeshvaranand Paramahansa, *First Steps to Higher Yoga*, Yoga Niketan Trust, New Delhi, 2001, p. 380

338 Swami Digambarji et al (eds & transl.), *Vasishta Samhita*, Kaivalyadhama, Lonavla, 1984, p. 39 (please note that page numbers in this edition occur twice and this is the second time this page number appears)

TECHNIQUE

First, we assume *Siddhasana*. With the left heel in the perineum, *Siddhasana* is the posture of choice to ignite *Mula Bandha*, the pelvic lock. Goraksha Natha and other authorities state that the left heel must be placed first to stimulate *Muladhara Chakra*. The characteristics of *Siddhasana* differ greatly from those of *Padmasana*, the posture of choice for *Yoga Mudra*. Whereas in *Padmasana* we bring the knees as close together as possible, in *Siddhasana* we take them apart as wide as possible. Initially, you may sit on a pad such as a folded blanket and later decrease its height as you gain proficiency. The pad will assist you in tilting the pelvis forward more.

From a sitting, straight-legged position (*Dandasana*), bend the left leg and place the heel against the perineum, the location of *Muladhara Chakra*, between anus and genitals. Now bend the right leg and place the right ankle on top of the left one so the right heel presses against the pubic bone. In males, the organ of generation is now between the left and right heels. Now insert the toes of the right foot between the calf and thigh of the left leg. Using both hands, move the calf and thigh of the right leg apart, reach through and pull the big toe of the left foot up so it is inserted between the calf and thigh of the right leg. Pay close attention to how this changes the location of the heel and what it does to the rotation of the left femur. It is only through this final action that the heel of the left foot comes into the right contact with the perineum. This is the position necessary for Kundalini-raising.

Please note, the easier variation of this posture for beginners, called *Ardha* (half) *Siddhasana,* is also a good meditation posture but is unlikely to be sufficient for *Maha Bandha Mudra*. Here, instead of stacking the heels on top of each other, they are placed in front of each other, with both feet on the floor. Use this posture only as a warm-up, and graduate to *Siddhasana* whenever possible.

Inhale now through both nostrils employing the *Ujjayi* sound, which enables us to take a deep and slow inhalation. Once you completed your inhalation to 80-95% of your respiratory capacity, perform *kumbhaka*. 100% respiratory capacity, i.e. inhaling as deeply as possible, is only used for activities like sprinting, where inhalation is immediately followed by exhaling. A *kumbhaka* preceded by such an inhalation would provide too much strain for the alveoli, as they cannot immediately recoil (through exhaling) and are kept in a stretched state. Therefore, even 95% respiratory capacity is only used by very experienced *pranayama* practitioners who know their limits.

Perform internal *kumbhaka* by lifting your chest and initiating *Jalandhara Bandha* by placing your chin on the raised sternum while swallowing and contracting the throat. As described under *Yoga Mudra*, *Jalandhara Bandha* needs to be of good quality. This is ascertained by trying to in- and exhale, and only if no air is passing your throat is the *bandha* properly executed. If you are not sure, please review the notes on *Jalandhara Bandha* in Section 2, *Mudra* 12. You may also wish to revisit the notes in contraindications for internal kumbhaka in Section 1, *Mudra* 3.

Maha Bandha Mudra **with internal** *kumbhaka*

Once *Jalandhara Bandha* is applied you can now add *Mula-*, and then *Uddiyana Bandha*. And *Jihva Bandha* is also a helpful add-on, however, the other *bandhas*, especially *Jalandhara Bandha*, are more important. All *bandhas* performed simultaneously constitute the great *bandha*, *Maha Bandha*, which gives this *mudra* its name. During the *kumbhaka* look towards the centre of the eyebrows (*Bhrumadhya Drishti*) or use *Shambhavi Mudra* (rolling the eyes backwards in the sockets), as described in Section 3, *Mudra* 16. Once you have established yourself in the techniques so far, start to slightly move the left heel to further stimulate the perineum and *Mula Bandha*. This helps with igniting Kundalini. I did not learn this last add-on from B.N.S. Iyengar, but after finding it repeatedly mentioned in *shastra*, I tried it out and found it helpful.

The hands in this *mudra* can be placed palms downwards on knees, if additional stability is required. The arms are kept straight. Alternatively the hands can be placed in *Jnana Mudra* with palms up. Repeat *Maha Bandha Mudra* initially three times, with a total of 21 times possible. Practice it always right after *Maha Mudra* and, once the learning phase is completed, perform the same number of rounds as *Maha Mudra*. Learn *Maha Mudra* first and establish yourself in that *mudra* before adding on *Maha Bandha Mudra*.

Chapter 23

MAHA VEDHA MUDRA
(Great Piercing Seal)

The *Maha Vedha Mudra* is sometimes called *Maha Bedha Mudra*. This is due to the great similarity of the letters 'v' and 'b' in the *Devanagari* script, which is the most common way Sanskrit is written. You can see the same play itself out in the many ways in which *Vrindavan*, the birthplace of Krishna is written. We encounter alternative spellings such as *Brindaban, Vrindaban* or *Brindavan*.

Maha Vedha Mudra forms a triad with *Maha Mudra* and *Maha Bandha Mudra* and is again one of the most prolifically mentioned mudras in *shastra*. Among other places we find it listed in the *Hatha Yoga Pradipika*[339], *Gheranda Samhita*[340], *Yoga Makaranda*[341], *Hathapradipika (10 chapters)*[342], *Kapala Kurantaka*

---

339 *Hatha Yoga Pradipika* III.26–31

340 *Gheranda Samhita* III.22-24 in the James Mallinson edition

341 T. Krishnamacharya, *Yoga Makaranda,* Media Garuda, Chennai, 2011, p. 106

342 Dr M.L. Gharote et al (eds. & transl.), *Hathapradipika of Svatmarama (10 chapters)*, Lonavla Yoga Institute, Lonavla, 2006, p. 113

Yoga[343], *Hathatatva Kaumudi of Sundaradeva*[344], *Dattatreya's Yogashastra*[345] and *Hathayoga Manjari of Sahajananda*[346].

The peculiar main method of *Maha Vedha Mudra* consists of sitting in *Padmasana*, performing *kumbhaka*, lifting oneself off the floor by means of one's arms, and repeatedly dropping back down, hence striking the floor with one's buttocks. I've seen a video in which this method was touted as the main method performed by certain Tibetan yogis, although this was never mentioned when I trained in Tibetan yoga myself. The Tibetan yogi in the video jumped up in the air and then landed on what appeared to be a thick plastic mattress. The video was replete with warnings this was no method for the uninitiated. The mattress, in this case, would mitigate the impact of a drop from great height, but even then, injury to the lumbar discs, sacroiliac- and knee joints could occur. It is not something I would recommend.

Maha Vedha Mudra is also like the so-called 'yogic flying', as performed by advanced practitioners of the Transcendental Meditation. Here one also sits in *Padmasana* on a mattress but pushes oneself off the ground by rapidly pressing the bent legs and knees into the floor, thus producing a hopping movement. Again there is a certain risk to the knee joints and I prefer the

---

343 Swami Maheshananda et al (eds. & transl.), *Kapalakurantaka's Hathabhyasa-Paddhati*, Kaivalyadhama, Lonavla, 2015, p. 93

344 Dr M.L. Gharote et al (eds. & transl.), *Hathatatvakaumudi*, The Lonavla Yoga Institite, Lonavla, 2007, p. 183

345 Dr M.M. Gharote (ed.), *Dattatreyayogasastram*, Lonavla Yoga Institute, Lonavla, 2015, p. 65

346 O.P. Tiwari (publ.), *Hathayoga Manjari of Sahajananda*, Kaivalyadhama, Lonavla, 2006, p. 42

Maha Vedha Mudra technique, as described in *shastra*. Introducing a mattress also necessitates the dropping from a much greater height to produce the same impact. The *Hatha Yoga Pradipika* in III.26 – 31 suggests performing *kumbhaka* in *Padmasana* with all three *bandhas*, place the hands down and lift off the floor. One then strikes or dashes the buttocks repeatedly, but gently on the floor. This moves the *prana* from the outer *nadis* into the central energy channel, *Sushumna*. The *Pradipika* advises this dropping does not occur from a great height or with great force.

Sahajananda's *Hathayoga Manjari* emphasises sitting in *Padmasana* with the right leg placed first, and to perform the method on an internal *kumbhaka*, i.e. holding the breath after inhalation[347]. Again, here is the emphasis on repeatedly striking the buttocks against the floor. The method of striking with one's behind is also confirmed in Shrinivasayogi's *Hatharatnavali*[348] and *Dattatreya's Yogashastra*[349]. Paramahamsa Yogeswaranand gives two methods by which *Maha Vedha Mudra* can be performed[350]. One is the conventional way of sitting in *Padmasana*, performing *kumbhaka* and repeatedly dashing the buttocks to the ground, which he describes as the superior method. Yogeshvaranand then offers a second method designed for those not ready to sit in *Padmasana*. Here one leg is placed on the opposite thigh

---

347 O.P. Tiwari (publ.), *Hathayoga Manjari of Sahajananda,* Kaivalyadhama, Lonavla, 2006, p. 42

348 Dr M.L. Gharote et al (eds. & transl.), *Hatharatnavali of Shrinivasayogi,* The Lonavla Yoga Institite, Lonavla, 2009, p. 61

349 Dr M.M. Gharote (ed.), *Dattatreyayogasastram,* Lonavla Yoga Institute, Lonavla, 2015, p. 65

350 Yogeshvaranand Paramahansa, *First Steps to Higher Yoga*, Yoga Niketan Trust, New Delhi, 2001, p. 380

and the heel of the other leg is used to repeatedly strike against that perineum, while holding oneself off the floor. I found this method extremely awkward and am unsure whether this way offers much in the way of improvement, should *Padmasana* be out of reach. Yogeshvaranand does say that when using *Padmasana*, the legs can be interchanged. This was something that also Krishnamacharya held. But both never went as far as B.K.S. Iyengar, who taught that the legs "should" be exchanged[351]. I'm a case of those who, albeit after a shaky start, practised *Padmasana* with the right leg first for most of my adult life, without ever feeling any form of imbalance or problem from that. Where then is the use for 'having' to change the order of one's legs? This makes only sense if practising the traditional method of placing the right leg first into *Padmasana* leads to problems.

Swami Muktibodhananda argues that if one cannot perform *Padmasana*, *Maha Vedha Mudra* cannot be performed properly, which is probably a sensible attitude[352]. She also confirms the inclusion of internal *kumbhaka* and *Jalandhara Bandha* but adds that the buttocks and the back of the thighs must touch the ground simultaneously. This is again sensible since if one would only strike the sit bones down, the impact on the spine would be everything but gentle, what the *Hatha Yoga Pradipika* calls for. Muktibodhananda suggests striking the buttocks 3 to 7 times and to repeat three rounds in total. Yet another variation of the method suggests sitting in a *Siddhasana*-like posture, with

---

351 Instruction givne to the author by B.K.S Iyengar at the Ramamani Iyengar Institute, Pune, Maharashtra, in 1993.

352 Swami Muktibodhananda, *Hatha Yoga Pradipika,* Yoga Publications Trust, Munger, 1993, p. 305

the left heel touching the perineum. One then lifts up with the arms and repeatedly drops the perineum down on the heel. The disadvantage here is that the strikes have to be performed precisely as this technique could otherwise lead to twisted sacroiliac joints. The *Padmasana* variation is still the preferred option.

Maha Mudra, *Maha Bandha Mudra* and *Maha Vedha Mudra*, although forming a sequence, should initially be learned individually, that is starting with *Maha Mudra* and then graduating to *Maha Bandha Mudra*. Only once these two are done proficiently, is *Maha Vedha Mudra* added to the mix. Once proficiency is gained, all three can be practised in sequence.

WHEN AND HOW OFTEN

A good time to initially learn all three *mudras* is right after one's asana practice. This is an obvious timeslot because the hips and shoulder joints are warmed up. Particularly with *Maha Mudra* care needs to be taken not to twist the SI-joints. However, the most logical time for the three-*mudra* sequence is after one's pranayama practice and before ones Kundalini-*chakra* meditation (the meditation could also be performed out of sequence at any time throughout the day). The three *mudras* constitute a practice that requires a certain success in synchronizing the lunar and solar *nadis* via alternate nostril breathing. This can easily be checked by making sure that one breathes roughly as much predominantly through the right nostril over a two-week period as one does so through the left one. This is a yogic sub-science that is generally called *Svara Yoga* and the *Shiva Svarodaya* is the authoritative text here[353]. Some yoga texts such as the 10-chapter

---

[353] Translated in Swami Muktibodhananda, *Svara Yoga*, Yoga Publications Trust, Munger, 1984,

edition of the *Hatha Yoga Pradipika*[354] and Sundaradeva's *Hathatatva Kaumudi*[355] suggest performing a set of 8 *Maha Vedha Mudra* rounds every 3 hours. This would be appropriate if we are desperate for a Kundalini event and are pursuing it in a monastic or retreat-type setting. It is exactly such a setting that some of the medieval *Hatha* texts, the *Hatha Yoga Pradipika* being one of them, are usually referring to, i.e. a person withdrawing from the world for an extended period to do only yoga. Contrary to that, T. Krishnamacharya taught yoga integrated into a householder setting where we can continue one's family and work responsibilities and therefore phase practices in over the long-term. This is the view taken in the *Yoga Yajnavalkya*, *Vasishta Samhita* and to some degree the *Gheranda Samhita*. From my experience, this method works better, as experiences phased in slowly are integrated more easily into one's life. However, the retreat setting is also worth consideration and will be described in more detail under *Shakti Chalana Mudra*.

INTERNAL OR EXTERNAL *KUMBHAKA*

The *Hatha Yoga Pradipika* clearly refers to *Maha Vedha Mudra* performed during internal *kumbhaka*[356]. The *Gheranda Samhita* is so ambiguous in its description there is an element of speculation to figure out what is meant. Sage Gheranda suggests that *Maha Vedha Mudra* means to perform *Uddiyana* during *Maha Bandha Mudra* position but seeing that *Uddiyana*

---

354 Dr M.L. Gharote et al (eds. & transl.), *Hathapradipika of Svatmarama (10 chapters)*, Lonavla Yoga Institute, Lonavla, 2006, p. 113

355 Dr M.L. Gharote et al (eds. & transl.), *Hathatatvakaumudi,* The Lonavla Yoga Institite, Lonavla, 2007, p. Lxxv

356 *Hatha Yoga Pradipika* III.26

is described in III.8 as the drawing backwards of the abdomen above and below the navel, we must assume that this refers to external *kumbhaka*[357]. The term *Uddiyana* in medieval *Hatha* texts is usually not consistent with the form of *Uddiyana Bandha* permanently applied by Ashtanga *vinyasa* practitioners during their *asana* practice. The Ashtanga *vinyasa* version of *Uddiyana Bandha* is applied throughout the entire breathing cycle and consists in engaging the lower part of the transverse abdominis muscle. During the *Hatha* version of *Uddiyana* the abdominal wall is relaxed and sucked inwards exclusively during external breath retention *(kumbhaka)*. We are thus confronted with two different methods that must not be confused.

T. Krishnamacharya taught *Maha Vedha Mudra* performed during external *kumbhaka*[358]. Swami Niranjanananda also teaches it that way[359], but Sahajananda's *Hathayoga Manjari* clearly refers to an internal *kumbhaka* during this *mudra*[360], which is also the way Swami Rama has it[361]. With this split among authorities, we are then left with performing it both during internal and external *kumbhaka* to figure out which one works best for the individual.

---

357 *Gheranda Samhita* III.18

358 T. Krishnamacharya, *Yoga Makaranda,* Media Garuda, Chennai, 2011, p. 106

359 Swami Niranjanananda Saraswati, *Yoga Darshan*, Yoga Publications Trust, Munger, 2009, p. 420

360 O.P. Tiwari (publ.), *Hathayoga Manjari of Sahajananda,* Kaivalyadhama, Lonavla, 2006, p. 42

361 Swami Rama, *Path of Fire and Light*, vol. 1, Himalayan Institute Press, Honesdale, 1988, p. 54

EFFECTS

The *Hatha Yoga Pradipika* in stanza III.24 suggests this *mudra* pierces the Brahma *Granthi*, the lowest of the three *granthis* blocking the *Sushumna*. It also mentions that the *mudra* moves the *prana* out of *Ida* and *Pingala* (the lunar and solar *nadi*) and thus produces immortality[362]. However, we must simply take this as a case of exaggeration (*stuti*) to reel practitioners in, a tendency for which the texts are known. In stanza 29-30 the *Hatha Yoga Pradipika* further ascribes to the *mudra* the capacity to overcome old age, grey hair and feebleness, and that it increases your appetite, too.

The *Hathatatva Kaumudi of Sundaradeva* argues that *Maha Vedha Mudra* pierces all three *granthis*[363]. This makes more sense because why would such piercing limited to the Brahma *Granthi* alone. The *Kaumudi* also suggests that *Maha Vedha Mudra* makes one happy forever[364], which is consistent with piercing the *granthis* because the *granthis* are *pranic* blockages that limits the expansion of our sense of self and our spiritual evolution. It is this limitation, which according to Indian philosophy, limits our happiness. The *Hathayoga Manjari of Sahajananda* states that *Maha Vedha Mudra* pierces all six *chakras* and awakens Kundalini[365]. This is consistent with *granthi* piercing because the *granthis* are only *pranic* blockages that prevent the Kundalini

---

362 *Hatha Yoga Pradipika* III.28

363 Dr M.L. Gharote et al (eds. & transl.), *Hathatatvakaumudi,* The Lonavla Yoga Institite, Lonavla, 2007, p. 183

364 Dr M.L. Gharote et al (eds. & transl.), *Hathatatvakaumudi,* The Lonavla Yoga Institite, Lonavla, 2007, p. 208

365 O.P. Tiwari (publ.), *Hathayoga Manjari of Sahajananda,* Kaivalyadhama, Lonavla, 2006, p. 42

from rising up through the *chakras*. It is a case of saying the same thing with different words. The *Hatharatnavali of Shrinivasayogi* promises that the three *mudras* in sequence give *siddhi*[366]. This sounds again like a case of *panem et circensis* (bread and games) for the gullible. The *Shiva Samhita* goes even further and covers all bases, promising us both freedom from death and decay, activation of the *chakras* and Kundalini, conquering of death within six months, *siddhi* and even all power[367].

TECHNIQUE

Padmasana's importance derives from the forward tilt of the pelvis, aligning the spine like that of a cobra ready to strike – necessary for the serpent power to rise. However, do not suddenly extend time spent in *Padmasana*. Add only a minute, or at most a few minutes, per week. The posture is extremely powerful, and long stints should be done only once we have reached competence in practices designed for *Padmasana*, i.e. *kumbhakas*, *kriyas*, *chakra*-Kundalini meditation and *mudras*. *Padmasana* is not an *asana* suitable for mere 'sitting'. You should not approach *Padmasana* out of ambition. Never force yourself into the position or forcibly stay in the posture if you suffer pain. Striking your buttocks down may place additional strain on your knees, so you need to be comfortably already employing *Padmasana* during *pranayama*, to take this additional step.

To enter the posture safely from a straight-legged position, flex the right knee joint completely drawing the right heel to the right buttock. The inability to touch the buttock with your

---

366 Dr M.L. Gharote et al (eds. & transl.), *Hatharatnavali of Shrinivasayogi*, The Lonavla Yoga Institite, Lonavla, 2009, p. 61
367 *Shiva Samhita* IV.25-30

heel would indicate that your quadriceps is too short to enter *Padmasana* safely. If you can touch your heel to your buttock, let the right knee fall out to the side, pointing and inverting the right foot. Now draw the right heel into the right groin to ensure that the knee joint remains completely flexed in this abducted position. From here, lift the right heel in towards the navel, bringing the knee closer to the centreline. Keeping the heel in line with the navel, place the ball of the foot into the opposite groin.

Repeat these steps on the left, as if the right leg were still straight. First, flex the knee joint completely until the underside of the thigh touches the back of the leg over its entire length. Drawing the knee far out to the left, first place the left ankle under the right ankle on the floor. From here, lift the left foot over the right ankle in towards the navel, while drawing the left knee out to the side. Do not lift the left foot over the right knee, as this would mean opening the left knee joint, which would induce lateral movement into the knee during the transition. Keep the left knee joint in the transition as flexed as possible, allowing you to move the femur (thigh bone) and tibia (shin bone) as a unity, with no gap between.

Now place the left foot into the right groin and then move both heels towards each other so they touch the navel area. Bring both knees close together so the thighbones become almost parallel (depending on the ratio of length between femur and tibia). Now inwardly rotate your femurs until the front edges of the tibias point downward and the soles and heels of the feet face upward. In this way, the knee joints are completely closed and protected. Do not sit in *Padmasana* while retaining the initial lateral rotation of the femurs used to enter the posture. The key to mastering *Padmasana* is to rotate your femurs internally, while being in the posture. This is difficult to learn by merely sitting in *Padmasana* itself without being warmed up. An ideal tool for learning this is the femur rotation pattern of the Primary Series as described in my book *Ashtanga Yoga: Practice and Philosophy*.

We will perform *Maha Vedha Mudra* first with an internal *kumbhaka*, which is less demanding. Inhale to capacity using the *Ujjayi* sound. Then lift the chest and drop the chin, while swallowing to induce the contraction of the throat. Place the chin into *Jalandhara Bandha* to perform *kumbhaka* as previously instructed. Now place your hands on the ground and lift your legs and hips off the ground as if you would practice *Utpluthi*, the last posture in the Ashtanga sequence, although, of course, during *Utpluthi* we do not perform *kumbhaka*. Lifting up is surprisingly easy when sitting in *Padmasana*, at least if the required arm and shoulder strength is present. Different to *Utpluthi*, here we do not hold ourselves up, but we let the thighs and buttocks drop back down. Do this initially even more gentle than seems reasonable. Reasons for that are not only to keep your knees and lumbar lower discs safe. Any impact could travel upwards to your neck and reach your cervical discs (intervertebral discs of the neck) and cause damage here. We want to avoid being overly zealous here.

Start the technique by performing on the first day only three strikes per *kumbhaka*, and one *kumbhaka* only. Once you have gauged over the next 24 hours that no adverse sensation is present in your neck, knees and low back, you can sensibly increase the number of the *kumbhakas* and strikes, and the velocity with which you let your body drop down, yet without casting prudence overboard. Remember that soft tissue and cartilage, such as that forming your lumbar and cervical intervertebral discs, does not contain nerves. Hence intervertebral discs cannot give you feedback right then when you overdo it. If unsure, you can always perform the *mudra* on a folded blanket to mitigate the impact.

Maha Vedha Mudra in *Padmasana*

The maximum is again 21 strikes per session. Some texts recommend doing 8 sets every 3 hours. How many strikes you can perform per *kumbhaka* also depends on your proficiency in *kumbhaka* practice. The differences between individuals are significant and little general guidelines can be given. It is suggested to perform the same number of repetitions in *Maha Mudra* and *Maha Bandha Mudra*. You can also try out the *Siddhasana* version, dropping down on one heel or striking the buttocks with one heel. Neither version worked very well for me, but they may do so for you.

Once you have gained a certain proficiency performing the *mudra* during an internal *kumbhaka*, try the same method with an external *kumbhaka*, which is more advanced. Because you will run faster out of oxygen (due to the empty lungs) it is harder to perform the same number of strikes per *kumbhaka*. Arguably though, during an external *kumbhaka* the technique is more powerful because the upward suction of the *Bahya* (external) *Uddiyana* provides additional pull on the Kundalini. Once you know the method well in both types of *kumbhakas*, choose the one you prefer and then always perform *Maha Vedha Mudra* in sequence with *Maha Mudra* and *Maha Bandha Mudra*. We are then practising all three *mudras* with an equal number of rounds and repetitions.

Chapter 24

ASHVINI MUDRA
(Horse Seal)

The next two *mudras* covered are the *Ashvini-*, and *Vajroli Mudras*, which are the rhythmic contracting/retracting inwards and subsequent releasing/ projecting outwards of the anal sphincter and the urethra, respectively. This is done to *pranically* seal both openings, which otherwise are responsible for losing solar *prana*. While the sense openings, i.e. eyes, ears, etc., are sealed to prevent the loss of lunar *prana* (*prana* responsible for powering the sense organs, the so-called *jnanendriyas*[368]), the present two *mudras* prevent loss of *prana* associated with extraversion of the organs of action (the so-called *karmendriyas*[369]). *Ashvini Mudra* is covered here, whereas *Vajroli Mudra* is dealt with under the next heading. *Ashvini Mudra* is named after the habit of horses to expand and contract the anus several times following defecation. One side effect of *Ashvini Mudra* is that it creates a better understanding of *Mula Bandha*, which is the contraction of the perineum.

The *Yoga Kundalini Upanishad* instructs us to induce prana into the *Sushumna* by performing *kumbhaka* in *Padmasana* with the

---

368 Lunar *prana* powers the olfactory, gustatory, visual, tactile and auditory senses.

369 Solar *prana* powers grasping, locomotion, speech, sexual intercourse, giving birth, urination and defecation

251

addition of *Ashvini Mudra*[370]. The *Upanishad* states that with this action fire (*agni*) and air (*vayu*) will mix and rise together in the *Sushumna* (central energy channel). Also, the *Gheranda Samhita* defines *Ashvini Mudra* as the repeated contraction and dilation of the anal sphincter until Shakti (i.e. Kundalini) is raised[371]. The anus and the act of defecation are closely associated with *apana*, the vital down current. *Apana* is holding down Kundalini and reversing *apana* back upwards is one of the main engines of conducting Kundalini. In stanzas III.49 – 51 the *Gheranda Samhita* further instructs that if Kundalini is asleep in the base *chakra*, *Muladhara*, we are mere animals and cannot attain true knowledge. Contrary to the *Yoga Kundalini Upanishad*, sage *Gheranda* espouses *Siddhasana* to apply *Ashvini Mudra* during *kumbhaka* to induce Kundalini to rise in the *Sushumna*[372].

Mid-20th century yoga pioneer Theos Bernard argues that *Ashvini Mudra* is a prerequisite for *Mula Bandha*[373]. He suggests learning *Ashvini Mudra* while being on one's hands and knees. One performs external *kumbhaka* with external *Uddiyana* and then tries to vigorously move anus and navel towards each other as often as one can. In another place, Bernard argues to practice *Ashvini Mudra* for 1 hour per day, after which it should be perfected in 2 weeks[374]. This seems to be excessive, but it must be noted that Bernard was known for excessive practices, holding headstands for up to 3 hours per day (albeit over

---

370 *Yoga Kundalini Upanishad* stanzas 83-84

371 *Gheranda Samhita* III.82

372 *Gheranda Samhita* III.54 – 56

373 Theos Bernard, *Hatha Yoga*, Rider, London, 1950, p. 70

374 Theos Bernard, *Heaven Lies Within Us*, Charles Scribner's Sons, New York, 1939, p. 249

separate sessions) and performing up to 1500 strokes per day each of *Nauli* and *Agnisara Kriya*. Performing similar feats may lead to Kundalini rising but also to cervical disc arthritis, brain aneurisms, severe *pitta* aggravation (through too much *Nauli*) and a visit to the mental ward. I strongly recommend to phase in any such practices slowly over the long-term and to forsake the seeking of spectacular short-term gains.

1960s yoga pioneer Andre Van Lysebeth agrees that *Ashvini Mudra* prepares for *Mula Bandha*[375]. He considers it necessary to create a strong pelvic diaphragm to deflect upwards pressure created by internal *kumbhakas*. This is a rationale for *Ashvini Mudra* not applicable to Ashtanga *vinyasa* practitioners (which neither Bernard nor van Lysebeth were), who are creating a strong pelvic diaphragm ready for *pranayama* by always engaging *Mula Bandha* during their *asana* practice. Van Lysebeth says *Ashvini Mudra* means to strongly contract the anus and suck it in then relax it and push it out. Each phase should last for 3 seconds[376].

The legendary *tantric* scholar Sir John Woodroffe was a British Raj Supreme Court Judge. While being ordained, he could not be seen to conspire with the ruled, and therefore, to keep his affinity with Indian culture under wraps, wrote under the pen name Arthur Avalon. Only once he retired from official duty did he publish many *tantric* texts under his legal name. Sir Woodroffe stated that *Ashvini Mudra* was to be repeated until

---

375 Andre van Lysebeth, A., *Die Grosse Kraft des Atems*, O.W. Barth, Bern, 1972, p. 223

376 Andre van Lysebeth, A., *Die Grosse Kraft des Atems*, O.W. Barth, Bern, 1972, p. 224

prana was induced into the *Sushumna*[377]. He also said that one of *Ashvini Mudra's* main applications was as an adjunct to *Shakti Chalana Mudra*, where it was preceded by *Nauli* in *Siddhasana*, and then combined with internal *kumbhaka* and *Shanmukhi Mudra*. We need to remember that Woodroffe made many of these statements in the late 1800s. A veritable trailblazer regarding Western understanding of yoga and *tantra*. Variations of *Shakti Chalana Mudra* will be explored more closely under *mudra* 27, the last *mudra* of Section 4.

Paramahansa Yogeshvaranand teaches *Ashvini Mudra* as the contraction and expansion of the anus in a seated position, which according to him needs to be done for several minutes and it then quickly raises the *prana* and awakens Kundalini[378]. Another important side effect of this *mudra* is its role during *Basti*, the yogic enema. In days of old Indian yogis performed enemas in open bodies of water such as rivers by simply dilating the anal aperture and then sucking in water using external *kumbhaka* with external *Uddiyana*. Once enough water was sucked in, a *Nauli*-like movement was performed, and the water was then expelled. With today's polluted waterways this cannot be performed in open bodies of water. On another note, even with clean water, the hygienic implications of such practice in open bodies of water in populated areas would have to be considered. A similar effect can, however, be achieved using an enema applicator kit.

---

377 Sir John Woodroffe, *The Serpent Power*, Ganesh & CO, Madras, 1995, p. 207

378 Yogeshvaranand Paramahansa, *First Steps to Higher Yoga*, Yoga Niketan Trust, New Delhi, 2001, p. 386

There are conflicting opinions on whether the *Ashvini* contractions should be performed during *kumbhaka* or during the inhalation and released during the exhalations or vice versa. Swami Kuvalayananda, the founder of the Kaivalyadhama Institute, argues the contractions should be initiated on the exhale. From my experience, Kuvalayanda is right but try out what is more effective for you. At which point of the breathing cycle exactly the *mudra* is initiated has not been specified in *shastra*. Scriptural references to it are generally rare, although most yogic schools teach it via oral tradition. Apart from the already quoted *Gheranda* passage the *mudra* is also mentioned in Jayatarama's *Jogapradipyaka,* but is here called *Samkshobhani Mudra*[379]. Jayatarama uses different names for most yoga techniques.

TECHNIQUE

Sit in *Padmasana* or *Siddhasana*. Alternate the dilation and pushing outwards of the anus with its contraction and sucking inwards. You may either start this beginning with the inhalation or the exhalation. This is initially done without *kumbhaka*. Alternatively you can also try being on all fours, performing external kumbhaka with external *Uddiyana* (sucking up the abdominal contents into the thoracic cavity) and moving anus and navel towards each other and apart. Start with practising either technique one minute daily and add one minute per week until you have reached 3 minutes. This is enough unless you perform the *mudra* in a *Shakti Chalana* context, which will be covered in Section 4, *Mudra* 27.

---

379 Swami Maheshananda et al. (eds & transl.), *Jogapradipyaka of Jayatarama,* Kaivalyadhama, Lonavla, 2006, p. 110

Additional practice, once *Vajroli Mudra* is also learned: alternate between *Ashvini Mudra, Mula Bandha* and *Vajroli Mudra*. Perform each of the three *mudras* by rapidly contracting and releasing for 1 minute before going on to the next, starting with *Vajroli Mudra,* then *Ashvini Mudra,* and finally *Mula Bandha.*

EFFECTS
Ashvini Mudra is a helpful adjunct in raising Kundalini, but is then performed within the context of *pranayama, chakra-*Kundalini meditation and *Shakti Chalana Mudra. Ashvini Mudra* helps establish *Mula Bandha.*

Chapter 25

VAJROLI MUDRA
(Thunderbolt Seal)

The *vajra nadi* (thunderbolt conduit) is the *nadi* that supplies *prana* to the urethra, bladder and reproductive system. Within yoga, *Vajroli Mudra* is one of the most tricky and unsatisfying subjects to write about. It is a great example of how twilight language backfired. In many Sanskrit treatises, twilight language (*sandhya*) is employed. Twilight language means there is more than one meaning to a phrase or choice of words. One of the meanings is usually more obvious and literal but leads to a misunderstanding, whereas the other meaning is often metaphorical, initially hidden, but reflects the true meaning of the stanza in question. The reason for this is that all yogic schools shrouded themselves in secrecy, lest their teaching should be discovered, watered down and bastardized by the uninitiated. Due to this concern, for millennia, the teachings were never written down, and when they finally were, they were written down only with double- and hidden meanings so nobody who wasn't personally induced into a lineage could cobble together the methods of the schools just because they simply got their hands on a manuscript. This tendency is further emphasized by the constant injunction in medieval texts that these methods must be kept secret at all costs and not be passed on to the uninitiated, as otherwise their value would be lost. Even the most important Indian texts, the *Vedas*, were not written down until the 19th century and then only via coercion through British Raj officials. Also, *Vedanta* philosophy, which we may today view as very non-esoteric and benevolent, until quite recently was not to be divulged to non-ascetics without invoking threats to one's live. The reason for this surprising fact lies in the belief that such radical teachings could shake the societal order of the day. Mansur al-Hallaj, in 14th century Baghdad Sufi mystic, was sentenced to death for uttering the today seemingly harmless sentence Ana-al-Haq, "I-am-the-Truth".

One of the most well-known examples of twilight language in yogic literature is the *Hatha Yoga Pradipika's* statement those who eat the flesh of the cow and daily ingest the immortal liquor are considered nobility and those who don't are a disgrace[380]. There are, of course, those who took this as an invitation to meat-eating and binge drinking, but any anthropologist could confirm that there is no proven statistical link between a carnivorous lifestyle and a drinking habit on the one hand and nobility on the other. So what does the stanza then mean? Brahmananda explains in his commentary on the *Pradipika* that the word *gau*, usually meaning cow, means tongue and eating here refers to "swallowing" the tongue, i.e. performing *Jihva Bandha* or *Khechari Mudra*[381]. This technique is done to arrest the mind and, with the mind as the source of all debauchery now suspended, nobility is the outcome. Immortal liquor is not alcohol but lunar *prana* exuding from the lunar storehouse of

---

380 Pancham Sinh, *The Hatha Yoga Pradipika,* Sri Satguru Publications, Delhi, 1991, p. 34

381 Kunjunni Raja (ed.), *The Hathayogapradipika of Svatmarama with the Commentary Jyotsna of Brahmananda*, The Adyar Library, Madras, 1972, p. 35

prana adjacent to the *Ajna chakra*, which is 'milked' by practising methods like *Khechari Mudra* or *Jihva Bandha*. We find here then that the deep meaning of the stanza is the exact opposite of the surface meaning, i.e. the stanza suggests a movement away from debauchery instead of towards it.

The problem here is like the Sufi literature of luminaries like Hafiz or Omar Khayyam. Superficially, their rapture can be taken as a call to become a winebibber, but when the Sufi poets talk about drunkenness, they mean drunken with love for the Divine, and when they talk about the tavern, they mean the community of worshippers or the state in which the Divine is seen. They simply clothed their teaching into colloquial terms to not be discovered and prosecuted for heretic spiritual teachings. Understandably, because sometimes they would be executed for such teachings.

In our present research subject, *Vajroli Mudra*, the case is more complex and the perfect translation for *sandhya* here would be not twilight language but double entendre. The term double entendre denotes a word or phrase open to two interpretations, one of which is often indecent, explicit or risqué. *Vajroli Mudra* used to simply be the same technique as *Ashvini Mudra*, however, this time applied to the urethra. The urethra was to be alternatingly contracted and sucked inwards versus dilated and pushed outwards. This becomes clear when examining the *Hathatatva Kaumudi of Sundaradeva*, where *Ashvini Mudra* (contracting and dilating the anus) is listed under the name *Vajroli* stage 1 and *Vajroli* stage 2 is *Vajroli* proper, which is to perform the same action with the urethra[382]. The same

---

382 Dr M.L. Gharote et al (eds. & transl.), *Hathatatvakaumudi*, The Lonavla Yoga Institite, Lonavla, 2007, p. 180

idea is described in Jayatarama's *Jogapradipyaka* but this time under the names *Bijarupini Mudra* and *Virajarupa Mudra*. These fancy names do not need to concern us. Jayatarama delights in giving new names to established techniques. What matters is that also here, we find the action of *Ashvini Mudra* applied to the generative organ[383]. The objective here is again to project solar *prana*, i.e. *prana* associated with an organ of action (here urination and/or sexual intercourse) to be projected back into the body. Medieval *shastra* authors and scribes then jumped on the opportunity to apply double entendre (*sandhya*) and made it sound as if *Vajroli Mudra* was indeed the key to endless carnal excesses, while at the same time advancing one's spiritually. Of course, that concept caught on like wildfire.

Modern commentators and teachers were quick to point out that taking these passages verbatim was contrary to the spirit of yoga. So says Shyam Sundar Goswami that *kumbhaka* and sex don't go together, and that *Vajroli Mudra* should be used to harness sexual energy rather than exploit it[384]. Dr M.L. Gharote, in his translation of the 10-chapter edition of the *Hatha Yoga Pradipika*, points out that descriptions of *Vajroli* employ twilight language and have nothing to do with sex[385]. The *Hatha Yoga Pradipika with Jyotsna Commentary* points out that the terms women, sexual intercourse and seminal fluid in the description of *Vajroli* cannot be understood literally, as yogis are expected to

---

383 Swami Maheshananda et al. (eds & transl.), *Jogapradipyaka of Jayatarama,* Kaivalyadhama, Lonavla, 2006, p. 115

384 Shyam Sundar Goswami, *Laya Yoga*, Inner Traditions, Rochester, 1999, p. 303

385 Dr M.L. Gharote et al (eds. & transl.), *Hathapradipika of Svatmarama (10 chapters)*, Lonavla Yoga Institute, Lonavla, 2006, p. Xxvi

adhere to *yama* and *niyama*[386] (code of ethics) and that the terms refer to an internal mystical process[387]. So far so good. This internal mystical process is exactly what we see when Hafiz of Shiraz or Omar Khayyam talks about wine, drunkenness and the tavern.

However, by that point, many yogis had already fallen for the corrupt reading of *Vajroli Mudra* and to avoid any confusion, more orthodox teachers such as T. Krishnamacharya stated this *mudra* should not be practised, lest it should corrupt us[388]. To understand Krishnamacharya's warning let's look into one of *Vajroli Mudra's* most concerning descriptions, which we find in *Kapala Kurantaka Yoga*[389]. The description begins with instructions for widening the urethra by inserting a particular green reed deeper and deeper into the penis. We are warned this could lead to severe pain and fever in which case intercourse with women (in the plural) is advised as remedy[390]. We are then told to make various thin tubes from horn, ivory, silver, and gold also inserted into the penis to make its opening wider so air and later water can be sucked up into the bladder (practically done

---

386 Kunjunni Raja (ed.), *The Hathayogapradipika of Svatmarama with the Commentary Jyotsna of Brahmananda*, The Adyar Library, Madras, 1972, p. 44

387 Kunjunni Raja (ed.), *The Hathayogapradipika of Svatmarama with the Commentary Jyotsna of Brahmananda*, The Adyar Library, Madras, 1972, p. 63

388 T. Krishnamacharya, *Yoga Makaranda,* Media Garuda, Chennai, 2011, p. 104

389 Swami Maheshananda et al (eds. & transl.), *Kapalakurantaka's Hathabhyasa-Paddhati*, Kaivalyadhama, Lonavla, 2015, p. 80

390 Swami Maheshananda et al (eds. & transl.), *Kapalakurantaka's Hathabhyasa-Paddhati*, Kaivalyadhama, Lonavla, 2015, p. 82

by performing *Madhyama Nauli*). Various herbs are then applied to the penis to heal the injuries inflicted by such actions[391]. Eventually sexual desire is awakened and again, intercourse with several women is practised[392]. When during intercourse one comes close to ejaculation, the semen is now sucked inwards. We are advised to choose for such interactions only beautiful women mad with desire and shunning passionless women we should select only passionate ones[393]. Advice such as these make the text a veritable zest pit of objectification of women. On the next page, we are glad to read that rape should not come into the equation, but if we do things right, we should, even without resorting to rape, be able to perform intercourse with 16 women per day, without developing any attachment to either of them[394]. So serial fornication is fine as long as we don't give a second thought for these women afterwards? This is reading like a gigolo's manual for wannabe ascetics, not like a yoga *shastra*. We should imagine for a moment if the sexes were exchanged. I will spare the reader vulgar terms that our culture directs towards women displaying such behaviour but for male spiritual aspirants, apparently, they are okay.

At the end of the *Kapala Kurantaka Yoga*, the translators are pointing out that the purpose of *Vajroli* is *brahmacharya* (often

---

391 Swami Maheshananda et al (eds. & transl.), *Kapalakurantaka's Hathabhyasa-Paddhati,* Kaivalyadhama, Lonavla, 2015, p. 84

392 Swami Maheshananda et al (eds. & transl.), *Kapalakurantaka's Hathabhyasa-Paddhati,* Kaivalyadhama, Lonavla, 2015, p. 87

393 Swami Maheshananda et al (eds. & transl.), *Kapalakurantaka's Hathabhyasa-Paddhati,* Kaivalyadhama, Lonavla, 2015, p. 89

394 Swami Maheshananda et al (eds. & transl.), *Kapalakurantaka's Hathabhyasa-Paddhati,* Kaivalyadhama, Lonavla, 2015, p. 90

translated as chastity or celibacy), and to destroy sexual desire. How sexual desire can be destroyed or reduced by first going through a process that involves cohabitating with over a dozen women per day is beyond my understanding. The translators point out that *Vajroli* has nothing to do with hedonism but fulfils the *Kurantaka's* definition of *brahmacharya*, which is defined as the ability to suck the ejaculate upwards (*bindorapatanam*) and to also suck the menstrual blood of the female up during intercourse (*raja adyarkarshanam*). Apart from the deeply sexist description that seems to utilize females, we are told that the male yogi who, once the urethra is sufficiently widened, achieves inward suction of the ejaculate, can have intercourse with as many women as available. As long as the reproductive fluids are sucked upwards the male yogi apparently is not in breach of *brahmacharya*!? How convenient! Anybody else who finds this unconvincing? It does remind me of the rationalizing of a high caste brothel owner who once told me that the negative *karma* of selling their bodies would only accrue to the female sex workers who toiled at his parlour. Because he always let the customers place the fee for the commercial sex acts directly on the counter in front of him, without physically touching him, the negative *karma* supposedly could not transfer to the brothel owner. And money itself could not transfer *karma* either. As we see, the theory of *karma* can even be modified to justify pimping.

If the terms semen and menstrual fluids are really representing internal mystical processes, as some writers suggest, then this was lost on the text's author, *Kurantaka* himself, or at least to the scribe who jotted down the *Kapala Kurantaka Yoga* in its present form. This text wastes almost 20% of its length on describing how to enlarge the penile duct. That's beyond *sandhya*, which is usually applied in a single word or phrase.

To recap, *Vajroli Mudra* initially was a technique like *Ashvini Mudra* but applied to the urethra. Double entendre (*sandhya*) was then applied to the description of *Vajroli Mudra* to make it harder to decipher. However, unfortunately sometimes even the authors and scribes of the texts themselves misunderstood this application of *sandhya* and took the descriptions as literal. They then came up with elaborate description that involved increasing numbers of women and fornications. The *Hathayoga Manjari of Sahajananda*, for example, describes *Vajroli Mudra* as initially the sucking of air into penis, a process that is later repeated with milk[395]. Through *Nauli* then during intercourse the ejaculate is drawn upwards, which will open the *Sushumna*. *Hatharatnavali of Shrinivasayogi* supports the importance of widening the urethra with a tube and claims that *Vajroli Mudra* brings success more quickly than *pranayama* and meditation[396].

The *Hatha Yoga Pradipka* starts its description of *Vajroli* with the statement that even a sensualist, shunning any form of (sexual) restraint can succeed with yoga through *Vajroli Mudra*[397]. Why then bother with restraint? We are told we need to procure an ingredient difficult to get, a woman behaving as desired[398], although in the next stanza, the *Pradipika* states the *Vajroli* can be performed by women, too. *Vajroli* is then described as drawing reproductive fluid back into the body during intercourse and

---

395 O.P. Tiwari (publ.), *Hathayoga Manjari of Sahajananda*, Kaivalyadhama, Lonavla, 2006, p. 52

396 Dr M.L. Gharote et al (eds. & transl.), *Hatharatnavali of Shrinivasayogi*, The Lonavla Yoga Institite, Lonavla, 2009, p. 71

397 *Hatha Yoga Pradipka* III 82

398 *Hatha Yoga Pradipka* III.83

here we find the use of a pipe or tube recommended to widen the urethra, and the introductory practise of sucking in air.

Also, in the *Shiva Samhita Vasu* we find *Vajroli* described and here the idea that through it even hedonists can gain emancipation[399]. The male practitioner is to suck the reproductive fluid of women (again plural) during intercourse up through the urethra. It is recommended to exercise suction first with milk and honey and, once proficient, with the male and female reproductive fluids, called *soma* and *rajas*[400]. The yogi is then to create their mystical union in his body. This passage switches back and forth from describing the method as sexual technique on the one hand and metaphorically as an internal, mystical process on the other. *Soma* and *rajas* are names for lunar and solar *prana*, balanced to create the precondition for entering *prana* into the central channel. Their balance is usually brought about through *pranayama*. Some texts have misappropriated the union of *soma* and *rajas* as the union of reproductive fluids during intercourse. Even the otherwise pious *Dattatreya's Yogashastra* advises us to approach "with utmost caution", "a lady engaged in yoga practice" but then leaves us to imagine the details[401]. The text then veers off into opaque esoteric descriptions and we are left off to wonder what to do with the "lady engaged in yoga".

Other texts, including the *Yoga Chudamani Upanishad*, have exclusively understood and described the union of *soma* and

---

399 *Shiva Samhita Vasu* IV. 54ff

400 *Shiva Samhita Vasu* IV. 58-59

401 *Dattatreya's Yogashastra stanzas 154-155, (p. 74-75 in the Lonavla edition)

rajas as an internal mystical process[402]. Dr M.L. Gharote in his translation of the *Yuktabhavadeva of Bhavadeva Mishra* summarizes that despite its elaborate descriptions, the practice of *Vajroli Mudra* is but for the ignorant and infatuated[403]. When I learned the *mudras* from B.N.S. Iyengar in the 1990s, the message was even starker. He taught that the method did in fact consist in inserting a pipe into the penis and practising the sucking up of water, milk, then honey and eventually the female genital fluid during intercourse. However, he insisted that it was a degenerate technique, and if I did do so, I would wind up in hell! On my varied travels, I did, however, meet several male yogis who told me they performed intercourse with as many women as possible and on those occasions practised what they believed to be *Vajroli Mudra*. No wonder then that in the *Gheranda Samhita* the method was changed to a *kumbhaka* during a handstand (described in this text as *Vajroni Mudra* under Section 1, *Mudra* 3) and that some teachers like T. Krishnamacharya discouraged *Vajroli* altogether.

I felt it necessary to give space here to unearth the confusing history of this *mudra*. Yoga is a great tool for transformation, but modern yogis are called upon to self-critically analyse our tradition and expose internal conflicts and misinterpretations. During the Middle Ages, the term yogi in India meant often little more than scoundrel, as yogis were often seen as sorcerers whose main aim was to hypnotize women into giving sexual

---

402 *Yoga Chudamani Upanishad* stanzas 57-62, (p. 209-211 in the Lonavla edition)

403 Dr M.L. Gharote et al, (eds & transl.), *Yuktabhavadeva of Bhavadeva Mishra*, Lonavla Yoga Institute, Lonavla, 2002, p. Lxxvii

favours. There is some healing here to do if we want to live up to the potential that yoga offers.

TECHNIQUE

Sit in *Padmasana* or *Siddhasana*. Contract the urethra as if wanting to stop urination. Alternate the dilation and pushing outwards of the urethra with its contraction and sucking inwards. You may either start this beginning with the inhalation or the exhalation. This is initially done without *kumbhaka*. Start with practising 1 minute daily and add one minute per week until you have reached 3 minutes. This is enough, unless you perform the *mudra* in a *Shakti Chalana* context, which will be covered in Section 4, *Mudra* 27.

Additional practice, once *Ashvini Mudr*is also learned: alternate between *Ashvini Mudra, Mula Bandha* and *Vajroli Mudra*. Perform each of the three *mudras* by rapidly contracting and releasing for 1 minute before going on to the next, starting with *Vajroli Mudra*, then *Ashvini Mudra,* and finally *Mula Bandha.*

Once you are comfortable with *kumbhaka* you can insert *Vajroli Mudra* into internal and external *kumbhakas*. You want to aim for and combining and alternating *Vajroli Mudra* with *Ashvini Mudra* in *Shakti Chalana Mudra*. This will often involve *kumbhaka*.

EFFECTS

Vajroli Mudra projects solar *prana* back into the body. It draws *apana*, the vital down current up, helping with the raising of Kundalini raising. It aids in gaining proficiency in the practice of *Mula Bandha*.

Chapter 26

PASHINI MUDRA
(Noose Seal)

According to the *Gheranda Samhita* this *mudra* is performed by placing both legs behind the head and crossing them behind the neck like a noose[404]. The *mudra* is said to awaken the Kundalini and give strength. However, sage *Gheranda* advises it should be practised with care. This is a typical example of a description that doesn't make sense without any further instruction. But how could it, seeing it consists of only two sentences. This *mudra* is to be performed only by yogis who are already advanced *asana* practitioners and proficient at performing leg-behind-head postures with great ease. Somebody who is not prepared through many years of *asana* practice could rupture the intravertebral discs in the low back when performing this difficult *mudra*. *Pashini Mudra* is performed by assuming *Dvipada Shirshasana* (both legs behind the head posture), lifting off the floor and then striking the buttocks on the ground. The striking action is like that performed in *Maha Vedha Mudra*. For that *mudra,* we were instructed to let the thighs strike the floor at the same time as the buttocks, to mitigate the impact. In *Dvipada Shirshasana* this is not possible as only the sit bones can be brought down to the floor. Any poor technique or sub-optimal

---

404 *Gheranda Samhita* III.84

alignment will mean that any impact caused by the striking will be absorbed by the low back discs.

TECHNIQUE

I have already described *Dvipada Shirshasana* in great detail in *Ashtanga Yoga The Intermediate Series*[405] and have given a number of warm-ups to improve one's performance of leg-behind-head postures. But even then, *Dvipada Shirshasana* usually occurs in the middle of one's *asana* practice, when one is thoroughly warmed up. To enter the posture more or less cold during *mudra* practice demands a different level of performance and excellent openness in one's hip joints. To attempt this *mudra,* we should be able to perform leg-behind-head postures such as *Ekapada Shirshasana* and better even *Durvasasana* and *Viranchyasana* A[406], on both sides with apparent ease. *Pashini Mudra* is contraindicated when sacroiliac joint problems, pelvic obliquity, previous low back injuries, weak neck muscles, and weak abdominal muscles are present.

To enter the posture, we sit on the floor, extending the right leg straight and the left leg on our left arm. We will proceed now to put first the left leg behind the head and then the right leg on top of the left one. The traditional way of performing double-sided leg-behind-head postures (including *Supta Kurmasana* and *Yoganidrasana*) is to bring first the left leg and then the right leg into position[407]. In this

---

405 Gregor Maehle, *Ashtanga Yoga The Intermediate Series,* New World Library, Novato, 2009, p. 144-146

406 Both are neck-snappingly difficult postures of the Advanced A Series of Ashtanga Yoga.

407 This does not apply in postures where only one leg at a time is placed

regard, double-sided leg-behind-head postures follow the same order as *Siddhasana,* in that first, the left leg is placed. These postures conflict with the arrangement in lotus postures, such as *Padmasana* or *Supta Vajrasana,* where first the right leg and then the left leg is brought into half-lotus. The reason we place the legs in this order and not the other way round is to accommodate the asymmetry of the abdominal and thoracic cavities. Especially regarding the order of the legs in all lotus posture variations many *shastras* are outspoken. However, T. Krishnamacharya insisted that the order of the legs could be exchanged to accommodate individual needs. This could be the case if a pelvic imbalance is present that makes the performance of the postures in the traditional way too difficult.

Flexibility and strength permitting, place the left leg behind your head by laterally rotating your thigh, using all the steps and precautions described in my book *Ashtanga Yoga The Intermediate Series* book under *Ekapada Shirshasana*[408]. This would take several pages to describe, and even then, it cannot be safely undertaken outside of context and without preparation. The further you get the leg down behind your neck, the easier it will be to carry the additional weight of the second leg. It will be impossible to carry both legs on the back of your head, whereas to carry them on or below C7 will be quite comfortable and safe. However, to draw the leg that far down behind the

---

behind the head, such as during *Ekapada Shirshasana, Kashyappasana, Bhairavasana* or *Durvasasana.* These postures follow a completely different energetic structure.

408 Gregor Maehle, *Ashtanga Yoga The Intermediate Series*, New World Library, Novato, 2009, p. 137-143

neck requires exceptional hip joint flexibility, which took me many years of *sadhana* to acquire. One should never just willy-nilly 'have a go' at such postures without acquiring the qualifications beforehand.

Arrest now the first leg in position by taking your head back and placing your left hand on the floor in front of you to hold your balance. Bend up your right leg, laterally rotating your thigh, and, using your right hand, take your ankle or, flexibility permitting, your calf closer to the knee.

Exhaling, bend forward somewhat and lift your right leg behind your shoulder and then your right ankle behind the left ankle. Keep sufficient tension in your neck so your left leg does not slip off from behind your head. You may allow that in the initial stage of getting used to the posture, but *Dvipada Shirshasana* is not properly executed until both legs are clearly arrested behind the head and stay there for the full breath count.

Drawing both legs as far down the back as possible will ensure that your shoulders carry part of their weight, rather than all of it is pressing onto your cervical spine. Once being proficient in the posture, point (plantar flex) both feet. In the initial stages, you might prefer to use flexion (dorsiflexion) of the feet, making it easier to hook the second foot onto the first. However, in the final version of the posture, the feet are ideally plantar flexed (pointed).

Once both legs are arrested behind the neck, engage your back extensors and straighten up as much as you can. Lift your chest and drop your pubic bone. Take your head back as far as possible, which will let your legs slide further down. Now place both hands on the floor in front of you and inhaling, straighten your arms and lift your sit bones off the floor. Try to keep your feet pointed here and breathe deeply into your chest. Use here the combined effort of your back extensors and trunk flexors to draw your sit bones down to the floor as the crown of the head extends upward, thus putting your spine into traction. Putting the spine into traction, although initially seemingly impossible, is the key to effective leg-behind-head postures as it increases the space between the vertebrae and thus improves the flow of Kundalini. The gaze is towards the forehead (*Brumadhaya Drishti*) and those at ease may use *Shambhavi Mudra*.

The next step now is to strike the sit bones down on the floor. This is done three times for those new to the method (reflecting the number of the *gunas*), seven times for those established in this *mudra* (one time for each *chakra*), or 21 times (number of *gunas* multiplied by the number of *chakras*) for advanced practitioners. While doing so, one must exercise caution to not use too much force as to not damage the lumbar or cervical intervertebral discs. The arms and shoulders must be strong enough to land lightly. Additionally, the hip joints have to be very flexible so that the low back is not too kyphotic, which would compromise the position of the lumbar discs and vertebrae. In either case, I suggest to initially perform *Pashini Mudra* on one or two folded blankets to mitigate the impact. If performing the *mudra* in sequence with other practices, it is ideally done after one's *asana* and *pranayama* practice but before one's *chakra*-Kundalini meditation. This is a powerful *mudra*, but it is questionable whether it is worth the risk to one's lumbar discs. My personal advise is to chose *mudras*, which are physically less demanding.

Pashini Mudra

EFFECTS

Awakens the Kundalini and gives strength.

Chapter 27

SHAKTI CHALANA MUDRA
(Power Conduction Seal)

Shakti Chalana Mudra is such a vast subject that an entire book could be written on it. I have divided this article into two sections, a theoretical section explaining why we are performing certain methods, and a practical section, describing what we are doing. The term *Shakti Chalana* means power conduction. What power is to be conducted? As you may have noticed, in this text, the terms Shakti and Kundalini, when occurring alone by themselves, have not been italicized. All Sanskrit terms besides names of people or names of the Divine have been italicized. Shakti and Kundalini are both names of the Divine Feminine, the Mother Goddess. Both terms are largely synonymous, but often Kundalini is the creative force of the Divine Feminine moving upwards within the body, whereas the term Shakti more often is used to describe the act of divine grace, that is a downward movement of the same energy. Shakti is also the name of the force that creates and sustains the whole of the universe. When learning or studying *Shakti Chalana*, we should give up on the idea that we deal only with a limited amount of physical energy, relegated to our small bodies. The Shakti is the Mother Goddess as she manifests in our bodies. In truth, all bodies, whether of sentient beings or celestial bodies such as stars, galaxies, black holes all matter, in the aggregate constitute Her body.

THEORETICAL SECTION

In many yogic schools, *Shakti Chalana Mudra* is the most important *mudra* because it represents each school's individual, usually jealously guarded, approach to power conduction. *Shakti Chalana Mudra* is usually not an individual *mudra*, a stand-alone technique, but it is the way how each school sequences the most powerful techniques it teaches so power conduction is assured. It usually involves a combination of *bandhas, kumbhaka, asana, kriyas* and other *mudras* and often *Maha Mudra* plays a role, too. So says the *Hathatatva Kaumudi* that the first step to *Shakti Chalana* is applying the five *bandhas*[409] and *Maha Mudra*[410]. Seeing that *Jalandhara Bandha* always involves breath retention, including *kumbhaka* is already apparent at the outset. The *Kaumudi* says that *kumbhaka* helped to rouse Shakti[411] and elsewhere that through the practice of *pranayama*, Shakti is aroused[412]. As I have described in my 2012 text *Pranayama The Breath of Yoga*, the culmination of *pranayama* also is called *Shakti Chalana Pranayama*[413], which in most schools consists of the sequential

---

409 The number here includes *bandhatraya* which is nothing but *Mula-, Uddiyana-,* and *Jalandhara Bandhas* plus *Jihva Bandha*.

410 Dr M.L. Gharote et al (eds. & transl.), *Hathatatvakaumudi,* The Lonavla Yoga Institite, Lonavla, 2007, p. 509

411 Dr M.L. Gharote et al (eds. & transl.), *Hathatatvakaumudi,* The Lonavla Yoga Institite, Lonavla, 2007, p. 407

412 Dr M.L. Gharote et al (eds. & transl.), *Hathatatvakaumudi,* The Lonavla Yoga Institite, Lonavla, 2007, p. 504

413 Gregor Maehle, *Pranayama The Breath of Yoga,* Kaivalya Publications, Crabbes Creek, 2012, p. 307ff

focus on all *chakras* during *kumbhaka* with *bandha* application. Also, this is confirmed by *Hathatatva Kaumudi*, which advises, among other approaches, *Shakti Chalana* as a compound of all five *bandhas* plus *kumbhaka* with a focus on the *chakras* added[414].

Also, other *mudras* are essential in this power conduction process, so the *Kaumudi*, since without *mudras*, *prana* will not enter *Sushumna*[415]. Theos Bernard asserts that *Shakti Chalana* can only be tackled when all other primary *mudras* in the *Hatha Yoga Pradipika* have been mastered[416]. Let's recall that this list included only ten *mudras*, with three of them being *bandhas*. Shyam Sundar Goswami agrees this is the most advanced *mudra* and that *Maha Mudra, Maha Bandha Mudra* and *Maha Vedha Mudra* have to be mastered beforehand[417]. This is so because these three *mudras* are essential in piercing the *granthis* without which *Shakti Chalana* cannot be attempted.

As we have learned in this volume, reversing the general downward flow of *apana* is one of the main objectives of *mudras*. In *Shakti Chalana* we need another important ingredient, fire (*agni*). Stirred by *apana* and *agni*, Shakti soon awakens, says *shastra* author Sundaradeva[418]. Elsewhere he adds that one should tread the avenue of *prana* (*apan*a is one of the five

---

414 Dr M.L. Gharote et al (eds. & transl.), *Hathatatvakaumudi*, The Lonavla Yoga Institite, Lonavla, 2007, p. 679

415 Dr M.L. Gharote et al (eds. & transl.), *Hathatatvakaumudi*, The Lonavla Yoga Institite, Lonavla, 2007, p. 141

416 Theos Bernard, *Hatha Yoga*, Rider, London, 1950, p. 72

417 Shyam Sundar Goswami, *Laya Yoga*, Inner Traditions, Rochester, 1999, p. 74

418 Dr M.L. Gharote et al (eds. & transl.), *Hathatatvakaumudi*, The Lonavla Yoga Institite, Lonavla, 2007, p. 505

major *pranas*, but the term here can refer more generally to *pranayama*, too) fire and mind[419]. The term mind here in this context applies to the pulling up of the Kundalini by means of mental concentration (focussing on Kundalini and the *chakras*). Again later in the *Kaumudi* Sundaradeva adds that the arousal of Shakti will not take place unless control over *prana* and fire (*agni*) is gained[420].

THE FUNDAMENTAL CONSTITUENTS: NAULI, BHASTRIKA, SURYA BHEDANA

Let's look at some elements of which *Shakti Chalana* is usually made up of. Prime ingredients for stoking fire are *Nauli, Bhastrika* and often *Surya Bhedana*. So says the 10-chapter edition of the *Hatha Yoga Pradipika* that Kundalini is roused by daily practising *Nauli, Bhastrika* and *Surya Bhedana*, each for 1.5 hours[421]. *Shitali* is then used to buffer against too much fire. This would lead to a total practice time of six hours. I list these extreme practices here only to be complete. They are not feasible as one would need to have practised decades of *asana, pranayama, kriya* and meditation to fortify oneself against the onslaught of the force created through such practice. My personal practice usually takes up about 4 hours per day, give or take. Of that, only 30 minutes is devoted to the above practices and the rest is spent with *asana, chakra*-Kundalini meditation and *samadhis*. Should

---

419 Dr M.L. Gharote et al (eds. & transl.), *Hathatatvakaumudi,* The Lonavla Yoga Institite, Lonavla, 2007, p. 513

420 Dr M.L. Gharote et al (eds. & transl.), *Hathatatvakaumudi,* The Lonavla Yoga Institite, Lonavla, 2007, p. 562

421 Dr M.L. Gharote et al (eds. & transl.), *Hathapradipika of Svatmarama (10 chapters)*, Lonavla Yoga Institute, Lonavla, 2006, p.170

I really devote 6 hours to the above practices my total practice time would be 10 hours per day. That's what I mean with not feasible.

Sahajananda's *Hathayoga Manjari* defines *Shakti Chalana* in a similar way[422]. We are to practice *Bhastrika* with *kumbhaka* for 1 hour 45 minutes, and then perform *Surya Bhedana* until both nostrils are equally open (which is recommended when attempting to induce *prana* into *Sushumna*), and Kundalini will rise. According to the *Hathayoga Manjari, Bhastrika kumbhaka* is the definite way to awaken Kundalini. *Bhastrika* is also listed as the prime method in many passages of the *Hathatatva Kaumudi of Sundaradeva*[423].

The *Hatha Yoga Pradipika with Jyotsna Commentary* takes a similar route[424]. We are to practice *Surya Bhedana* and *Nauli* in the morning and evening for 1.5 hours each. *Siddhasana* is then used to stimulate *Mula Bandha* and subsequently *Bhastrika* is performed. The four-chapter edition of the *Hatha Yoga Pradipika* also espouses the combination of extreme, multi-hour stints of *Bhastrika* and *Nauli*[425]. The *Pradipika* then emphasizes sexual restraint, a moderate diet and the constant application of *asana, pranayama, bandhas* and other *mudras* to support these extreme

---

422 O.P. Tiwari (publ.), *Hathayoga Manjari of Sahajananda,* Kaivalyadhama, Lonavla, 2006, p. 54

423 Dr M.L. Gharote et al (eds. & transl.), *Hathatatvakaumudi,* The Lonavla Yoga Institite, Lonavla, 2007, p. 516, 518, and 521

424 Kunjunni Raja (ed.), *The Hathayogapradipika of Svatmarama with the Commentary Jyotsna of Brahmananda,* The Adyar Library, Madras, 1972, p. 57-58

425 *Hatha Yoga Pradipika* III.108-115

practices[426]. We find *Nauli* again recommended in the *Hathatatva Kaumudi of Sundaradeva*, but here the advice is even to practice for several *muhurtas* (a *muhurta* is one-and-three-quarter hours)[427]. The importance of *Nauli* is also confirmed by Theos Bernard, who recommends practicing first *Surya Bhedana* for 1.5 hours, then *Bhastrika* followed by *Nauli* for 1.5 hours each[428]. Bernard follows the *Pradipika* closely. This is a formidable practice, and he again confirms in the same text that 100s of rounds of *Nauli* have to be performed[429].

SURYA VERSUS CHANDRA BHEDANA

The medieval *Hatha* texts display a preponderance towards *Surya Bhedana*[430] (rather than *Chandra Bhedana*) for Kundalini raising. This is due to fact that *Surya*, the solar *nadi*, increases fire (*agni*), one engine for powering Kundalini. Besides the many passages already quoted, the *Hathatatva Kaumudi of Sundaradeva*, also suggests initiating *Shakti Chalana* by inhaling through *Surya*, the right nostril, for 90 minutes in the morning and evening[431]. We find this approach also espoused in the 10-chapter edition of the

---

426 Kunjunni Raja (ed.), *The Hathayogapradipika of Svatmarama with the Commentary Jyotsna of Brahmananda*, The Adyar Library, Madras, 1972, p. 59

427 *Hathatatva Kaumudi of Sundaradeva* XLIV.11

428 Theos Bernard, *Hatha Yoga*, Rider, London, 1950, p. 74

429 Theos Bernard, *Hatha Yoga*, Rider, London, 1950, p. 303

430 The pranayama method during which all inhalations are taken throguh the right nostril and all exhalations through the left nostril.

431 Dr M.L. Gharote et al (eds. & transl.), *Hathatatvakaumudi*, The Lonavla Yoga Institite, Lonavla, 2007, p. 513

Hatha Yoga Pradipika[432], and again in the *Hathatatva Kaumudi of Sundaradeva*[433]. Many other instances could be quoted, but these shall suffice.

However, we should not let ourselves be duped that the opposite technique, *Chandra Bhedana*, is never advised. During *Chandra Bhedana* all inhalations are taken through the left nostril and all exhalations through the right. This method reverses the arrangement of *Surya Bhedana*. So says the *Hathatatva Kaumudi* that a yogi should always practice through the left nostril, which controls *amrita*, the nectar of immortality[434], and that the left nostril is the lord of the mind. The *Kaumudi* also says that the right nostril leads to overheating and toxins[435]. Similarly, the *Khechari Vidya of Adinatha* in stanza II.46 states that *Surya*, the right nostril, is the bearer of poison, while *Chandra*, the left nostril is the bearer of nectar. One should, therefore, always inhale through the left and exhale through the right[436]. Also, the *Yoga Kundalini Upanishad* teaches a *Shakti Chalana* approach that involves *Chandra Bhedana*, *kumbhaka*, *Jalandhara Bandha* and *Khechari Mudra*[437]. Several additional passages are in the *Hathatatva Kaumudi of Sundaradeva* (XLIV.21 & 47), which among

---

432 *Hatha Yoga Pradipika* (10-chapter edition) V41-42

433 Dr M.L. Gharote et al (eds. & transl.), *Hathatatvakaumudi*, The Lonavla Yoga Institite, Lonavla, 2007, p. 518

434 Dr M.L. Gharote et al (eds. & transl.), *Hathatatvakaumudi*, The Lonavla Yoga Institite, Lonavla, 2007, *p.* 526

435 Dr M.L. Gharote et al (eds. & transl.), *Hathatatvakaumudi*, The Lonavla Yoga Institite, Lonavla, 2007, *p.* 366

436 James Mallinson (ed. & transl.), *Khecarividya of Adinatha*, Indica Books, Varanasi, 2010, p. 125

437 Dr. M.M. Gharote et al (eds. & transl.), *Critical Edition of Selected Yogopanisads*, Lonavla Yoga Institute, Lonavla, 2017, p. 111

other statements include the injunction that a yogi should always practice through the lunar, left nostril, through which the nectar flows[438]. In the next verse, stanza 48, the *Kaumudi* then suggests that practice through the left nostril brings success in yoga. Why then this discrepancy between all these passages?

One disadvantage of the *Surya nadi* is that it creates too much heat. In all fairness, we can mitigate much of that heat through *Shitali* and *Kaki Mudra*. However, we may need these two techniques already to balance excess heat created through *Kapalabhati* and *Nauli*, the last of which we may have to perform excessively. If three heat-producing techniques are produced side-by-side, even *Shitali* and *Kaki Mudra* may not be enough to balance the aggravated *pitta* and *agni*.

To understand which method of both, *Surya* or *Chandra*, we need to employ, we need to look at how both influence brain and mind. Let's look at *Surya Bhedana* first. The *pranayama* technique through which all inhalations are taken through the right nostril and exhalations are performed through the left nostril powers the solar *pranic* storehouse, which is adjacent to the *Manipura Chakra* (navel or power *chakra*). The term power *chakra* comes from the fact that there are two storehouses of life force in the body, the solar storehouse, associated with the navel *chakra* and the lunar storehouse, associated with the third eye *chakra*. The solar *pranic* storehouse and with it the navel *chakra*, power the following functions:

- Left analytical brain hemisphere
- Right solar nostril

438 Dr M.L. Gharote et al (eds. & transl.), *Hathatatvakaumudi*, The Lonavla Yoga Institite, Lonavla, 2007, p. 519, also p. 526 stanza XLIV.47

- Fundamentalist mind
- Sympathetic nervous system
- Extraversion
- Efferent (outgoing) nerve currents
- Motor-neurons
- Catabolism (breaking down tissue)

This solar *pranic* storehouse powers functions that are more male in nature than the lunar *pranic* storehouse. This reflects that many cultures give the sun a male natural gender and the moon a female natural gender. Notice that most primate and human societies, are male dominated. Under the sway of the navel *chakra* our society also became more science-oriented and empirical. To be outgoing rather than introverted is esteemed in our culture. Modern life is becoming more and more stressful due to the overload of the sympathetic nervous system (which activates the fight, flight and freeze reflex, whereas rest-and-relaxation are receding into the background). Because our efferent (outgoing) nerve currents are overloaded, we suffer from sleep depletion. It is expected of us to have a strong physical presence, and people who don't, are rarely elected as leaders, even if they are ethically and intellectually highly developed. Our entire culture is highly catabolic (breaking down tissue, and by extension, any structure) and therefore destructive of nature and traditional communities. Through our unsustainable activities our culture is breaking down the entire biosphere, with many species of plants and animals on a daily base being made extinct. Rather than caused by fate or being predetermined, the imbalanced state of modern humanity came about through the cultural choices we have made over the recent millennia, influenced by the power *chakra* and the *Surya nadi*. The navel *chakra* and solar *pranic* battery have shaped a society in which production facilities are male-dominated, and, while everybody in a position of power believes that we need to dissemble and dissect the world, extract minerals, build factories and make profit (all male catabolic concepts), the idea that the whole planet is one living organism that needs to be nurtured (an anabolic concept linked to feminine spirituality), a process that may impinge on profitability, is still considered too intuitive and right-brained by many.

If you imagine India 500 to 800 years ago, the above-described solar tendency would have been considered innovative progress. If you, for example, look at Paramahamsa Ramakrishna's upbringing (1836-1886), he grew up in a society that was still absorbed in magical and mythical thinking. What we would today consider fairy tale creatures were still readily perceived by Indian peasants, who were still much closer to what we would today consider indigenous culture. In those days the practice of *Surya Bheda*na was considered very important. The individual yogi had to pull themselves out of superstition, excessive dependence on community and opinion of others, and had to increase will power and discipline. *Shakti Chalana* is a system quite comparable to a scientist withdrawing into their laboratory to conduct long experiments, while their social and community life suffers. Only in the case of the yogi, the laboratory consists of the body and psyche of the scientist, rather than being an external set-up.

Today, however, after a 1000-year long process during which the world became more and more solar, the tables have turned. The dark side of the solar *nadi* means that if it becomes aggravated (i.e. too much *pranic* charge in the solar versus the lunar *nadi*), the yogi may turn into a Type-A personality, ego megalomaniac, potentially phallic-narcissistic go-getter.

Our societies are already dominated by this white, male personality type, which we can see from the fact that more and more wealth becomes concentrated in fewer and fewer hands every year. As I am writing this, the 100 wealthiest individuals hold as much wealth as the poorer 50% of humanity. While inequality is on the rise, the working-class masses must toil every year more hours to simply get by. And this takes place against a backdrop of environmental destruction and mass extinction of life. Note that most murderous activities in history have been performed by men (who are more solar), whereas women who carry and bring forth new life are archetypically more lunar, empathetic and community oriented. That doesn't mean they cannot perform atrocities, too.

Humanity's aggravated *Surya nadi* has caused us to pursue competition, warfare, capitalism, and the systematic conversion of nature and human relationships into money, thus bringing ourselves closer and closer to the yawning abyss of environmental holocaust and ecocide. This does not mean there is never a case when *Surya Bhedana* is appropriate. A yogi should start *pranayama* through the *solar nadi* if she does suffer from a lunar aggravation. India, for most of the last 2000 years, did suffer from a lunar aggravation. We may say that during the last 2000 years India was the lunar mother culture of the planet. But during the 300 years of Mogul rule and the subsequent centuries of British Raj, India as a response became more and more solar. This process became completed when after acquiring home rule India adopted Western Science, capitalism and subsequently IT. I am not suggesting that India did not have the right to do this; we could speculate that it had to do so to liberate itself from Western colonialism. Looking from the vantage point of global balance, however, that the previous lunar mother culture of the plant has turned solar, has radically accelerated global imbalance and natural destruction.

Now only a few remaining bastions of lunar culture remain on the planet, most indigenous cultures. As a result the planet heats up (courtesy of solar aggravation) and environmental destruction and mass extinction of life accelerates. If we want to tread the path towards healing and balance, we need to prevent any further rise of the *Surya nadi*. In this case, most people will need to practice lunar *pranayama,* i.e. *Chandra Bhedana.* Yoga can make a huge and healing contribution to shaping future society.

Let's look now at what influence the lunar *nadi* and *Chandra Bhedana* have on the brain and mind. Applying this method, all inhalations are taken through the left nostril and all exhalation performed through the right nostril. This process charges the lunar storehouse of *prana,* or lunar *pranic* battery, which is adjacent to the third eye *chakra,* (*Ajna chakra*). The third eye *chakra's* function is female, nurturing and anabolic. The lunar *pranic* battery powers the following functions:

- Right holistic brain hemisphere
- Left lunar nostril
- Relativistic mind
- Parasympathetic nervous system
- Introversion
- Afferent (incoming) nerve currents
- Sensory neurons
- Anabolism (building up tissue)

Kundalini can be raised through both the left or right nostril. To raise it through the right nostril was important 500 years ago when the age of Enlightenment and the industrial and scientific revolution was still ahead of us. Now we are facing a different situation, which requires different solutions. *Chandra Bhedana* activates the right holistic brain hemisphere. This is important for big-picture thinking, but also for coming up with solutions for modern society's problems completely outside the box. The right brain-hemisphere is responsible for intuitive and holistic thinking. In this context this, for example, means that we realize that the value of a single species like the Monarch butterfly or the Delta Smelt must include all complex interactions that it has with all other species in its biotope, which in final analysis interacts with all the other biotopes on the planet. Small changes, caused by the extinction of species such as the above, may be acceptable to the analytical left brain-hemisphere. However, the right, holistic, intuitive hemisphere recognizes how little we know. It also recognizes that each species has the right to exist, a right with which we humans have no right to impinge on. Speciesism, the belief that one species (usually the human) is superior to another, will, like previously sexism and racism, fall away once the right brain-hemisphere is fully activated. If we are to survive, hundreds of years from now we will look at our speciesism of today with the same shame and guilt we are now objecting slavery to. All life is an emanation of the Divine, not just the human one.

Chandra Bhedana also shifts our mind away from fundamentalism towards relativism. Socrates' statement, "I know that I know nothing", is the epitome of relativism. With this maxim, we are always ready to listen to others, to learn more, and our curiosity remains active. The various forms of religious fundamentalism have received significant criticism. What is less investigated is how much scientific and economic fundamentalism destroys our world and nature. According to these two forms of fundamentalism one has to first proof how a particular policy reduces CO2 or increases jobs, for it to attract any funding. For example, in my home country Australia, we are still destroying the Great Barrier Reef, the largest organism on Earth (and the only organism large enough to be seen from space). We do so because the Great Barrier Reef provides less profit than the giant coal mines located near to it. As I am writing this, new coal mining leases are given out, more canals are being dredged through the reef to provide shipping access, a giant new coal port is being built, and each time large rainfalls occur, run-off from the mines is polluting the reef. All the while obsolete industries are being kept alive through government subsidies and scientific studies showcasing their destructive nature lose their funding.

The fundamentalist mind, caused by a solar aggravation, reduces the many truths to one truth. Once it has done that, it disregards whatever goes counter to that one truth. When suffering from solar aggravation, I may follow a particularly narrow set of rules, such as, for example, profit-maximization, and may become closed off and arrogant towards anything outside of my reality tunnel. I may then hold the position that indigenous shamanism and animism, who hold that everything is a form of spirit and therefore deserves respect and being listened to, is bugaboo. While on the surface the scientific paradigm may hold all the trump cards, why then did a mere 300 years of scientific revolution destroy most of the natural world and make Millions of species extinct. Why did cultures like the Australian Aborigines, who were according to the Western Scientific paradigm until recently treated as fauna, caused in over 60,000 years of habitation less damage to this continent than white, scientific people did in 200 years?

The relativistic mind, empowered by *Chandra Bhedana*, knows that we know little and is always prepared to listen and learn more. When we maintain this openness, new insights can come from the most unexpected directions. A disclaimer here: I do not propose that we should ignore Western Science. The advantage of Western Medicine, with surgery and infectious diseases, cannot be disputed. What I am arguing against is the philosophy of Western Science, materialistic reductionism, i.e. the fundamentalist argument that Western Science alone is the path to knowledge and that everything that is not based on empirical data can be disregarded.

Chandra Bhedana also powers the parasympathetic nervous system. When Paramahamsa Ramakrishna was asked how came he so easily entered *samadhi,* his answer was "by totally receiving it". One problem with the solar *nadi* is that it gives you the impression that progress can be made only by discipline, hard work, practice, will power and control. While that is an important part of yoga, the opposite, the attitudes of receptiveness and surrender, is also necessary for success in yoga. This is confirmed by *Yoga Sutra* I.12, which says, "suspension of mind comes through the dual means of practice and disidentification". Patanjali here talks about the importance of balance between the solar and lunar *nadis*. Disidentification means to let go of any all-to-narrow definitions of who we are. Through such letting go we become receptive and open to receiving the knowledge that cannot be obtained with hard work. To have the attitude that only hard work and nothing else will yield fruit, leads to developing rigid beliefs about who we are. I'm not saying here that hard work has no place. It does. But we need to balance discipline and effort on one hand, and rest, relaxation, letting go, receptiveness and surrender on the other. *Chandra Bhedana* can help here because it opens us up to receiving.

Our society demands of a successful person to be extravert, outgoing, jolly, to have a strong physical presence and to be interested in sports and competition. The corporate Briggs-Myers personality test even surveys job applicants for some of these traits. The problem with extraversion is that we set ourselves up to depend on external and sensory stimulus. The lunar *pranic* storehouse powers introversion, sensory neurons and afferent (incoming) nerve currents, with the three obviously being closely connected. All three direct us towards the fact that happiness and freedom can be found within and can be made to radiate out from there and transform our personality. *Chandra Bhedana*, therefore, guides us to become less reliant on sensory and external stimulus. This is an important prerequisite for higher yoga. All addictions, for example, are based on the misconception that lasting happiness and freedom are to be found outside of us. This is erroneous because everything outside of us is in constant flux, everything changes, nothing lasts. *Chandra Bhedana* turns the focus inwards.

The lunar *pranic* storehouse also powers anabolism, the part of our metabolism that builds up tissue. Catabolism, the ability to break down cells into constituents (which are then rebuilt by the anabolic cycle into new cells), and anabolism need to form a balance in a functioning metabolic system. There is also an important mental dimension to these terms. For example, look at how much of our entertainment, particularly the movie industry, and violent sports, are based on catabolic concepts, i.e. those of destruction. How much do we all enjoy seeing the villain punitively beaten up and ultimately killed? We are teaching ourselves and our children that violence and coercive measures are a viable aspect of conflict resolution. Then this plays into our readiness to go to war. I vividly remember watching 9/11 interview footage featuring people on the street yelling into the camera, "Mr. President, send the bombers!" Where to send the bombers was not asked at that moment. It was not considered important. What was important was the procurement of a sacrificial victim, a scapegoat. In that moment, any ethnic population anywhere in the world seemed good enough to complete the cycle of retributive violence. This is learned via our choice of entertainment and our worship of competitiveness via competitive sports. This choice of entertainment, with our hyper-competitive capitalist economy, has fostered a situation where today as a society we collectively have too much *prana* in our solar *nadis*, i.e. our entire society suffers from a solar aggravation.

Collectively, as a society, we need to steer towards activating the lunar component of our psyche, the one that engenders listening, empathy and compassion for all species. Only then can we avoid descending into the abyss of ecocide and environmental holocaust. This must lead us to the conclusion that for most of us today, *Chandra Bhedana* is more important than *Surya Bhedana*.

Which of both techniques we perform, depends, of course, on the situation of the individual, i.e. if the individual practitioner tends to lunar or solar aggravation. The easiest test for this is to determine whether over a 14 or 28-day period you breathe roughly for the same duration through the left nostril than through the right. To make a test, close one of your nostrils with a finger or thumb and breathe exclusively through the other. Notice the amount of restriction or free flow. Then reverse the exercise and close the other nostril. Again check for restriction and congestion versus unrestricted flow. You'll notice that in 99% of cases one nostril is more restricted than the other. Mentally note which one is open. Repeat this check every 2 hours. At the end of a 14 or 28-day period compare whether both nostrils were balanced or if there is an imbalance in one or the other direction. Usually there is. Most modern people have a solar aggravation, that is the right nostril is open more often than the left. In this case, use *Chandra Bhedana* for Kundalini raising. For more details on how to diagnose and balance a lunar-solar imbalance please study my text *Pranayama The Breath of Yoga* and particularly the chapters on *nadi* purification[439] and *Chandra*[440] and *Surya*[441] *Bhedana*.

WHY NOT NADI SHODHANA DURING SHAKTI CHALANA MUDRA?

The yoga *shastras* are surprisingly silent about the option of raising Kundalini through *Nadi Shodhana Pranayama*, the *pranayama* method that combines both *Chandra* and *Surya Bhedana* in each single respiratory cycle. Here one first inhales through the left nostril, then exhales through the right, followed by an inhalation through the right and an exhale through the left. After that, the cycle starts again with an inhalation through the left nostril, etc. *Kumbhakas* are ideally performed after each in- and exhalation. *Nadi Shodhana* is the

439 Gregor Maehle, *Pranayama The Breath of Yoga*, Kaivalya Publications, Crabbes Creek, 2012, p. 233ff

440 Gregor Maehle, *Pranayama The Breath of Yoga*, Kaivalya Publications, Crabbes Creek, 2012, p. 289ff

441 Gregor Maehle, *Pranayama The Breath of Yoga*, Kaivalya Publications, Crabbes Creek, 2012, p. 283ff

method preferred if there is no major imbalance of the *nadis*. If so, then *Nadi Shodhana* practice is gradually dialled up and extreme, lopsided efforts to raise Kundalini are considered unnecessary.

As I will describe in more detail in the practical section, *Shakti Chalana Mudra* is an extreme practice to be performed for a relatively short period in a retreat period. However, it is still necessary to phase this extreme practice in and out. If the *nadis* are relatively balanced, we would not go towards the retreat scenario but gradually intensify *Nadi Shodhana Pranayama* over years. This is the scenario that T. Krishnamacharya preferred and practised, too. In a person, however, in which imbalance continues to persist, even after reasonable counteracting efforts have been made, we would consider going to a retreat situation. We would then supercharge the *nadi* opposite to our general preponderance and raise Kundalini in one major effort, performed over several weeks or months.

Is one or the other method to be preferred? Is there a significant advantage to raising Kundalini slowly and gradually over years of practice through *Nadi Shodhana* or is the retreat option with an intense practice burst of *Chandra-* or *Surya Bhedana* to be preferred? In reality, we do not really have a choice. A person with little imbalance for whom *Nadi Shodhana* suffices, is usually equipped with a personality that makes them disinclined to intense, short bursts of practice effort. And generally, they don't need to as it is enough for them to gradually chip away on obstacles. But a person who despite efforts continues to live with significant imbalances, often experiences a certain amount of suffering in their life. This suffering then powers thirst and desire for intense practices. It is this drive and intensity that will eventually get a person to decide that a retreat situation to raise Kundalini is appropriate.

WHICH POSTURE TO CHOSE FOR SHAKTI CHALANA?

There is a lengthy discussion across *shastras* whether to prefer *Siddhasana* or *Padmasana* for the actual act of raising Kundalini. The difference of opinion reflects the fact where various authorities place the so-called *kanda* (bulb), the seat of the Kundalini. Some authorities identify the *kanda*, the seat of Kundalini, with *Muladhara Chakra* and in this case, they usually prefer *Siddhasana*, which stimulates the *Muladhara* with the left heel. The schools that see the *kanda* in the *Svadhishthana Chakra* usually prefer *Padmasana*, as this posture can press the lower abdomen with both heels. Shyam Sunder Goswami taught that the *kanda* is in the perineum (i.e. in the *Muladhara*) and therefore recommends *Siddhasana* [442]. He sticks to the traditional method of using the left heel to stimulate the *kanda* in the perineum[443]. Theos Bernard also learned from his teacher, the Maharishi, that *Siddhasana* is the preferred posture to rouse Kundalini[444]. These contemporary teachers take their inspiration from the *siddha* Goraknath, who in the *Goraksha Shataka* displayed a clear preponderance to *Siddhasana*.

Sundaradeva, in his *Hathatatva Kaumudi*, also displays a preference for *Siddhasana* with the Kaumudi even heretically

---

442 Shyam Sundar Goswami, *Laya Yoga*, Inner Traditions, Rochester, 1999, p. 169

443 Shyam Sundar Goswami, *Laya Yoga*, Inner Traditions, Rochester, 1999, p. 74

444 Theos Bernard - *Heaven Lies Within Us,* Charles Scribner's Sons, New York, 1939, p. 304

suggesting placing the right heel into the perineum[445]. I know, this throws the cat of uncertainty among our pigeons of neatly established *shastric* order, but I prefer to authentically report what the *shastras* say rather than just omitting evidence that doesn't reconcile with my views. Sundaradeva shows that his suggestion of using the right heel was not a whimsical mistake or chance omission, by again in a different passage recommending the right-side-first version of Siddhasana, this time with *Kaki-*, and *Shanmukhi Mudras*[446].

When I studied *mudras* with B.N.S. Iyengar it was clearly *Padmasana*, which was the preferred posture and Iyengar placed the *kanda* in the lower abdomen. Kundalini was to be stimulated with both heels in lotus posture. *Hathatatva Kaumudi of Sundaradeva* has it both ways and in stanza XLIV.5 confirms *Padmasana* as the posture for *Shakti Chalana*[447]. Sundaradeva does so again in stanza XLIV.21 and many other passages [448]. T. Krishnamacharya also taught *Shakti Chalana Mudra* in *Padmasana*, rather than *Siddhasana*[449]. This is also confirmed by the *Hatha Yoga Pradipika*, which teaches to assume *Vajrasana* (another name of *Padmasana*), in which the *kanda* then will

---

445 Dr M.L. Gharote et al (eds. & transl.), *Hathatatvakaumudi,* The Lonavla Yoga Institite, Lonavla, 2007, p. 683

446 Dr M.L. Gharote et al (eds. & transl.), *Hathatatvakaumudi,* The Lonavla Yoga Institite, Lonavla, 2007, p. 684

447 Dr M.L. Gharote et al (eds. & transl.), *Hathatatvakaumudi,* The Lonavla Yoga Institite, Lonavla, 2007, p. 514

448 Dr M.L. Gharote et al (eds. & transl.), *Hathatatvakaumudi,* The Lonavla Yoga Institite, Lonavla, 2007, p. 519

449 T. Krishnamacharya, *Yoga Makaranda,* Media Garuda, Chennai, 2011, p. 109

be near the heels, with whom it should be stimulated[450]. The dispute between schools of thought is to some extend moot because both *chakras*, the *Muladhara* and the *Svadhishthana* are seats of Kundalini, so both postures could be used. This is confirmed by Theos Bernard who wrote that his teacher advised him both postures were suitable[451]. From my experience, it is not a choice of one over the other, but both postures need to be actively used, as they both bring unique qualities into the mix. My preferred approach is to use *Padmasana* for all sessions involving *pranayama* and *kumbhaka*, and *Siddhasana* for all those focussing on *chakra*-Kundalini meditation.

THE ROLE OF CHAKRA MEDITATION

Which brings us to the role of *chakra* meditation. I see *Shakti Chalana* and other *mudras* as an alternative for those who, for whatever reason, may shy away from long-term commitment to extensive *pranayama* and *chakra*-meditation. What I mean with that is the commitment to spend around two hours per day on the compound of *pranayama* and *chakra*-meditation, typically 30 minutes for *pranayama* and around 90 minutes for *chakra*-Kundalini meditation. Long-term commitment to *chakra*-meditation seems easy of those with a more cerebral orientation, but it can be challenging for those more kinaesthetically inclined. With the *mudra* and *Shakti Chalana* approach our method fulfils to a greater extent the needs of the kinaesthetically inclined, i.e. the need to feel body sensations as a confirmation that something is happening spiritually. One needs to be on one's guard though, regarding the need to feel an energetic,

---

450 *Hatha Yoga Pradipika* III.107.

451 Theos Bernard, *Heaven Lies Within Us*, Charles Scribner's Sons, New York, 1939, p. 301

kinaesthetic sensation as a confirmation for spiritual progress. As said, the Kundalini is a spiritual and not a physical force and that only changed behaviour initiated through spiritual experiences confirms that we really have experienced something spiritually. Many people, however, have a strong kinaesthetic orientation and compute with their bodies. This can go as far that some people can't think inspirational thoughts or have realizations and revelations without moving their bodies to compute kinaesthetically. They have to almost 'feel' themselves into spiritual states. In the past our education system in general and yoga in particular have often labelled such people as learning disabled and closed their doors to them by insisting on the maintenance of a rigidly frozen posture as a base camp for cerebral, spiritual pursuit. If yoga truly wants to change our society, it is time to disavow these rigid tendencies. The point here is to neither encourage students to further go into that direction but also not to discourage them to explore if that is their existing tendency.

Mudra practice can give us the opportunity to reduce time spent performing *chakra*-Kundalini meditation; however, that doesn't mean we can dispose of it entirely. A minimum of *chakra*-meditation practice still needs to be maintained because whatever method we employ to raise Kundalini, we will still use short *chakra*-meditation sessions to place and maintain Kundalini in the particular *chakra* required for our particular purpose during that session[452]. So does, for example,

---

452 Which type of *samadhi* we enter is determined by which *chakra prana* is held during our *samadhi* practice, similarly to the way in which the turning of a radio receiver's dial determines the radio station. The skill of holding *prana* in a particular *chakra* is gained through *chakra*-Kundalini meditation.

Jayatarama's *Jogapradipyaka* call *Shakti Chalana* by the name *Dravani Mudra* and describes it as consisting of *Khechari Mudra* (to be described in Section 5, *Mudra* 31) and the focus on the six *chakras*[453]. The same is confirmed by Sir John Woodroffe, who says that in the ritual called *bhuta shuddhi* (another name for *chakra*-meditation), ascent and descent are imagined only[454]. When perusing this peculiar wording we must remember that the book was written in the late 1800s. With "imagined only" Woodroffe means it is a mental act, rather than a physical act. Woodroffe again states that Kundalini is awakened by meditating on the *chakras* sequentially[455]. Also, Theos Bernard describes how during each *kumbhaka* he mentally went through awakening Kundalini by leading it through the *chakras* until it became united with consciousness[456].

ASHVINI MUDRA

Continuing to research constituents of *Shakti Chalana*, we go now on to *Ashvini Mudra*. As a stand-alone technique, this *mudra* was already described in Section 4, *Mudra* 24. The *Gheranda Samhita* in stanza III.4 recommends *Ashvini Mudra* to stimulate the Kundalini in *Shakti Chalana*[457]. The connection of *Ashvini*

---

453 Swami Maheshananda et al. (eds & transl.), *Jogapradipyaka of Jayatarama*, Kaivalyadhama, Lonavla, 2006, p. 110

454 Sir John Woodroffe, *The Serpent Power*, Ganesh & CO, Madras, 1995, p. 242

455 Sir John Woodroffe, *The Serpent Power*, Ganesh & CO, Madras, 1995, p. 206

456 Theos Bernard, *Hatha Yoga*, Rider, London, 1950, p. 95

457 James Mallinson, *The Gheranda Samhita*, YogaVidya.com, Woodstock, 2004, p. 74

Mudra with *Shakti Chalana* is also confirmed by Yogeshvaranand Paramahansa who advocates this *mudra* to induce *prana* into *Sushumna* during *kumbhaka*[458]. However, he also recommends manipulating the *kanda*, which he locates between navel and generative organ, i.e. in the *Svadhishthana Chakra*. He also suggests the use of both heels, for which again *Padmasana* is the best posture. *The Serpent Power* also endorses *Ashvini Mudra*[459]. Its author suggests performing *Ashvini Mudra* combined with *Nauli* in *Siddhasana* and *Shanmukhi Mudra*, until *prana* manifests in the *Sushumna*. And Theos Bernard emphasises the role of *Ashvini Mudra* as the tool of choice to conduct *apana* upwards[460]. *Ashvini Mudra*, as we will soon find out, for maximum effect it is practised in turns with *Vajroli Mudra*.

SHANMUKHI MUDRA (YONI MUDRA)

This brief passage only covers *Shanmukhi Mudra's* relevance as a component of *Shakti Chalana*. As a stand-alone technique, this *mudra* will be covered in Section 5, *Mudra* 29. The *Yoga Chudamani Upanishad* suggests combining *Shanmukhi Mudra*, *Vajroli Mudra* and *Ashvini Mudra* to close all nine *pranic* gates of the body[461]. The nine gates include the eyes, ears, nostrils, mouth, genital and anus. Through these gates the body loses *prana* and *mudras* rectify and reverse this. *Vajroli-*, and *Ashvini*

---

458 Yogeshvaranand Paramahansa, *First Steps to Higher Yoga*, Yoga Niketan Trust, New Delhi, 2001, p. 384

459 Sir John Woodroffe, *The Serpent Power*, Ganesh & CO, Madras, 1995, p. 207

460 Theos Bernard, *Heaven Lies Within Us*, Charles Scribner's Sons, New York, 1939, p. 299

461 *Yoga Chudamani Upanishad* stanza 107

Mudras were already covered. *Shanmukhi Mudra* is a technique in which all the facial orifices are closed with one's fingers. The efficacy of *Shanmukhi Mudra* in this process is also confirmed in Sir John Woodroffe's *The Serpent Power*[462]. Woodroffe teaches *Shakti Chalana* as comprising of *Nauli* in *Siddhasana*, after which internal *kumbhakas* are performed with *Shanmukhi-*, and *Ashvini Mudras*.

SHAKTI CHALANA PRACTICAL SECTION

The above theoretical section was designed to source the primary elements of *Shakti Chalana* and conduct an inquiry into *shastra* regarding which techniques might be promising. Some schools list opaque or unusual approaches. If there was too little scriptural evidence, I have ignored these as otherwise, the theoretical section would have become unwieldy. With the above analysis we have now a powerful toolbox, which includes all potent methods helpful for power conduction. Before stringing the methods together we need to first look into what needs to already be in place to start this process.

PREREQUISITES FOR SHAKTI CHALANA

Shakti Chalana is not a beginner's subject but an advanced subject of yoga. One should not start yoga with the expectation to raise Shakti early on. This may seem clear to some readers, however, quite regularly I am contacted by novice practitioners with insufficient yogic background who ventured into these techniques and now ask for advice how to handle the forces

---

462 Sir John Woodroffe, *The Serpent Power*, Ganesh & CO, Madras, 1995, p. 207

they summoned. To use *Shakti Chalana Mudra* safely, readiness in three areas must be obtained firsthand.

Firstly, the prerequisites pertaining to practice must be fulfilled. This includes establishment in the daily practice of *asana, Nauli, pranayama* with internal and external *kumbhakas*, including all *bandhas*, and *chakra*-Kundalini Meditation including *mantra* and sun/moon visualization. This sounds like a serious ask, but many students who have worked for a few years with my previous books and integrated their teachings will already qualify here. Regarding *asana* a daily long-term practice comprising of 60-90 minutes per day for several years is required. 60 minutes are usually enough for an older person, whereas a younger person requires a longer daily *asana* practice. Consistency is more important than the ability to perform fancy postures. Most important are proficiency in *Padmasana, Siddhasana, Shirshasana* and *Sarvangasana*. A daily practice of 3 minutes of *Nauli* and 5 minutes of *Kapalabhati*, both comprising of several hundreds of strokes, is important. Also, a daily practice of 3 minutes of *Bhastrika* and approximately 20 minutes of slow breathing pranayamas such as *Nadi Shodhana, Chandra-*, or *Surya Bhedana*[463] is important, preferably with internal and external *kumbhakas* in the same breath cycle. At least five minutes of *chakra*-Kundalini meditation per day, performed over several years is required. More extensive daily meditation practices are better, of course, but let's not forget that we are exploring here an avenue that might replace long-term,

---

463 All these methods were described in nauseating detail in my text *Pranayama The Breath of Yoga.* As the descriptions go into several hundred pages, I cannot repeat them here and shortcutting the descriptions would do these magnificent techniques little justice.

extensive *chakra*-Kundalini meditation for those not so inclined. These guidelines are not set in stone, and variations depending on personal situation are possible, but personally I would not approach *Shakti Chalana* without all these systems in place. The main reason for that is once *Shakti Chalana* practice commences, we will use the above practices as a stepping stone, plateau, or base camp from which to venture higher. If these systems are not in place, we have no base from which to take off. For those who still doubt let me again quote the unintended inventor of the Kundalini-accident and spontaneous-awakening genres, Gopi Krishna, who stated that you need to be established at least in *asana, kriya* and *pranayama* to prepare for Kundalini rousing[464].

The next prerequisite is readiness pertaining to stage of life, i.e. *ashrama*. An example will elucidate this point. If you have three small children to care for, additionally run a business while doing a PhD on the side, with mortgage repayments breathing down your neck, this is not the time of life to commence *Shakti Chalana*. Again this may seem obvious to some, but the valued reader would be surprised to hear how many high achievers in exactly the situation above have approached me for technical support for Kundalini raising.

Shakti Chalana is a typical *vanaprashta* practice, this being the third stage (ashrama) of life. Preferably your children would have become self-sufficient, you are debt-free and can therefore reduce your professional duties, so you don't have too many responsibilities. You will need extra space in your life and available mental bandwidth to deal with *Shakti Chalana*. You also

---

464 Gopi Krishna, *Kundalini The Evolutionary Energy in Man*, Shambala, Boston & London, 1997, p. 130

need to consider that afterwards, your life may take a different direction. You need to have the freedom to change direction if required, as otherwise, there might not be a point to start with *Shakti Chalana* in the first place. Do not expect for *Shakti Chalana* to provide the energy for a high-roller or high achiever lifestyle. It could turn out that you are heading right the other way.

The third and last requirement is spiritual readiness. The purpose of *Shakti Chalana* is to place yourself into the service of a power greater than you, that is, to place yourself into the service of the Divine. While this undertaking of surrender (*ishvara pranidhana*) is strongly amplified through the process of *Shakti Chalana* itself, it needs to be started beforehand. You need to know why you do this, i.e. ideally, you already have an inkling of what service to the Divine you are providing, for which you need power conduction. You don't want to practice *Shakti Chalana* as an experiment, that is with the idea, "Let's get the energy and then see what to do with it once we have it". There is peril in using Kundalini for spiritually manipulating others and playing guru, which can easily happen if one has unresolved narcissistic issues, or one simply just wants to be loved or wants others to recognize one's greatness. These are common issues for human beings, but they have no place in *Shakti Chalana*. One needs to enter power conduction with a readiness to serve the Divine, to serve nature and to serve others, rather than wanting to achieve greatness and self-aggrandisement. The key to this is that one has found freedom in giving and serving the progress of others. For this finding freedom in giving and serving, one needs to have overcome the *need to receive*. This attitude forms the bedrock of a spiritual process I have described in *How To Find Your Life's Divine Purpose – Brain Software For a New Civilization*.

RETREAT SITUATION

Shakti Chalana is not a process continued ad infinitum, but it is an intense short burst in one's practice, possibly lasting for several weeks or months. It is not done permanently but only until the desired result is achieved. Once power conduction has taken place, we then enter a period in which we stabilize Kundalini, and efforts can be gradually phased down. As I have written, this scenario is not suitable for everybody. For some practitioners staying long-term at a medium intensity practice is more suitable. For others practising high-intensity power conduction practice for a few weeks or months is the better option. The retreat scenario is more suitable for people with a strong drive and intensity, which is usually powered by continued *karmic* suffering. With that I do not mean those who suffer from mental health issues but those who practice what the Armenian mystic G.I. Gurdjieff called conscious suffering.

SHAKTI CHALANA ELEMENTS

These are the primary elements of power conduction:

1. Advanced level *Nauli* and *Bhastrika* to create the fire and air to move Shakti. We would start this practice at 3 minutes each daily and dial it up to 5, 10, 15, 20 minutes each daily. Please ensure that all prerequisites are met.

2. The compound *Maha Mudra, Maha Bandha Mudra* and *Maha Vedha Mudra* to pierce the *granthis*. This must be preceded by an intermediate level long-term practice of *Bhastrika* combined with *Nadi Shodhana* including internal and external *kumbhakas*.

3. *Chandra* or *Surya Bhedana* with internal and external *kumbhaka* and all *bandhas*. Preferably this is done in *Padmasana* including *Ashvini* and *Vajroli Mudras* until

Shakti rises. Stimulate the *kanda* in the *Svadhishthana Chakra* by gently moving both heels.

4. When Kundalini rises use *chakra*-Kundalini meditation in *Siddhasana,* including *Ashvini* and *Vajroli Mudras* to consolidate. Also, here the heel of the lower foot is gently moved to stimulate, in this case, the *Muladhara Chakra* in the perineum.

5. Practice *Kaki Mudra* and *Shitali* to remove any excess *agni* and *pitta*. This could take 15, 20 or more minutes on its own.

ORDER OF TECHNIQUES

The order of techniques does not have to occur in exactly this order. For example, I am practising *Nauli* every morning first thing. The *agni* created through the technique is present for the whole day. It is advisable to conduct a long *Bhastrika* session right before the main *pranayama* session involving *Chandra* or *Surya Bhedana*. The compound of *Maha Mudra, Maha Bandha Mudra* and *Maha Vedha Mudra* can be practised before or after *pranayama*. I find it helpful to practice my *chakra*-Kundalini meditation early in the morning right after *Nauli*. Then my mind is fresh and receptive.

A good argument can be made to practice both the compound of *Maha Mudra, Maha Bandha Mudra* and *Maha Vedha Mudra* and the *Chandra* or *Surya Bhedana* with internal and external *kumbhaka* and *Ashvini* and *Vajroli Mudras* straight after one's *asana* practice. It is helpful to conduct the *Kaki Mudra/ Shitali* session last. Monitor every day for heat- and burning sensations or interrupted sleep. In this case, *Kaki Mudra/ Shitali* need to be dialled up or *Nauli* dialled down. Don't let excess *agni* let your mental balance deteriorate. The huge advantage of using *Chandra Bhedana* over *Surya Bhedana* is that the former does not aggravate *agni,* whereas the latter does. This means that if you chose *Chandra Bhedana* your *Kaki Mudra/ Shitali* practice will only have to balance extra fire created through *Nauli.* Including *Shitali* also means you cannot practice *Shakti Chalana* in a metropolis with bad, polluted air. *Kaki Mudra/ Shitali* requires premium air quality, i.e. no air pollution. If you practice *Kaki Mudra/ Shitali* in poor, polluted air you are likely to get a throat and chest infection. This is another reason *Shakti Chalana* is usually performed in a retreat situation somewhere out in nature, because this enables you to select a place with excellent air quality, a significant advantage for advanced *pranayama* practice.

NAULI

This is a simplified technical description of *Nauli.* It was necessary to include it into this account of *Shakti Chalana Mudra* as it is an essential part of it. You will find a more extensive essay on *Nauli* in my book *Pranayama the Breath of Yoga*[465]. *Nauli* is the churning of the abdominal muscles. The abdominal recti are isolated and then a wavelike motion is initiated, which first churns vertically up and down, then from the right to the left and then from the left to the right. The *Hatha Yoga Manjari* states that *Nauli* helps to turn the *chakra*s upwards[466]. The *chakra*s are always facing the Kundalini. In a person who has not awakened Kundalini, the *chakra*s, thought of as lotus flowers, hang with their heads down facing the Kundalini in the *Muladhara* (base *chakra*). *Nauli* is an

---

465 Gregor Maehle, *Pranayama The Breath of Yoga*, Kaivalya Publications, Crabbes Creek, 2012, p. *176*
466 *Hatha Yoga Manjari of Sahajananda* II.48

important exercise in raising Kundalini; hence Sahajananda, the author of the *Hatha Yoga Manjari*, remarks it assists in turning up the lotuses. There are many other benefits to *Nauli*. However, their discussion is not essential in *Shakti Chalana Mudra*.

NAULI CONTRAINDICATIONS

Nauli should not be practised if hyperacidity occurs and not for six weeks after giving birth. And it should not be done during pregnancy and menstruation or if suffering from high blood pressure, heart problems, ulcers, hernia or glaucoma. Due to the intense pressure exchange, *Nauli* should not be practised during a time when women wish to conceive. If you suffer from an aggravated *pitta* condition, do less *Nauli*, particularly stage 1. However, *Nauli* is part of the parcel of techniques used to purify *pitta/agni*. *Nauli* is taught here in four stages. *Nauli*'s first stage in yogic literature is variously called *Agnisara* (fanning of digestive fire) or sometimes even *Uddiyana*. Since this present technique forms a necessary prelude to the more advanced stages of *Nauli*, I will simply call it *Nauli* stage 1.

NAULI STAGE 1

The action should be performed on an empty stomach and after the evacuation of the bowels. The early morning is ideal – before other yoga practices such as *asana* and *pranayama*. *Nauli* can be done in *Padmasana* or a similar meditation posture, but it is most easily learned standing. Place your feet hip-width apart and your hands on your thighs just above the knees. Now stoop forward and look at your abdomen. It is helpful to bare your abdomen so you see and understand the effect of your actions.

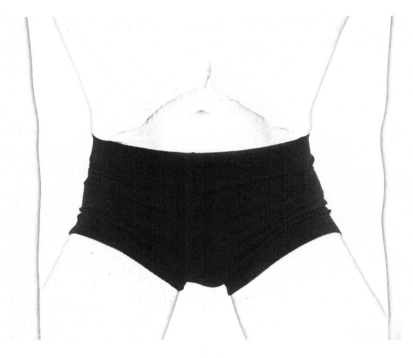

Bahya Uddiyana

Now exhale fully, and at the end of the exhalation, use the contraction of your abdominal muscles to expel the last bit of air. Lock and contract your throat and completely relax your abdominals. Keeping the throat firmly contracted, perform a faked inhalation. This means you act as if you are inhaling but can't since your throat is locked. A limited expansion of the ribcage ensues with the intercostal muscles. And lift the ribcage upwards to the head. The effect of these combined actions is that the vacuum in the lungs will suck the lungs up towards the clavicles. This raises and stretches the diaphragm, which now sucks the contents of the abdominal cavity into the thoracic cavity with all the pressure- changing effects this has for the abdominal organs. You will understand now that you need to be of average health (not of poor health) and without major disorders of the abdominal and thoracic organs to perform this intense action.

If you are comfortable with and accustomed to external *kumbhaka*s, suddenly release the intercostal muscles, latissimus dorsi and lower trapezius, and let go of the upward suction of the lungs. Your diaphragm will suddenly drop, and the abdominal organs return to their original position. The action is performed without engaging the abdominal muscles, but only through creating and releasing suction with the thorax and the lungs. Once the abdominal organs have returned to their place of origin, you have completed one stroke of stage 1 *Nauli*. Once this is achieved one learns to repeat one stroke after another, while maintaining *kumbhaka*, which will create a flapping, vertical wave-like motion of your abdominal wall. Once you have come to the end of your capacity release your throat, inhale gently and come up to standing. The number of strokes per *kumbhaka* is gradually increased until around 60 strokes in a single round can be performed. During that process, do not sacrifice amplitude of the strokes for increased frequency. Make sure that each individual stroke is vigorous, as otherwise, the exercise becomes impotent. A fast increase of strokes and rounds is not recommended during summer, particularly during a heatwave. Gradually build up your practice until you can perform three of such rounds, each constituting an external *kumbhaka* including 60 strokes of *Nauli*. This makes 180 strokes of *Nauli* stage 1, which is part of our long-term baseline practice from which we may eventually ascend to the summit of *Shakti Chalana*.

NAULI STAGE 2, MADHYAMA

Once you are firmly established in stage 1, additionally practice stage 2. *Nauli* stage 2 starts in the same way as stage 1. Stand in the same position, exhale, lock your throat and perform a faked inhalation so the contents of the abdominal cavity are being sucked up into the thorax. Without reducing the suction thus created, press down with latissimus dorsi, trapezius and the lower part of the diaphragm, and press on your knees with your arms. Now engage the two sides of the rectus abdominis and push it out while you continue to lift the thorax upwards.

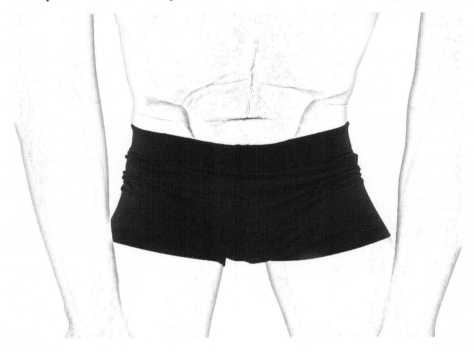

Madhyama Nauli

You will now see that the two sides of rectus abdominis stand out while the more lateral parts of the frontal abdominal wall, where the obliques abdominis muscles are located, are being sucked inwards. This is because by pushing out the recti a vacuum is created behind them. It is this vacuum we will use in *Nauli*. Initially do one *kumbhaka* only and slowly build up to three rounds, bringing you to a total of six external *kumbhakas* (this includes the three of *Nauli* stage 1). This stage of *Nauli* is called *Madhyama* (middling) because the abdominal muscles are popping out in the middle.

NAULI STAGE 3, VAMA AND DAKSHINA

Once you have practised stage 2 and are comfortable with it, move to stage 3. Stage 3 initially starts like stage 2. While standing, bend forward and perform external *kumbhaka* with external *Uddiyana*. Keeping the abdominal contents sucked upwards, pop out the abdominal recti in the middle (*Madhyama*) by pressing down with your arms on your knees, as in stage 2. Make sure that you never actually contract the abdominal mucles by pushing them out. The abdominal muscles are relaxed and are only contracting as a result of pressing with the arms down on the knees. This point is important as otherwise you will use all four layers of the abdominal muscles to brace rather than isolating the rectis abdominis only. Now lean to the left and push down with your left arm on the left knee while you relax your right arm. You may exaggerate initially by lifting the right hand off the right knee. This action relaxes the right side of the rectus abdominis, and you will now notice that the right side retreats and is sucked back into the abdomen, while only the left side protrudes. This is called *Vama Nauli*, i.e. *Nauli* on the left side. Hold it for the length of your *kumbhaka* and keep engaging the left side of your rectus, bearing down on your left knee only. Now relax your throat, inhale gently and come up to standing.

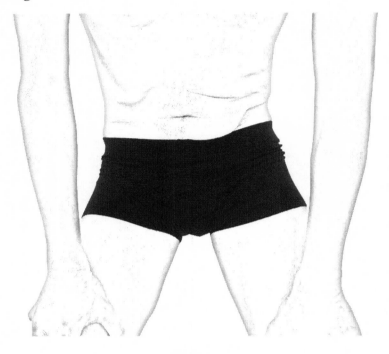

Vama Nauli

Now reverse left for right and perform the exercise on the right. First, perform external *kumbhaka* with *Madhyama Nauli*. Then relax the rectus on the left and continue to engage the rectus on the right by leaning into the right arm, pressing down on the right knee. Again, hold it during the external *kumbhaka*. Once accustomed to the exercise, take your time to isolate the two sides of the muscle by repeating the exercise once or twice. You may now discontinue *Nauli* stage 2 *Madhyama*, as you always enter *Vama* and *Dakshina Nauli* through *Madhyama*. In the early stages what is important is not how many repetitions you can do but the intensity and precision of your isolation. Continue with *Nauli* stage 1 as per above.

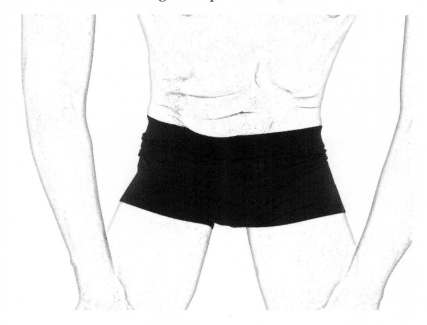

Dakshina Nauli

NAULI STAGE 4, ROLLING, FULL VERSION

Stage 4 is the horizontal *Nauli* proper. Once it is learned, stages 2 and 3, which are for didactic purposes only, are to be discontinued. However, stage 1 is to be continued. Bending forward, perform external *kumbhaka* with external *Uddiyana*. Now engage the rectus abdominis in the middle, performing *Madhyama Nauli*. Next, take the pressure off the right arm and perform *Vama Nauli*, engaging the rectus on the left. After you have clearly isolated the rectus on the left, take the weight off both arms, relax the rectus completely and suck the abdominal contents back into the thoracic cavity performing full external

Uddiyana. Hold this for a second and then press down on the right arm and engage the rectus on the right (*Dakshina Nauli*). This is the first time you access *Dakshina Nauli* straight from external *Uddiyana* and not from *Madhyama Nauli*. It may take a few rounds to get used to that. Then go on from *Dakshina Nauli* to *Madhyama Nauli*, which constitutes one churning. Take a breath and then repeat the exercise in the same order: *Bahya Uddiyana, Madhyama, Vama, Uddiyana, Dakshina* and *Madhyama*. What is essential is that you keep properly isolating each position and not concerning yourself with how fast you can do it.

Now repeat the exercise in reverse order. First, perform *Bahya* (external) *Uddiyana*, then pop out the middle (*Madhyama*), from here, go over to the right (*Dakshina*), suck back in with *Bahya Uddiyana* and go over to the left (*Vama*) and back to the middle (*Madhyama*). Come up, take a few breaths and then do a second *kumbhaka*, again churning to the right. Repeat this daily for a while, if necessary for a few weeks, until you have full control of all stages.

Once you can isolate all the positions, perform two and more churnings in one *kumbhaka*. As you slowly get more proficient and faster with the exercise, you will notice a wave-like motion going across your abdomen. However, do not achieve this effect by losing precision. The order to the left is: *Kumbhaka, Bahya Uddiyana*, pop out *Madhyama*, then *Vama*, then back to *Bahya Uddiyana*, then *Dakshina*, then *Madhyama*, from here, straight over to *Vama* and back to *Uddiyana*, out on the right, *Dakshina*, back into the middle, *Madhyama*. Then take a few breaths and take another *kumbhaka*'s worth of rolling to the left, performing as many churnings as you are comfortable with without losing the precision of the isolation. The goal is again to perform three *kumbhakas* or rounds, with each consisting of 60 strokes, i.e. 180 strokes of *Vama Nauli*, distributed over three *kumbhakas*.

Then perform the same quantity on the right, *Kumbhaka*, *Bahya Uddiyana*, *Madhyama*, *Dakshina*, *Bahya Uddiyana*, *Vama*, *Madhyama*, *Dakshina*, *Bahya Uddiyana*, etc. Again the goal is to reach 180 strokes of *Dakshina Nauli*, distributed over three *kumbhakas*. Our total baseline practice of *Nauli* consists now of 540 strokes, distributed evenly across *Nauli* stage 1, *Nauli* stage 4 *Vama* and *Nauli* stage 4 *Dakshina*.

BHASTRIKA

This is again a simplified technical description of *Bhastrika*, without which *Shakti Chalana Mudra's* account would not have been complete. For a more extensive description, please consult my book *Pranayama the Breath of Yoga*[467]. *Bhastrika* is a rapid-breathing technique with the largest breath volume and the most powerful *pranayama* method. It is used to supercharge the entire organism with *prana*. It simultaneously reduces and ejects all three *doshas* (humours), *vata*, *pitta and kapha*. Thus it can be practised, similarly to *Nadi Shodhana*, without creating an imbalance in the humours. Properly introduced into the practice of a well-prepared yogi, it will accelerate spiritual growth quickly. If it is mishandled, however, it can comprehensively backfire.

PREREQUISITES

Bhastrika is the most athletic *pranayama*. For *Bhastrika* practice, you need to be proficient in *Kapalabhati* and *Nadi Shodhana*. You

---

467 Gregor Maehle, *Pranayama The Breath of Yoga*, Kaivalya Publications, Crabbes Creek, 2012, p. 263

also need to be proficient in a high-quality meditation posture, ideally *Padmasana*. The better your general *asana* practice, the further you can go in *Bhastrika*. It is also advisable to be proficient in long inversions.

CONTRAINDICATIONS

Bhastrika is contraindicated during pregnancy and menstruation and in cases of high blood pressure, epilepsy, stroke, heart disease and deep-vein thrombosis. Do not practise *Bhastrika* when your nostrils are blocked or almost blocked. The strain placed on the tender alveoli could eventually lead to emphysema.

TECHNIQUE

To perform *Bhastrika* you need to sit in a proper meditation/ *pranayama* posture with your knees on the floor, palms and soles of the feet facing up and spine, neck and head in a straight line, preferably *Padmasana*. During *Bhastrika* keep the whole body absolutely still. Don't lift your shoulders when inhaling and also keep your head steady. Do not rock your torso back and forth or from side to side.

Advanced *Bhastrika* consists of a complete yogic breathing cycle with increased volume and accelerated speed. However, to come to terms with the increased volume, we will not initially increase the speed. Take a few breaths to establish the complete yogic breathing cycle[468]. Exhale all air available and exhale it from all areas of the torso. When inhaling, fill all available areas of the torso and inhale close to the maximum volume (without

---

468 In a nutshell this term refers to the practice of using your entire breath volume on in and exhalation, but at the same time to breathe really slowly.

brimming or straining). Be especially particular about the upper lobes of the lungs.

The next step is to add *Bhastrika*'s native breath wave, the two-stage up-and-down wave[469]. All rapid breathing methods need to be exercised using a two-stage wave since when you breathe fast, you cannot isolate the three levels of the torso[470]. We will start *Bhastrika* slowly and it will seem to you as if you could use a three-stage wave. This is impossible will become apparent once you use higher respiratory rates. In distinction from *Kapalabhati*, we will here use the thorax for bellowing. This means we will actively expand the thorax to breathe in and actively compress it to pump air out. Once a high respiratory rate is achieved, it appears as if only the thorax is used, and the abdomen remains static.

Using the two-stage up-and-down wave, fill up the torso from the pubic bone to the collarbones and then eject the air starting from the uppermost part. To learn this movement without tensing up it is necessary to slow it right down. Most students start *Bhastrika* much too fast and therefore never learn it properly. If the average person breathes about 16 times per minute, each breathing cycle takes on average 3.75 seconds.

I suggest starting with *Bhastrika* below that, taking about 6 seconds per breath (i.e. 3 seconds for inhalation and 3 seconds for exhalation) so you will take only 10 breaths per minute. If

469 This term refers to taking the first half of the inhale into the abdomen and the second half into the thorax and to reverse this order when exhaling, i.e. exhaling first from the chest and then from the abdomen. For more information see *Pranayama The Breath of Yoga,* p. 200ff.

470 A three-staged wave, compartmentalizing three separate areas of the torso, is used for all slow-breathing *pranayama* techniques such as *Nadi Shodhana, Chandra Bhedana, Surya Bhedana* and *Shitali.*

you combine that with the fact that you will use close to your maximum breath volume, after 90 seconds or 15 breaths, you will already feel a clear effect.

Initially even just 15 breaths with such a huge volume may make you light-headed, a sign that *prana* is entering your head. There are two ways to prevent that. One is not to breathe all the way up to the collarbones. Instead of that you may breathe up to about the third or fourth rib. Do so until the light-headedness abates. The other method is to slightly contract your throat, as you would do in *Ujjayi*, but to a lesser extent. This method, suggested by Swami Sivananda, will limit the volume of air breathed and thus prevent light-headedness[471]. Its disadvantage is that it puts strain on the alveoli. I found this method helpful for *Bhastrika* in the beginning, but the throat should be constricted only mildly, with the breath barely discernible audibly. Also, to prevent putting strain on the alveoli, it is preferable this method be faded out once your organism has adjusted to the increased oxygen and decreased amount of carbon dioxide in your blood.

If each breathing cycle is to be 6 seconds, each inhalation and each exhalation will be 3 seconds long. While under normal circumstances, it may not be that difficult to time a breathing cycle to exactly 6 seconds, you will find it a different story altogether when experiencing the onslaught of huge amounts of oxygen. I found the use of a metronome made *Bhastrika* much more accessible, and it enables you to replicate a certain exercise every day under similar conditions without a lot of fluctuations. If you set your metronome to 20 ticks per minute, there will be one tick per 3-second inhalation and one tick per 3-second

---

471 Swami Sivananda, The Science of Pranayama, BN Publishing, 2008, p. 79

exhalation. I found this to be a good initial setting, which allows you to distribute your breath volume evenly over the 3 seconds.

For some students, it will be enough to take 10 full high-volume breaths in this fashion to reach their capacity. If so, stay at this level but perform the exercise daily. Other students will be comfortable with 15 breaths. Do not go beyond the 2-minute mark in the first few days. Initially, your intercostal muscles may get sore, and you need to prepare them slowly for this vigorous exercise. In the second week you may go to 2.5 minutes of practice, in the third week to 3 minutes, but you may also progress much more slowly if you prefer. At this early point 3 minutes should be the limit for an uninterrupted session of *Bhastrika*.

Once you can practise 3 minutes of *Bhastrika* with a breathing cycle length of 6 seconds there are several ways to intensify your practice. The first and most obvious is to expand your breath volume by breathing further up into the chest and making sure that all air is exhaled subsequently. The second step is to increase your breath ratio. At a breath ratio of 10 breaths per minute, we are looking at a very introductory practice of *Bhastrika*. I suggest increasing that slowly and step by step. You should have a teacher to check your progress and determine whether you are ready to increase speed.

The next step now is to increase your breath ratio during the bellowing. So far, we have worked with a breathing-cycle length of 6 seconds, leaving 3 seconds for each inhalation and exhalation respectively. This equates to 20 ticks on the metronome per minute. Now change your metronome to 21 ticks. This reduces the breathing cycle from 6 to approximately 5.7 seconds, and it means you will, for example, fit 10.5 breathing cycles instead of only 10 into 1 minute. This is only a slight increase, but if you proceed at this level your increases will eventually compound to an incredible practice, whereas otherwise, you might discontinue your practice for one reason or another. What is important is that you do not sacrifice breath volume for speed; otherwise, there is no point in increasing the breath ratio. Maintain your volume and increase speed in small increments. If you are not yet ready to increase your count, stay here and wait until you can again accelerate the breath ratio. Setting your metronome to 22 ticks per minute, each inhalation or exhalation will now be 2.73 seconds long and a full breathing cycle 5.45 seconds. You will now fit 22 full-volume breaths into 2 minutes or 11 into 1 minute. This is still very slow for *Bhastrika*, but you need to get used to this powerful practice before accelerating too fast.

Slowly, slowly, over months of practice, increase your breath ratio until you hit 60 strokes/breaths per minute and increase your breath count accordingly. The maximum breath count for *Bhastrika* is said to be 120 strokes per minute, but I found this unrealistic unless one lets the breath become shallow. This, however, would be counterproductive. The art is to gradually increase speed while maintaining breath volume. When using *Bhastrika* in a conventional *pranayama* practice combined with *kumbhakas* we would bellow for 2 minutes and then perform a single round of alternate nostril breathing combined with *kumbhakas*. We would then repeat this cycle several times. Another powerful way of using *Bhastrika* is to practice it for 3 -5 minutes straight after *Kapalabhati* and then go into an extended session of *Nadi Shodhana* or one of its half-cycles with both types of *kumbhakas*. This is the way I prefer to use *Bhastrika*. In our present case of using *Bhastrika* as an element of *Shakti Chalana*, however, we will use a single, uninterrupted, mammoth-session of *Bhastrika* to supply the air element to the already present fire, accumulated with *Nauli*. We would again start from a basecamp practise of *Bhastrika*, which may be 5 minutes of uninterrupted bellowing at around 60bpm (beats per minute). Several years of practice are required to reach this level. Once this level is reached the practice can rapidly ratcheted up in a retreat-type situation of several weeks or months duration. One needs to be sensitive to not exceed one's capacity and adequately adjust the other components (*Nauli, Maha Mudra, Shitali, kumbhaka, chakra*-Kundalini meditation, etc.) to achieve the desired effect. A good gauge for one's capacity is to watch out for deterioration of sleep quality, headaches, agitation, short fuse, etc.

SECTION 5:

SAMADHI MUDRAS

I need to start this section with a dampener. Despite its flamboyant name, *Samadhi Mudras*, this group of *mudras* will achieve little in a person, whose mind does not already gravitate towards *samadhi*, a quality created through ongoing *sadhana*. The *mudras* of this group lack any propensity to lead to *samadhi*, if the mind of the practitioner using them does not already gravitate towards *samadhi*. Such gravitation is common in the so-called *nirodha* (suspended) type of mind. As the *Yoga Sutra* states, 'Only through long-term, uninterrupted practice, employing a devotional attitude, can practice succeed' [in cultivating samadhi][472]. In a novice these *mudras* may do little to nothing, whereas when utilized by an ancient soul the impetus they provide may be enough to push us over the edge into *samadhi* [473]. I have outlined the qualities of Patanjali's eight *samadhis* in my 2015 text *Samadhi The Great Freedom*. To delve into them here is beyond the scope of this inquiry.

---

472 *Yoga Sutra* I.14

473 The term "ancient soul" is shorthand for a person that has matured through *sadhana* across many lifetimes.

The *Yoga Sutra's* approach to the eight limbs, including *samadhi*, is that it describes their outcome but not the exact method by which this outcome is achieved. The exact method was to be filled in by the particular school of yoga. This has led to many misunderstandings. Some believe there is no complex system of *asana, pranayama* or meditation underlying the *Yoga Sutra* because Patanjali doesn't describe it. But he doesn't describe any methods because it's simply not within the scope of a text comprising just 195 stanzas. A much bigger text would be required. A different approach is shown in the *Gheranda Samhita*. In Chapter 7 of this text six *samadhis* are listed, but sage Gheranda does not differentiate them according to level or depth of contemplation but according to type or avenue of access[474]. The six ways of accessing *samadhi* are as follows:

- *Dhyana* Yoga through *Shambhavi Mudra*
- *Nada* Yoga through *Bhramari Mudra*
- *Rasananda* Yoga through *Khechari Mudra*
- *Laya* Yoga through *Yoni Mudra* (alternative name for *Shanmukhi Mudra*)
- *Bhakti* Yoga
- *Kumbhaka* (breath retention)

Of these, I have covered the *kumbhaka* approach in my earlier text *Pranayama The Breath of Yoga*. *Bhakti* Yoga I intend to cover in an upcoming volume. *Shambhavi Mudra* has been described in Section 3 of this present text. This *mudra* can also serve as a stand-alone technique to induce *samadhi* in a mind that already gravitates towards it. However, its role as one of the

---

474 *Gheranda Samhita* VII.5-6

prime *pratyahara mudras*, supporting *pranayama* and meditation techniques, is so essential that it needed to be covered in that section. I will, however, describe here an extension of *Shambhavi Mudra*, called *Jyoti Mudra*, which rarely doubles up as a *pratyahara mudra*.

This leaves us to cover in this section the following *mudras*:
Bhramari Mudra
Shanmukhi Mudra (Yoni Mudra)
Jyoti Mudra
Khechari Mudra

Chapter 28

BHRAMARI MUDRA
(Black Bee Seal)

As already mentioned, this *mudra* is listed in the *Gheranda Samhita* as one of the six access paths to *samadhi*. Many other texts list this technique not among *mudras* but in the *kumbhaka* section[475]. If they do so, they then call the method *Bhramari Kumbhaka*. The *Kapala Kurantaka Yoga* mentions the technique briefly under the name of *Bhramari Kumbhaka* and says about it only that on the inhale, we need to produce the sound of a bee[476]. The *Kumbhaka Paddhati of Raghuvira* in stanza 169 gives a very precise description of *Bhramari Kumbhaka* with breath retention[477]. We are to rapidly inhale, producing the sound of the black bee, and exhale slowly, again producing the same sound, interspersed by breath retention. The *Hathatatva Kaumudi of Sundaradeva* in stanza X.18 gives more detail[478]. It defines *Bhramari* as a forceful inhalation, producing the sound of the

---

475 *Hatha Yoga* texts usually refer to *pranayama* techniques as *kumbhakas* rather than pranayamas. This tendency persists to some extent among contemporary Hindu ascetics.

476 Swami Maheshananda et al (eds. & transl.), *Kapalakurantaka's Hathabhyasa-Paddhati*, Kaivalyadhama, Lonavla, 2015, p.78

477 Dr M.L. Gharote, *Kumbhaka Paddhati of Raghuvira*, Lonavla Yoga Institute, Lonavla, 2010, p. 56

478 Dr M.L. Gharote et al (eds. & transl.), *Hathatatvakaumudi*, The Lonavla Yoga Institite, Lonavla, 2007, p. 126

male bee, combined with a very slow exhalation, emulating the sound of the female bee. We are getting close now but still have not heard how such sound is to be produced. The 10-chapter edition of the *Hatha Yoga Pradipika* finally gives us that missing clue[479]. While stanza IV.59 gives the same information regarding forceful inhale/ male bee versus slow exhale/ female bee, in the notes to the stanza, we learn that a nasalized sound like the one in the word *ganga* is produced during inhale and exhale. The *Hatharatnavali of Shrinivasayogi* in stanza II.26 contains almost the same wording as the *Pradipika* and here the translator, Dr M.L. Gharote, suggests using nasalization as in *ganga* to produce the bee-like sound[480]. In his own textbook, *Pranayama,* Dr Gharote recommends pronouncing a sound like "king" to produce the bee sound during inhale and exhale[481]. I have experimented with various "ng" sounds and they pretty much all work, as long as they are nasalized. However, our *Bhramari* technique is still incomplete. In the *Gheranda Samhita* stanzas V.73-77 we find *Bhramari* described as a *kumbhaka* in which the ears are blocked using both hands[482]. We are then to listen to inner sounds (*nadanusandhana*), which will induce *samadhi*. The association

---

479 Dr M.L. Gharote et al (eds. & transl.), *Hathapradipika of Svatmarama (10 chapters)*, Lonavla Yoga Institute, Lonavla, 2006, p. 92

480 Dr M.L. Gharote et al (eds. & transl.), *Hatharatnavali of Shrinivasayogi*, The Lonavla Yoga Institite, Lonavla, 2009, p. 50

481 Dr M.L. Gharote, *Pranayama: The Science of Breath*, Lonavla Yoga Institute, Lonavla, 2003, p. 75

482 James Mallinson, *The Gheranda Samhita*, YogaVidya.com, Woodstock, 2004, p. 107-8

of *Bhramari* with listening to inner sound is also mentioned in Jayatarama's *Jogapradipyaka*[483].

TECHNIQUE

Since we are using the technique here simply as a *mudra* to induce *samadhi* rather than a full-blown *pranayama* technique, we need not concern ourselves with the *kumbhaka* part. The scriptures agree that the *mudra* consists of producing the sound of the male black bee during inhalation and of the female black bee during exhalation. This is a very different technique than *Ujjayi*. During *Ujjayi,* a hissing or whispering sound is produced by slightly closing the glottis. Engaging the vocal cords during *Ujjayi* is shunned. However, here in *Bhramari* the vocal cords are engaged. Let's start with the exhalation; it's much easier. Produce a nasalized 'ng' sound, like the one in *ganga,* or at the end of the French *garçon,* or at the end of the English "gong" or "king". In Sanskrit this sound is called *anushvara,* meaning nasalization. One intonates the sound by using as a clue one of the above words and then continues to hum it throughout the exhalation. This is the sound of the female bee.

Once the exhalation is complete, continue the 'ng' sound, but this time by forcefully inhaling. The sound will continue only if you rapidly suck the air in, which means you cannot sustain it for long because your lungs will fill up quickly. When you produce the sound, you will notice it is much higher pitched. This represents the sound of the male black bee. The male black bee sound flimsier than the female. This might be due to the females performing all the hard work maintaining the hive, while the males function

---

483 Swami Maheshananda et al. (eds & transl.), *Jogapradipyaka of Jayatarama,* Kaivalyadhama, Lonavla, 2006, p. 101

exclusively as gigolos. I would not think that we can extrapolate this state of affairs to the human species in general, or yogis in particular, although I have seen anecdotal evidence of that.

Close your ears with your thumbs, place your index fingers on your forehead for resonance, and place the remaining fingers on your closed eyes and cheekbones. Now produce the sound continuously on the inhalation and exhalation while keeping any external visual and audio impressions shut out. To perform the *mudra* for an extended period, it may help to sit on the floor and rest your elbows on a chair or low table in front of you so your arms don't get tired.

Bhramari Mudra

Focus your mind completely on this sound and follow the sound inwards, letting go of any concept and memory of the outside world. Following the sound inwards to the core of your being, memories of the world will quickly fall away, and you will arrive at a state of primordial, pure being-ness. Of course, this is pending on whether the force of introversion and internalization of the mind is already strong. Most yogic practices are preparations for that state and this *mudra* is a good indicator of how far we have come. By itself, *Bhramari Mudra* will only work if there is already a strong karmic or subconscious preponderance for internalization.

Another way of performing the *mudra* for an extended period is to use earplugs instead of one's thumbs and, instead of using the fingers to close the eyes, one may look at the rising full moon. The moon is the symbol of lunar *prana*—the power that internalizes and introverts the mind. This method also works well for people who find it difficult to progress in yoga due to excessive extroversion.

Chapter 29

SHANMUKHI MUDRA
(Six-Headed Seal)

This *mudra* is also known under the name *Yoni Mudra*, but I learned it as *Shanmukhi Mudra*, under which name it also is listed in many scriptures. *Shanmukhi* means six-headed, and the name refers to the *mudra* being ideal for venturing into meditating on the six *chakras*. The *chakras* are often listed as six, ignoring the thousand-petalled lotus, which is added later because it is supra-cranial and outside of the breathing cycle. In Jayatarama's *Jogapradipyaka*, for example, we find *Shanmuhki Mudra* explicitly used to meditate on the six *chakras* to raise Kundalini[484]. This is also confirmed in *Gheranda Samhita* stanzas III.33-38, but here the method is called *Yoni Mudra*[485]. We are to block the ears with the thumbs, the eyes with the index fingers, the nostrils are closed with the middle fingers and the remaining fingers place on the upper and lower lips. The inhalation is then performed via *Kaki Mudra*, described in Section 2, *Mudra* 14, and sequential meditation on the six *chakras* is then performed.

Also, in the *Hathatatva Kaumudi of Sundaradeva* we learn that when performing *Shanmukhi Mudra*, we are to inhale through

---

484 Swami Maheshananda et al. (eds & transl.), *Jogapradipyaka of Jayatarama*, Kaivalyadhama, Lonavla, 2006, p. 127

485 R.B.S. Chandra Vasu (transl.), *The Gheranda Samhita*, Sri Satguru Publications, Delhi, 1984, pp. 37 – 44

the mouth and perform *kumbhaka*[486]. The inhalation through the mouth here is performed via *Kaki Mudra*, which the *Kaumudi* calls *Kaka Cancuka*, crow beak. The mouth is to be pointed and the tongue sticks out akin to *Shitali pranayama*. *Kaki Mudra* forms an intricate part of *Shanmukhi Mudra* and according to the *Hatha Tatva Kaumudi* the practice of both raises Kundalini[487]. That *Kaki Mudra* is part of *Shanmukhi Mudra* is also confirmed by T. Krishnamacharya in *Yoga Makaranda*[488].

In the 10-chapter edition of the *Hatha Yoga Pradipika* we find that adopting *Shanmukhi Mudra* leads to inner sound manifesting in the central energy channel (*Sushumna*)[489]. This constitutes the *Pradipika*'s main pathway to accessing *samadhi*. The same statement also occurs in stanza IV.68 of the *Hatha Yoga Pradipika with Jyotsna Commentary*[490]. In the *Shiva Samhita* we find a rather bizarre introduction to *Yoni Mudra*. In stanza IV.3 we are introduced to *chakra* meditation, but *Yoni Mudra*, as the name of the technique, is only mentioned in stanza IV.5[491]. In the then following stanzas we are informed this *mudra* is so

---

486 Dr M.L. Gharote et al (eds. & transl.), *Hathatatvakaumudi,* The Lonavla Yoga Institite, Lonavla, 2007, p. 683

487 Dr M.L. Gharote et al (eds. & transl.), *Hathatatvakaumudi,* The Lonavla Yoga Institite, Lonavla, 2007, p. 684

488 T. Krishnamacharya, *Yoga Makaranda,* Media Garuda, Chennai, 2011, p. 108

489 Dr M.L. Gharote et al (eds. & transl.), *Hathapradipika of Svatmarama (10 chapters),* Lonavla Yoga Institute, Lonavla, 2006, p. 234

490 Kunjunni Raja (ed.), *The Hathayogapradipika of Svatmarama with the Commentary Jyotsna of Brahmananda,* The Adyar Library, Madras, 1972, p. 74

491 R.B.S. Chandra Vasu (transl.), *The Shiva Samhita,* Sri Satguru Publications, Delhi, 1986, pp.41-42

powerful that it even protects us from the *karmic* backlash that follows upon murdering our spiritual teacher or fornicating with his wife! I want to cast doubt on the accuracy of this passage lest readers should get dubious ideas. This and similar passages praise the power of a particular technique rather than instructing us on how to get away with murder.

The *Shiva Samhita* then describes the actual technique of the *mudra* a chapter further down at stanza V.22, and peculiarly without further mentioning the name of the *mudra*[492]. A typical case of scriptures conveying things veiled. Unless one knows what to look for, such passages rarely make sense. This is no accident but done purposefully. Scriptures are often more akin to lecture notes for teachers, rather than stand-alone manuals for students. The exact hand position during *Shanmukhi Mudra*, as per *Shiva Samhita* is identical to that in *Gheranda Samhita*, but no instruction regarding inhalation, *kumbhaka*, or the object of meditation is given here. Only a few stanzas further down we learn that the result of the *mudra* is the perception of inner sound, which is used here as an access key to *samadhi*[493].

The *Mandala Brahmana Upanishad* in stanza 2.2 2. also lists *Shanmukhi Mudra*, but only informs that one needs to perform it with the fingers of both hands[494]. We are instructed to perform *kumbhaka* and here we are told this would lead to the conceiving of inner sound, removing us from the shackles of

492 R.B.S. Chandra Vasu (transl.), *The Shiva Samhita*, Sri Satguru Publications, Delhi, 1986, p. 57

493 R.B.S. Chandra Vasu (transl.), *The Shiva Samhita*, Sri Satguru Publications, Delhi, 1986, p. 57

494 Dr. M.M. Gharote et al (eds. & transl.), *Mandalabrahmanopanisad and Nadabindupanisad,* Lonavla Yoga Institute, Lonavla, 2012, p. 87

karma. However, this time, no gory details are given what acts we could perform without karmic recourse, if thus indemnified. *Yoni Mudra* is also listed in *Yoga Chudamani Upanishad* and is here utilized for revitalization after lunar *prana* is burned in the gastric fire[495]. Also, here, no technical details are given. The *Trishikhi Brahmana Upanishad* praises *Shanmukhi Mudra* for bringing the mind under control but tells us about the technique only that it consists of closing the ears and other sense orifices with the fingers of one's hands[496].

The *Jogapradipyaka of Jayatarama* recommends *Shanmukhi Mudra* in case *pranayama* becomes obstructed[497]. Here closing the seven doors, i.e. eyes, ears, nostrils and mouth, with the fingers is mentioned. Amongst *Vedic* yoga text *Shanmukhi Mudra* is described in the *Yoga Yajnavalkya* in stanza VI.50-53, including the precise hand position but additionally with focusing on the crown of head[498]. Such focus, so sage Yajnavalkya, will lead to bliss. I have discussed the focussing on the crown on the head when analysing Gopi Krishna's case and his adverse Kundalini experiences. This is a good time to briefly revisit the subject. Sage Yajnavalkya taught focussing on the crown of the head in his treatise two thirds down the track of chapter six. Chapter one deals with the prerequisites of yoga, while chapter two lists the ethical rules.

---

495 *Yoga Chudamani Upanishad,* (p. 142 in the Satyadharma translation, p.253-5 in the Lonavla edition

496 Dr. M.M. Gharote et al (eds. & transl.), *Critical Edition of Selected Yogopanisads,* Lonavla Yoga Institute, Lonavla, 2017, p. 77-78

497 Maheshananda, Sw. et al. (eds & transl.), *Jogapradipyaka of Jayatarama,* Kaivalyadhama, Lonavla, 2006, p. 131

498 A.G. Mohan (transl.), *Yoga Yajnavalkya,* Ganesh & Co., Madras, p. 83

Chapter three is devoted *to asanas*, with chapter four dealing with subtle anatomy and the theoretical aspects of *pranayama*. In chapter five we then find Yajnavalkya's method of *nadi* purification without which according to him nobody should start *pranayama*. It is the same method which I have taught in *Pranayama The Breath of Yoga*, citing the sages Yajnavalkya and Vasishta as ancient authorities. I want to make sure that no novices take the above stanza from Yoga Yajnavalkya as an excuse to focus on the crown of the head. The positioning of the stanza in which sage Yajnavalkya instructs to focus on the crown of the head, the sixth chapter, clearly identifies the technique as a very advanced practice.

The *Vasishta Samhita* without mentioning its name lists *Shanmukhi Mudra* in stanzas III.37-38, but it describes the required hand position accurately[499]. Also, here the result is listed as inner sound (*nada*), which occurs when *prana* enters *Sushumna*. *Shanmukhi Mudra* also is mentioned in Sir John Woodroffe's *The Serpent Power*, where it is combined with *Ashvini Mudra* (Section 4, *Mudra* 24 here in this text) and *Nauli* in *Siddhasana* to execute *Shakti Chalana*[500]. There are interesting variations of *Shanmukhi Mudra*. Yogeshvaranand Paramahansa, besides offering the conventional variation[501], also teaches modifications where the

---

499 Swami Digambarji et al (eds & transl.), *Vasishta Samhita*, Kaivalyadhama, Lonavla, 1984, p. 39 (please note that page numbers in this edition occur twice and this is the second time this page number appears)

500 Sir John Woodroffe, *The Serpent Power*, Ganesh & CO, Madras, 1995, p. 207

501 Yogeshvaranand Paramahansa, *First Steps to Higher Yoga*, Yoga Niketan Trust, New Delhi, 2001, p. 384

inhalation is done through the nostrils instead of the mouth[502], and one where alternate nostril breathing is integrated into the *mudra*[503]. Yogeshvaranand Paramahansa holds that the *mudra*, if done with internal breath retention (*antara kumbhaka*), still requires us to apply *Jalandhara Bandha*. This rule uniformly applies to all internal *kumbhakas* with a length over ten seconds. *Jalandhara Bandha* protects us from air pressure, building up in the thoracic cavity due to the breath retention, entering the cranial cavity where it could do damage. This rule is sometimes neglected by some contemporary teachers who believe that just because we close all sensory gates via *Shanmukhi Mudra*, we are somehow protected from rising *vayu* (vital air). Don't fall for such teaching. It is negligent.

TECHNIQUE

Close the ears with the thumbs, the eyes with the index fingers, and the nostrils with the middle fingers. Now place the ring fingers on the upper lip and the little fingers on the lower lip. The prime method to perform the inhalation is the *Kaki Mudra*, which includes sticking out the preferably rolled tongue to moisten the inhaled air. This method will increase *kapha* in our system and it is not preferred for those with excess *kapha*. *Kapha*, *vata* and *pitta* are the three bodily humours according to *Ayurveda*. They are sometimes translated as phlegm, wind and bile, respectively, but these terms are so truncated and tendentious that it is better

---

502 Yogeshvaranand Paramahansa, *First Steps to Higher Yoga*, Yoga Niketan Trust, New Delhi, 2001, p. 342

503 Yogeshvaranand Paramahansa, *First Steps to Higher Yoga*, Yoga Niketan Trust, New Delhi, 2001, p. 337

to keep using the Sanskrit terms, which may remind us we haven't yet completely comprehended the subject.

If you already understand the three *gunas, tamas, rajas* and *sattva,* then this can help to get a handle on the humours, too. The *gunas* can be quite aptly translated as mass-particle, energy-particle and intelligence particle. They also form the three qualities of mind, which crystallize into the body because mind forms body. The body influences the mind, too, but mind comes first because evolution works from the inside out, from the subtle to the gross. *Tamas* (mass-particle) crystallized as body becomes *kapha. Rajas* (energy-particle) if applied to the body becomes *vata. Sattva* (intelligence-particle), when manifesting in the body becomes *pitta.* Remember that the *gunas,* when applied to the body become vitiated, i.e. they are not in their elemental form anymore. Most yogic techniques, and those taught in this volume are no exception, increase *agni* (fire) which can lead to a depletion of *kapha* or, if not careful, aggravation of *pitta.* The extra *kapha,* potentially created by *Kaki Mudra,* usually is not a hindrance but helpful in balancing any aggravated *pitta.*

Lift the ring fingers from the upper lip and the little fingers from the lower lip, then perform *Kaki Mudra* and inhale. Once the inhalation is completed to about 80-90% of respiratory capacity, place the two fingers back on the mouth, lift the chest, drop the chin on the chest, swallow and, contracting the throat, perform *Jalandhara Bandha* and internal breath retention. Once you held the *kumbhaka* to capacity, lift the head, lift the middle fingers blocking the nostrils, release the *bandha* and exhale through the nose. This constitutes one round and can be continued until the effect is reached.

Shanmukhi Mudra

Regarding the inner work two approaches stand out. The first one is to go down the avenue of *nadanusandhana*, that is listening to inner sound. Once inner sound manifest one focusses on it, which leads to *samadhi* (in a mind that already gravitates to *samadhi*). The second avenue is to contemplate the six *chakras* in sequential order, pronounce the appropriate root syllables, and finally raise Kundalini to the higher *chakras*. I described these techniques in my previous text *Yoga Meditation*. This is a complex multi-stage exercise, and a description would go beyond the scope of this volume. To bring about the raising of Kundalini one can also add a *Nauli*-like rotational movement of the abdominal muscles, while in *kumbhaka*.

EFFECTS
Raises Kundalini and induces *samadhic* trance.

Chapter 30

JYOTI MUDRA (Light Seal)

Jyoti Mudra is closely related to Shambhavi Mudra. We could call it an extension thereof. *Shambhavi Mudra* was already included among the *pratyahara mudras*, therefore, it is not included in the present section. It is, however, listed in the *Gheranda Samhita* as a *samadhi mudra*. *Shambhavi Mudra* is described in the *Hatha Yoga Pradipika* in stanzas IV.35-38[504]. The *Hatha Yoga Pradipika* takes a different approach to other texts in describing *Shambhavi Mudra* as seemingly looking outward, while the mind is absorbed in an internal object. This internal object, according to Brahmananda's *Jyotsna Commentary,* is the heart *chakra*[505]. In stanza IV.39 of the *Hatha Yoga Pradipika, Jyoti Mudra* is then described as directing the eyes towards the light and raising the eyebrows[506], whereas the mind is still concentrated on the heart *chakra*. We find a similar description in the 10-chapter edition of the *Hatha Yoga Pradipika,* stanzas VII.40-42[507]. We are told to direct the inner

---

504 Kunjunni Raja (ed.), *The Hathayogapradipika of Svatmarama with the Commentary Jyotsna of Brahmananda*, The Adyar Library, Madras, 1972, p. 67-68

505 *Jyotsna Commentary* to the *Hatha Yoga Pradipika* stanzas 37 and 38

506 Kunjunni Raja (ed.), *The Hathayogapradipika of Svatmarama with the Commentary Jyotsna of Brahmananda*, The Adyar Library, Madras, 1972, p. 69

507 Dr M.L. Gharote et al (eds. & transl.), *Hathapradipika of Svatmarama (10 chapters)*, Lonavla Yoga Institute, Lonavla, 2006, p. 221

vision towards the light (*jyoti*) by raising the eyebrows, while otherwise maintaining *Shambhavi Mudra*.

The same approach is taught in *Sundaradeva's Hathatatva Kaumudi* stanza XLIX.28[508]. Also, here we are taught that while in the state of *Shambhavi*, seemingly looking outward, we are directing the vision towards the internal light by raising the eyebrows a little. Stanza 30 in the same chapter tells us that such gazing suspends the *Ida* and *Pingala* (the lunar and solar energy channels, which power the dichotomizing mind) and enables us to see the ultimate reality in that intensely luminous internal light. Thus one attains *samadhi* (if one's mind already gravitates towards this state).

Jyoti Mudra also gets a kind mention in *Amanaska Yogah*, a *Vedantic* text that, although its name includes the term yoga, otherwise makes short shrift of yogic technique[509]. Stanza 1.8 of *Amanaska Yogah* teaches to fix the gaze at the internal light (meant is here the *Sushumna*, the central energy channel) and raise the eyebrows a little[510]. This brings about the *unmani* state. *Unmani*, i.e. supramental state, is a term that medieval *Hatha* texts often use instead of objectless *samadhi*, that is a *samadhi* on

---

508 Dr M.L. Gharote et al (eds. & transl.), *Hathatatvakaumudi,* The Lonavla Yoga Institite, Lonavla, 2007, p. 615

509 Just because yoga is written on it, doesn't mean there's yoga in it. Another text that follows this pattern is the illustrious Yoga Vashishta. Also this text refers to yoga in its title but the content is actually *Vedantic*. That doesn't make either of this texts wrong or inferior but it means that the reader and modern yogi needs to be aware that in vital elements these texts depart from Patanjali's *yoga darshana* (the classical yogic system of philosophy).

510 Dr M.M. Gharote et al (eds. & transl.) *Amanaska Yogah- A Treatise On Laya Yoga*, Lonavla Yoga Institute, Lonavla, 2019, p. 8

consciousness itself. This is confirmed in stanza II.7 of *Amanaska Yogah,* which states that the light to focus on (*jyoti*) is at the centre of *Sushumna*[511]. When *Ida* and *Pingala* are suspended and *prana* is inducted into *Sushumna,* then *samadhi* on consciousness is possible. We find a similar understanding in the *Shandilya Upanishad*[512]. Also, here we are told while being in *Shambhavi Mudra* to focus on the light by elevating the eyebrows a little to enter the *unmani* state.

TECHNIQUE

First, assume *Shambhavi Mudra,* as described in Section 3, *Mudra* 16. Here we gradually learned to roll the eyeballs up and backwards in the sockets until the gaze is directed towards the third eye *chakra.* Please note, this is a gradual process and cannot be done all at once. The ocular muscles are to be slowly trained to keep the eyes in this challenging position. Once this step has become easy, we now raise the eyebrows, thus wrinkling the forehead. This gives additional impetus to raise the *prana* to the higher *chakras.* At the same time we focus on the light of the *Sushumna.* In the original *Upanishads,* such as the *Chandogya Upanishad,* the terms *hrt* (for core or heart), heart *chakra,* and *Sushumna,* were not yet differentiated. To some extent they are not different but talk about the same phenomenon from a different angle. When the Indian sage Ramana Maharishi talked about the heart, he did not mean the romantic heart but our core, the *Sushumna,* which in psychological terms represents the consciousness.

---

511 Dr M.M. Gharote et al (eds. & transl.) *Amanaska Yogah- A Treatise On Laya Yoga,* Lonavla Yoga Institute, Lonavla, 2019, p. 61
512 *Shandilya Upanishad* stanza 34

Jyoti Mudra

Chapter 31

KHECHARI MUDRA
(Space Movement Seal)

Khechari Mudra is the reverting of the tongue onto itself and directing it back and up along the soft palate towards the nasopharyngeal orifice. The tongue is another outlet of subconscious activity. By arresting it, the subconscious activity relating to the tongue and gustation is arrested, too. The *mudra* arrests *prana* in the throat *chakra* (*Vishuddha*) and third eye *chakra* (*Ajna*). Like *Shambhavi Mudra*, it needs to be introduced slowly. The oncoming of a headache could be an early symptom of strain. An integrated approach would use both *mudras* simultaneously when attempting to access *samadhi*. Even any advanced form of *chakra*-Kundalini meditation should come with both of those *mudras*. *Khechari Mudra* reduces respiratory speed, thus enabling longer *kumbhakas*. It makes *prana* steady and thus steadies the mind.

The name of this *mudra* (*kha* = space and *chari* = movement) originally referred to moving of tongue up to the space above and behind the palate. So says the *Dhyana Bindu Upanishad* that when via *Khechari Mudra* the tongue enters the space (kha) above the palate then the mind moves in the element space (*akasha*)[513]. The meaning of this is that the mind expands into infinity which is the definition of Patanjali's fifth samadhi (*ananda samadhi*).

---

513 *Dhyana Bindu Upanishad* stanzas 81(b)-83(a)

However, in later centuries, yoga became more and more mystified and magical thinking became included, bringing it closer to witchcraft and sorcery. It was then taken to mean that by employing this *mudra* you could fly through space. So says the *Hatha Yoga Pradipika* that by means of *Khechari* both mind and tongue reach *akasha* [514]. *Khechari Mudra* is an important *mudra* that can access *samadhi*. Unfortunately, similarly to *Vajroli Mudra*, twilight language and the intent to veil the true meaning of instruction from uninitiated, prying eyes, took on a life of itself and confusing teachings originally introduced to conceal the correct teaching began to be taken at face value.

DISAMBIGUATION

Khechari Mudra is like *Nabho Mudra* and *Jihva Bandha* in that regard that all three constitute a manipulation of the tongue. Some texts and schools do not clearly mark delineations of the three techniques. After extensive consultation of *shastras* and traditional teachings, I have settled on these definitions: *Jihva Bandha* is a simple turning up on itself of the tongue and immobilizing it against the soft palate. It is as an ancillary technique supporting *pranayama* and meditation by arresting gustatory *prana*. *Jihva Bandha* is described in Section 3, *Mudra* 15. *Nabho Mudra* is a stand-alone technique that often involves *kumbhaka* and absorbing secretions from the so-called moon, the lunar *pranic* storehouse. Similarly to *Jihva Bandha*, it does not include the elongation of the tongue. The purpose of *Nabho Mudra* is *sthirata*, fortitude. It is described in Section 1, *Mudra* 5. Like *Nabho Mudra*, so also *Khechari Mudra* is usually a stand-alone technique, but its purpose is accessing *samadhi*. It involves

---

514 *Hatha Yoga Pradipika* III.41

methods to elongate the tongue and sometimes includes *kumbhakas*. It is considered *rasananda* yoga, i.e. accessing ecstasy through taste. This does not mean eating sumptuous meals but the collecting of secretions of the lunar storehouse of *prana*.

TEXTUAL EVIDENCE

Khechari Mudra is one of the most widely described *mudras*. It is listed in *Dattatreya's Yogashastra*[515], the *Mandala Brahmana Upanishad*[516], the *Yoga Chudamani Upanishad*[517], the *Yoga Kundalini Upanishad*[518], the *Kapala Kurantaka Yoga*[519], the *Yoga Gorakshataka*[520], the *Gheranda Samhita*[521], the *Hatharatnavali of Shrinivasayogi*[522], the *Shiva Samhita*[523], the *Hathatatva Kaumudi of*

515 Dr M.M. Gharote (ed.), *Dattatreyayogasastram*, Lonavla Yoga Institute, Lonavla, 2015, p. 66

516 Dr. M.M. Gharote et al (eds. & transl.), *Mandalabrahmanopanisad and Nadabindupanisad*, Lonavla Yoga Institute, Lonavla, 2012, pp 91, 95, 96

517 Dr. M.M. Gharote et al (eds. & transl.), *Critical Edition of Selected Yogopanisads*, Lonavla Yoga Institute, Lonavla, 2017, p. 206

518 Dr. M.M. Gharote et al (eds. & transl.), *Critical Edition of Selected Yogopanisads*, Lonavla Yoga Institute, Lonavla, 2017, p. 139-144, also p. 148-154

519 Swami Maheshananda et al (eds. & transl.), *Kapalakurantaka's Hathabhyasa-Paddhati*, Kaivalyadhama, Lonavla, 2015, p. 94

520 Swami Kuvalayananda (ed.), *Goraksasatakam*, Kaivalyadhama, Lonavla, 2006, p. 297

521 *Gheranda Samhita* III.25 – 32, pp. 24, 25 in the Chandra Vasu translation, pp. 68-69 in the James Mallinson translation

522 Dr M.L. Gharote et al (eds. & transl.), *Hatharatnavali of Shrinivasayogi*, The Lonavla Yoga Institite, Lonavla, 2009, p. 85

523 *Shiva Samhita* IV.31

Sundaradeva[524], the *Jogapradipyaka of Jayatarama*[525], the *Hathayoga Manjari of Sahajananda*[526], *Hatha Yoga Pradipika with Jyotsna Commentary*[527], the *Yoga Makaranda*[528], the 10-chapter edition of the *Hatha Yoga Pradipika*[529], the *Shandilya Upanishad*[530] and the *Dhyana Bindu Upanishad*[531]. Almost the entire second chapter of the *Yoga Kundalini Upanishad* deals with *Khechari* and there is even a *shastra* dealing with it exclusively, being the *Khechari Vidya of Adinatha*[532].

DIFFERING OPINIONS

It is therefore clear this is one of the prime *mudras*; however, opinions on it differ widely. The *Gheranda Samhita* in stanzas III.25 lists it as one of six paths of entering *samadhi*. Due to this, it has been included here in Section 5. The 10-chapter

524 Dr M.L. Gharote et al (eds. & transl.), *Hathatatvakaumudi,* The Lonavla Yoga Institite, Lonavla, 2007, p. 159

525 Swami Maheshananda et al. (eds & transl.), *Jogapradipyaka of Jayatarama,* Kaivalyadhama, Lonavla, 2006, p. 126

526 O.P. Tiwari (publ.), *Hathayoga Manjari of Sahajananda,* Kaivalyadhama, Lonavla, 2006, p. 43

527 Kunjunni Raja (ed.), *The Hathayogapradipika of Svatmarama with the Commentary Jyotsna of Brahmananda,* The Adyar Library, Madras, 1972, p. 45

528 T. Krishnamacharya, *Yoga Makaranda,* Media Garuda, Chennai, 2011, p. 104

529 Dr M.L. Gharote et al (eds. & transl.), *Hathapradipika of Svatmarama (10 chapters),* Lonavla Yoga Institute, Lonavla, 2006, p. 115 & 125

530 *Shandilya Upanishad* stanzas 32-62

531 *Dhyana Bindu Upanishad* stanzas 1.79-86

532 James Mallinson (ed. & transl.), *Khecarividya of Adinatha,* Indica Books, Varanasi, 2010

edition of the *Hatha Yoga Pradipika* considers *Khechari* to be the foremost of *mudras*[533]. The *Hatha Yoga Pradipika with Jyotsna Commentary* considers this *mudra* similarly praiseworthy by stating that when properly executed it would conquer death in 15 days[534]. Elsewhere the four-chapter edition of the *Pradipika* states that even turning the tongue up briefly would save one from disease, death and old age, and free us from hunger, sleep and *karma*[535]. These effects are completely exaggerated and the reason for mentioning them is simply to get yogis to practice it. For example, stanza III.44 of the *Pradipika* claims that *Khechari* will protect you from the venom of snakes. I wouldn't try that out. From today's viewpoint we would consider such claims counterproductive, as inevitably practice will fall short of expectations.

The *Shiva Samhita* argues that even briefly practising *Khechari Mudra* would reserve us rebirth into a family of aristocrats, and if practised diligently, would make one near immortal[536]. However, not everybody shares the joy. T. Krishnamacharya's *Yoga Makaranda* recommends to practice *mudras* with exception of *Khechari* and *Vajroli*[537]. T. Krishnamacharya's rejection of *Khechari* was based on a peculiar development in the history

533 Dr M.L. Gharote et al (eds. & transl.), *Hathapradipika of Svatmarama (10 chapters)*, Lonavla Yoga Institute, Lonavla, 2006, p. 134

534 Kunjunni Raja (ed.), *The Hathayogapradipika of Svatmarama with the Commentary Jyotsna of Brahmananda*, The Adyar Library, Madras, 1972, p. 44

535 *Hatha Yoga Pradipika* III.38-40

536 The *Shiva Samhita* IV.33-35

537 T. Krishnamacharya, *Yoga Makaranda*, Media Garuda, Chennai, 2011, p. 104

of the *mudra*, which is that many *shastras* suggest cutting the tendon (frenum) of the tongue. The *Jogapradipyaka of Jayatarama* warns of this action by stating that cutting the frenum may lead to dumbness[538]. Additionally, Jayatarama argues that sages have declared that one has to undergo 12 years of suffering when cutting the tongue[539]. James Mallinson, translator and editor of the *Khechari Vidya of Adinatha,* when researching the *mudra* found that the majority of those practising it said that cutting frenum was unnecessary.[540] Surprisingly, this opinion was held even by those with their tongues cut. And Sir John Woodroffe, tantric scholar and author of many important books on *tantra* held that the cutting interfered with withdrawing the tongue.

One would think that cutting a part of the body with a blade or knife would constitute a form of self-violation and therefore contradict *ahimsa*, the dictum of harmlessness. So states, for example, Lord Krishna in the *Bhagavad Gita*, "Those ignorant and of demoniac nature, hypocrites and egotists, driven by desire and attachment, practice severe austerities without following the scriptures, and senselessly torture the body, including also Me who dwells within the body"[541]. This is a reference to the fact that the *Gita*, a dialogue between Krishna and Arjuna, on a psychological level is a dialogue between the higher or true

---

538 Swami Maheshananda et al. (eds & transl.), *Jogapradipyaka of Jayatarama,* Kaivalyadhama, Lonavla, 2006, p. 18

539 Swami Maheshananda et al. (eds & transl.), *Jogapradipyaka of Jayatarama,* Kaivalyadhama, Lonavla, 2006, p. 123

540 James Mallinson (ed. & transl.), *Khecarividya of Adinatha,* Indica Books, Varanasi, 2010, p. 201

541 *Bhagavad Gita* XVII.5-6

self (represented by Krishna), and the lower or phenomenal self (represented by Arjuna). So, if there are such strong opinions against self-harm, how did it come that the advice of cutting tongue was taken literally?

TWILIGHT LANGUAGE

Again here we have a case where twilight language and double entendre backfired. Initially, the *shastras* were purposely written containing opaque and confusing language, lest somebody should circumnavigate the community of the initiated and simple practice *sadhana* as found in some texts they accidentally got hold of. As previously stated, the famous example is the *Hatha Yoga Pradipika*'s stanza III.46, which states that noble are those who eat the flesh of the cow and drink the immortal liquor daily. Stanzas 47-48 however explain that the Sanskrit used for cow also means tongue and eating it means to insert it into the nasopharyngeal orifice. Further we are informed that the immortal liquor is only the *prana* exuding from the moon (*Chandra*), the lunar storehouse of *prana* in the centre of the cranium. The *Dhyana Bindu Upanishad* adds that once *Khechari* is achieved the yogi will not lose his vital essence even if embraced by a passionate woman[542]. As found with the case of *Vajroli Mudra*, these terms originally described an internal mystical process. The "embrace of the passionate woman" was a code for the arousal of Kundalini, a manifestation of the divine feminine. When the above passage was composed nobody seriously believed that it would kickstart a fashion according to which yoga became identified with unrestrained fornication. Such an interpretation in days of yore was considered unfeasible

---

542 *Dhyana Bindu Upanishad*, stanza 83(b)-84

because yoga originally was firmly built on the bedrock of *yama* and *niyama* (restraints and observances, code of conduct). An important part of these was *brahmacharya*, according to sage Vasishta defined as having intercourse only with one's lawful partner[543].

So, let's see whether we can find a path through the many differing instructions regarding *Khechari* and whether we can locate what is essential and what are confused later add-ons. Dr M.L. Gharote writes there are four or even five different types of *Khechari Mudra*[544]. Some include *kumbhaka* or focus on conducting *prana* to the third eye[545]. There is even a version where we are to raise *prana* only to the throat *chakra* but additionally meditate on Shakti with an upturned face[546]. The most seminal description we find in the four-chapter edition of the *Hatha Yoga Pradipika*, which defines *Khechari* as folding the tongue back, inserting it into the cavity above the palate and fixing the gaze between the eyebrows[547]. The *Shiva Samhita* teaches *Khechari* as sitting in *Padmasana*, in a secluded place, fixing the gaze between the eyebrows, and placing the tongue carefully into the cavity above the palate, thus performing *kumbhaka*[548]. The

---

543 Swami Digambarji et al (eds & transl.), *Vasishta Samhita,* Kaivalyadhama, Lonavla, 1984, p. 9 (please note that page numbers in this edition occur twice and this is the second time this page number appears)

544 Dr M.L. Gharote et al (eds. & transl.), *Hathapradipika of Svatmarama (10 chapters),* Lonavla Yoga Institute, Lonavla, 2006, p. Xxvii

545 Dr M.L. Gharote et al (eds. & transl.), *Hathapradipika of Svatmarama (10 chapters),* Lonavla Yoga Institute, Lonavla, 2006, p. 115

546 Dr M.L. Gharote et al (eds. & transl.), *Hathapradipika of Svatmarama (10 chapters),* Lonavla Yoga Institute, Lonavla, 2006, p. 132

547 *Hatha Yoga Pradipka* III.32

548 *Shiva Samhita* IV.31

Jogapradipyaka by Jayatarama is more elaborate[549]. This text first insists on the importance of making the six *chakras* bloom. This is a metaphorical term alluding to the fact that the *chakras* are often labelled as lotus flowers. They are conceived as closed buds when inactive and as blossoming flowers when their potential is activated and available. The importance of *Khechari*, so the *Jogapradipyaka*, is that the *Sushumna* is the *nadi* that pertains to the tongue. The *Sushumna* is called *Khechari* at the region of tongue and *samadhi* can be obtained by culturing the tongue, so *Jayatarama*. Culturing is a nice term. No word here about cutting into it.

The connection of *Khechari* to the *chakras* is also confirmed by the *Shandilya Upanishad*[550]. According to this *Upanishad*, *Khechari Mudra* is in the *Akasha Chakra* in the head, between sun and moon. Sun and moon are here code for the *nadis*, which begin at the right and left nostril, respectively. The tongue, once placed in *Khechari*, can manipulate the flow of *prana* through these nadis as required. The *Akasha Chakra* is a sub-*chakra* of the *Ajna*, above the soft palate. There are six of these sub-*chakras*, but their knowledge is not essential and usually for simplicity they are grouped together as the *Ajna* (third eye) *chakra*. The *Shandilya Upanishad*, like other *shastras*, also confirms the connection between both mind and tongue, which are both together to be moved into *Akasha* (referring to the space above the palate when related to the tongue and the element space when relating the term to the mind).

---

549 Swami Maheshananda et al. (eds & transl.), *Jogapradipyaka of Jayatarama*, Kaivalyadhama, Lonavla, 2006, p. 158
550 *Shandilya Upanishad* stanza 59

EFFECTS

The *Shandilya Upanishad* states that *Khechari* brings about the supramental state (*unmani*)[551]. The same is claimed in the *Hatha Yoga Pradipika*, which adds that pure consciousness, in the *Upanishads* called *turiya*, the fourth state, is experienced[552]. James Mallinson, translator and editor of the *Khechari Vidya of Adinatha*, found that among his research subjects *Khechari Mudra* was used for extended *samadhi*[553]. One of the important effects of *Khechari* is on the breath. So says Swami Sadhananda Giri that *Khechari* reduces respiratory speed[554]. Theos Bernard goes even as far as saying it overcomes the urge to breathe[555].

TEMPORAL ASPECTS

This section deals with when and for how long *Khechari* needs to be practised. The *Hathatatva Kaumudi of Sundaradeva* states that success in *Khechari* is obtained within 12 years[556]. That's an important statement as often this *mudra* is touted as some shortcut. But there is a shortcut to the twelve-year-long shortcut. The *Jogapradipyaka of Jayatarama* confirms that to succeed with the *mudra* takes very long indeed but that with adding the right *mantra* success is possible

---

551 Shyam Sundar Goswami, *Laya Yoga*, Inner Traditions, Rochester, 1999, p. 87

552 *Hatha Yoga Pradipika* IV.46-47

553 James Mallinson (ed. & transl.), *Khecarividya of Adinatha*, Indica Books, Varanasi, 2010, p. 233

554 Swami Sadhananda Giri, *Kriya Yoga*, Jujersa Yogashram, Howrah, 2005, p. 103

555 Theos Bernard, *Hatha Yoga*, Rider, London, 1950, p. 69

556 Dr M.L. Gharote et al (eds. & transl.), *Hathatatvakaumudi*, The Lonavla Yoga Institite, Lonavla, 2007, p. 159

within 6 months[557]. But Swami Rama taught that *Khechari* could be practised only after *pranayama* is mastered[558]. That's again a statement that should deter us from believing that *Khechari* is a quick fix. As a measurement of success, the *Yoga Kundalini Upanishad* promises that by drawing up the tongue for six months, it would externally reach the third eye, i.e. when sticking the tongue out, we could raise it up all the way to the third eye[559]. In the following three stanzas the *Upanishad* then makes the outlandish claims that within three years the tongue should go up to the hairline and after another 3 years to the crown of the head. We will later revisit the question what the objective of that could be, if any.

CUTTING

The *Hatha Yoga Pradipika* argues that to achieve *Khechari* the tongue is to be lengthened by cutting the frenum lingae, (i.e. the tendon that fixes the tongue to the floor of the mouth)[560]. As we have heard, this is one reason for reducing the value of the *Pradipika* in the eyes of some authorities, T. Krishnamacharya being one of them. The *Pradipika* recommends the use of a sharp, smooth and clean instrument to cut the frenum of the tongue by a hair's thickness at a time. This should be repeated at every seventh day, with the total process, after which the tendon should be completely severed, lasting six months[561]. We find the same procedure and

557 Swami Maheshananda et al. (eds & transl.), *Jogapradipyaka of Jayatarama,* Kaivalyadhama, Lonavla, 2006, p. 126

558 Swami Rama, *Path of Fire and Light*, vol. 1, Himalayan Institute Press, Honesdale, 1988, p. 138

559 *Yoga Kundalini Upanishad* II.33

560 *Hatha Yoga Pradipika* III.33.

561 *Hatha Yoga Pradipika* III.35-36

timeframes also in the *Yoga Kundalini Upanishad*[562]. The *Hathayoga Manjari of Sahajananda* even talks of the six limbs (*shatangas*) of *Khechari,* which are pulling, cutting, inserting, meditation, churning and *mantra*[563]. The *shastras* suggest the application of various herbs and minerals to the cut. So says, for example, the *Hatha Yoga Pradipika* that a mixture of rock salt and myrobalan should be used[564], whereas the *Yoga Kundalini Upanishad* relies on a mixture of rock salt and sea salt[565].

Scanning practical accounts, Theos Bernard used a razor blade to cut the frenum, but also his own teeth by sticking the tongue out and drawing it left and right over the teeth[566]. James Mallinson confirms that the frenum can be scraped away using the lower teeth, but most of his informants, including those who had done it themselves, claimed that the cutting or scraping was unnecessary [567]. Sir John Woodroffe similarly was not in favour of cutting as it interfered with the withdrawing of the tongue. Mallinson also notes that some people can insert their tongue into the cavity above the palate with no preparation, and he found cases in which the cutting resulted in difficulties when speaking and eating[568]. The big question, so asks Mallinson, is

---

562 *Yoga Kundalini Upanishad* II.29-31

563 O.P. Tiwari (publ.), *Hathayoga Manjari of Sahajananda,*
Kaivalyadhama, Lonavla, 2006, p. 43

564 *Hatha Yoga Pradipika* III.35

565 *Yoga Kundalini Upanishad* II.30

566 Theos Bernard, *Hatha Yoga*, Rider, London, 1950, p. 67

567 James Mallinson (ed. & transl.), *Khecarividya of Adinatha,* Indica
Books, Varanasi, 2010, p. 201

568 James Mallinson (ed. & transl.), *Khecarividya of Adinatha,* Indica
Books, Varanasi, 2010, p. 202

if the tongue can be inserted into the cavity above with little preparation, which place then is a tongue, which can reach externally the crown of the head, supposed to reach internally[569]? The cavity above the palate is surrounded by bone all around. There is nowhere to go inside of the head that would necessitate a tongue of such enormous length.

PULLING AND INSERTING

An important aspect of *Khechari Mudra* is the pulling and stretching of the tongue to elongate it. The *Khechari Vidya of Adinatha* suggests for this purpose to catch the tongue with a linen towel and then to pull on it[570]. This does not happen all at once. Initially, little progress is made. Theos Bernard advised practicing the pulling of the tongue twice per day until it is long enough so it can be swallowed all day long[571]. With swallowing, Bernard means to insert it into the cavity above the soft palate. The tongue cannot actually be swallowed, a term implying its insertion into the oesophagus.

When inserting the tongue into the nasopharyngeal orifice, the entry passage is quite narrow, viz. it is only designed for air to pass. The soft palate is ideally loosened and pulled forward to make space for the tongue to enter. The *Khechari Vidya* suggests using the right thumb for loosening the soft palate. To do this, one hooks the right thumb behind the soft palate and draws it forward to facilitate

---

569 James Mallinson (ed. & transl.), *Khecarividya of Adinatha*, Indica Books, Varanasi, 2010, p. 206

570 James Mallinson (ed. & transl.), *Khecarividya of Adinatha*, Indica Books, Varanasi, 2010, p. 203

571 Theos Bernard, *Heaven Lies Within Us*, Charles Scribner's Sons, New York, 1939, p. 39

the entry of tongue[572]. I don't know how it works for my readers, but my right thumb is a much too course and cumbersome tool for this purpose and initiates a gag response very quickly. Theos Bernard was taught to use a bent teaspoon for this purpose, which I cannot recommend lest somebody should swallow the spoon. After the soft palate is gently pulled or dragged forward, one uses then the fingers of the other hand to push the tongue backwards until it can be inserted into the opening[573]. This is possible only if the tongue is already lengthened enough. The *Jogapradipyaka by Jayatarama* advises a similar course of action, using the thumbs and fingers of both hands[574].

AMRTA AND RASA

Some texts put a lot of emphasis on the various tastes (*rasas*) sampled by the tongue in the cavity. So says, for example, the *Gheranda Samhita* that *Khechari Mudra* leads to *samadhi* through taste[575]. The *Shiva Samhita* states that the practitioner should drink the nectar daily as by this absorption of *amrita* all yogic powers are obtained[576]. The *Khechari Vidya* goes into more detail describing different tastes such as an icy milky taste or the sweet, cool taste akin to that of sugar cane juice[577]. I do take these tastes

---

572 James Mallinson (ed. & transl.), *Khecarividya of Adinatha,* Indica Books, Varanasi, 2010, p. 201

573 James Mallinson (ed. & transl.), *Khecarividya of Adinatha,* Indica Books, Varanasi, 2010, p. 127

574 Swami Maheshananda et al. (eds & transl.), *Jogapradipyaka of Jayatarama,* Kaivalyadhama, Lonavla, 2006, p. 124

575 *Gheranda Samhita* VII.5-6

576 *Shiva Samhita* IV.32.

577 *Khechari Vidya of Adinatha* II.65

as metaphorical expressions. If you look at the qualities of icy, milky, sweet, cool, they are all adjectives describing qualities of the lunar *prana* held in the third eye *chakra*. As I have argued in my earlier text on *pranayama* that the term *amrita* is only a poetic code for lunar *prana*, which powers introversion, etc.

MANTRA

No discussion of *Khechari Mudra* would be complete without *Khechari mantras*. As the *Jogapradipyaka of Jayatarama* states, without *mantra Khechari Mudra* takes long to attain. The *Jogapradipyaka* teaches as a suitable mantra, *Hrām Hrīm Hrūm Hraim Hraum Hrah*[578]. The *Khechari Vidya's* teaching on *mantra* are complex as the *mantras* are only obliquely referred to and need to be inferred similarly as when playing detective. After lengthy analysis James Mallinson concludes that the *Khechari bija* (short *mantra*) is *Hrīm* or *Kraum*[579]. The long *mantra* is described in stanzas 30 to 40 of the first chapter of the *Vidya*, but again it is not simply listed but described so it is very open to interpretation. Mallinson does a great attempt trying to decipher the code of the long mantra, but even the Indian ascetics he interviews cannot agree on it. However, it could be like *gam sam nam mam pham lam* or *ham sam mam yam sam ksham*, nowhere near close to the *Jogapradipyaka's mantra*. For more options please study Mallinson's text[580].

---

578 Swami Maheshananda et al. (eds & transl.), *Jogapradipyaka of Jayatarama,* Kaivalyadhama, Lonavla, 2006, p. 127

579 James Mallinson (ed. & transl.), *Khecarividya of Adinatha,* Indica Books, Varanasi, 2010, p. 199

580 James Mallinson (ed. & transl.), *Khecarividya of Adinatha,* Indica Books, Varanasi, 2010, p. 200

TECHNIQUE

After accepting the *Bhagavad Gita*'s injunction against self-harming, T. Krishnamacharya's rejection of *Khechari* due to its inclusion of cutting, and Jayatarama's warning that cutting the tongue could lead to idiocy, I have outlined here steps that can be taken to elongate the tongue to the length required without resorting to cutting it. As Mallinson heard from his subjects, the cavity inside the skull is not actually that deep it requires an extraordinarily long tongue.

Step 1

Some schools call this first step *Rajadanta*, but it is not identical with the *Rajadanta* method that constitutes a watered-down version of *Jihva Bandha*. In this technique, here we are using suction to adhere the tongue to the upper front teeth and the hard palate just behind the teeth. Use as much suction as you can so the tongue adheres to the teeth and palate. Once you have achieved this, slowly drop your lower jaw while maintaining the suction. You will now feel a stretch of the frenum lingae, which can be quite uncomfortable depending on its existing length. This length largely fluctuates between individuals. At some point, once you drop your jaw far enough, the tongue will disconnect with a smacking sound. As you progress with *Rajadanta,* you will become better at keeping the connection of the tongue and the upper front teeth/ hard palate right at the point before adhesion is lost. Even so, you will need to daily practice *Rajadanta* extensively to make an impact.

Step 2

Utilizing a small cotton towel, such as a tea towel, stick the tongue out and catch it with the towel. B.N.S. Iyengar suggested to me to grease the tongue with butter and then catch it with a plier and pull it. I found this unrealistic, as the tongue is much too slippery, and the butter does nothing to alleviate it. And one needs to apply firm pressure with the plier, which can easily lead to harm. The towel, however, does work. Slowly pull on the tongue, holding it with the towel, and once you have reached the maximum stretch you can tolerate, hold it for as long as possible. The tongue is surprisingly un-elastic and if you pull on it too much you will develop nausea pretty quickly. Avoid auto-aggression and a self-harming attitude. Do not yank on the tongue but use a gentle and consistent pull. Remember that ultimately the long-term goal of all spiritual practice is to realize God as limitless love for all beings. Any form or self-torture for ego-aggrandisement will only set you back. Repeat several times to capacity. Combine steps 1 and 2 for maximum effect and practice both daily.

Step 3

The soft palate is quite rigid and the opening in its normal form is usually too small to receive the tongue. Prepare and soften the soft palate by massaging it with your thumb. For this purpose you need to guide your thumb as far back as you can tolerate. Inevitably this will induce a gag reflex, to which some tolerance needs to be built up.

Step 4

Once the soft palate is gently drawn forward with the fingers of one hand, use the fingers of the other hand to gently push the tongue backwards and insert it up into the orifice.

Remember, this is a *samadhi*-inducing technique that only works if the mind has been made *samadhic*. It is not a miracle technique, and it is not suitable for novices. The anatomical structure of the tongue also varies widely between individuals. For one person it might be relatively easy to insert the tongue whereas somebody else even after years of preparation might struggle to do so. This needs to be considered when working on this technique. To that regard *Khechari Mudra* is like some advanced asana groups such as deep backbending or leg-behind-head postures. There is benefit in doing these postures, but for many students they are structurally so inaccessible that one would get a poor return on invested time and effort if one would keep plodding away at them. The frenum can be stretched to some extent, but if you start out with an extremely short frenum you may never be able, even after years of stretching, to put the tongue into the right position. Note also that merely placing the tongue into the right place does not guarantee spiritual progress. Again there is similarity with the subject *asana* here. And as long as the frenum is not actually severed, it will always recontract when it is not regularly stretched and lengthened. Also, in that regard the *mudra* is like certain advanced *asanas*.

EFFECTS
Khechari Mudra reduces respiratory speed, thus enabling longer *kumbhakas*. It makes *prana* steady and thus steadies the mind. It can serve as an entry point for *samadhi*.

Epilogue

Use this book on *mudras* as a companion as you slowly graduate through the eight limbs of yoga. *Mudras* are not a limb of yoga, but for almost every limb there are *mudras* that can deepen and accelerate its practice. *Mudras* constitute integral, structural elements of *pranayama* and *pratyahara*, without which the practice of these two limbs would become ineffective. *Asana* and *dharana* practice can be significantly accelerated by supplementing with the stand-alone *mudras*, described in this text. By far the most important *mudras* described here are the Kundalini-raising *dharana mudras*. Remember that significant yoga practice must be in place before tackling these.

A word on secrecy. Today many of the here quoted yoga *shastras* can be downloaded from the web and websites describe *mudras*, often relying only on a single source of information. Descriptions often lack vital detail. It is hoped that the here offered scientific approach of giving as much detail as possible, including discussing potential dangers, makes the practice of the *mudras* safer.

In this 21st century humanity faces a crisis it has brought onto itself by turning its back onto nature, spirituality and *dharma* (right action). The *Vedic* idea is that abundance on all levels does not come from being smart, cunning and competitive, but by acting *dharmic*, that is in all one's actions one is motivated by the common good, and by giving rather than receiving. We can find the motivation to do this through a return to earth-based spirituality, where our actions benefit all life on Earth, not just ourselves and not just human life. For this we need to spiritually evolve and in this context yoga in general and *mudras* specifically can be of great service.

Bibliography

Aranya, H., Sw., *Yoga Philosophy of Patanjali with Bhasvati*, 4th enlarged edn, University of Calcutta, Kolkata, 2000.

Aurobindo, S., *A Synthesis of Yoga*, Lotus Press, Twin Lakes, 1993.

Bernard, T., *Hatha Yoga*, Rider, London, 1950.

Bernard, T., *Heaven Lies Within Us*, Charles Scribner's Sons, New York, 1939.

Bhagwan Dev, A., *Pranayama, Kundalini & Hatha Yoga*, Diamond Books, New Delhi, 2008.

Chandra Vasu, R.B.S. (transl.), *The Gheranda Samhita*, Sri Satguru Publications, Delhi, 1984.

Chandra Vasu, R.B.S. (transl.), *The Shiva Samhita*, Sri Satguru Publications, Delhi, 1986.

Chapple, C. (transl.), *The Yoga Sutras of Patanjali*, Sri Satguru Publications, Delhi, 1990.

Das, S.K., *Divine Light*, New Age Books, New Delhi, 2002.

Desikachar, T.K.V. (transl.), *Nathamuni's Yoga Rahasya*, Krishnamacharya Yoga Mandiram, Chennai, 1998.

Desikachar, T.K.V. (transl.), *Yoga Taravali*, Krishnamacharya Yoga Mandiram, Chennai, 2003.

Desikachar, T.K.V., *Health, Healing & Beyond*, Aperture, New York, 1998.

Deussen, P. (ed.), *Sixty Upanisads of the Veda*, transl. V.M. Bedekar & G.B. Palsule, 2 vols, Motilal Banarsidass, Delhi, 1997.

Digambarji, Sw. (ed. & comm.), *Vasishta Samhita*, Kaivalyadhama, Lonavla, 1984.

Evans-Wentz, W.Y. (ed.), *The Tibetan Book of the Dead*, Oxford University Press, London, 1960.

Digambarji, Sw. et al (eds. & transl.), *The Gheranda Samhita,* Kaivalyadhama, Lonavla, 1978.

Fitzgerald, E. (transl.), *Rubaiyat of Omar Khayyam,* Bloomsbury, 2016.

Gambhirananda, Sw., *Bhagavad Gita with Commentary of Sankaracarya,* Advaita Ashrama, Kolkata, 1997.

Gharote, Dr M.L., *Pranayama: The Science of Breath,* Lonavla Yoga Institute, Lonavla, 2003.

Gharote, Dr M.L., *Yogic Techniques,* Lonavla Yoga Institute, Lonavla, 2006.

Gharote, Dr M.L. (ed. & transl.), *Kumbhaka Paddhati of Raghuvira,* Lonavla Yoga Institute, Lonavla, 2010.

Gharote, Dr M.L. et al (eds & transl.), *Yuktabhavadeva of Bhavadeva Mishra,* Lonavla Yoga Institute, Lonavla, 2002.

Gharote, Dr M.L. et al (eds. & transl.), *Brhadyogiyajnavalkyasmrti,* Kaivalyadhama, Lonavla, 1982.

Gharote, Dr M.L. et al (eds. & transl.), *Hatharatnavali of Shrinivasayogi,* The Lonavla Yoga Institite, Lonavla, 2009.

Gharote, Dr M.L. et al. (eds & transl.), *Hathatatvakaumudi of Sundaradeva,* Lonavla Yoga Institute, Lonavla, 2007.

Gharote, Dr M.L., et al (eds. & transl.), *Hathapradipika of Svatmarama (10 chapters),* Lonavla Yoga Institute, Lonavla, 2006.

Gharote, Dr M.M. (ed.), *Dattatreyayogasastram,* Lonavla Yoga Institute, Lonavla, 2015.

Gharote, Dr M.M. et al (eds. & transl.) *Amanaska Yogah- A Treatise On Laya Yoga,* Lonavla Yoga Institute, Lonavla, 2019.

Gharote, Dr M.M. et al (eds. & transl.), *Critical Edition of Selected Yogopanisads,* Lonavla Yoga Institute, Lonavla, 2017.

Gharote, Dr M.M. et al (eds. & transl.), *Mandalabrahmanopanisad and Nadabindupanisad*, Lonavla Yoga Institute, Lonavla, 2012.

Gharote, Dr M.M. et al. (eds), *Therapeutic References in Traditional Yoga Texts*, Lonavla Yoga Institute, Lonavla, 2010.

Gosh, S. (transl., ed. & comm.), *The Original Yoga*, 2nd rev. edn, Munshiram Manoharlal, New Delhi, 1999.

Goswami, S.S., *Laya Yoga*, Inner Traditions, Rochester, 1999.

Gupta, R.S., *Pranayama: A Conscious Way of Breathing*, New Age Books, Delhi, 2000.

Krishnamacharya, T., *Yoga Makaranda*, rev. English edn, Media Garuda, 2011.

Krishna, G., *Kundalini The Evolutionary Energy in Man*, Shambala, Boston & London, 1997.

Kuvalayananda, Sw., *Pranayama*, 7th edn, Kaivlayadhama, Lonavla, 1983. Kuvalayananda, Sw. & Shukla, Dr S.A. (eds and transl.), *Goraksasatakam*, Kaivalyadhama, Lonavla, 2006.

Kunjunni Raja (ed.), *The Hathayogapradipika of Svatmarama with the Commentary Jyotsna of Brahmananda*, The Adyar Library, Madras, 1972.

Madhavananda, Sw. (transl.), *The Brhadaranyaka Upanisad*, Advaita Ashrama, Kolkata, 1997.

Maheshananda, Sw. et al. (eds & transl.), *Jogapradipyaka of Jayatarama*, Kaivalyadhama, Lonavla, 2006.

Maehle, G., *Pranayama The Breath of Yoga*, Kaivalya Publications, Crabbes Creek, 2012.

Maehle, G., *Ashtanga Yoga: Practice and Philosophy*, New World Library, Novato, 2007,

Maehle, G., *Ashtanga Yoga: The Intermediate Series*, New World Library, Novato, 2009,

Maehle, G., *Chakras, Drugs and Evolution – A Map of Transformative States*, Kaivalya Publications, Crabbes Creek, 2021.

Maehle, G., *How To Find Your Life's Divine Purpose*, Kaivalya Publications, Crabbes Creek, 2020.

Maehle, G., *Samadhi The Great Freedom*, Kaivalya Publications, Crabbes Creek, 2015.

Maehle, G., *Yoga Meditation: Through Mantra, Chakras and Kundalini to Spiritual Freedom*, Kaivalya Publications, Crabbes Creek, 2014.

Maheshananda, Sw. et al (eds. & transl.), *Kapalakurantaka's Hathabhyasa-Paddhati*, Kaivalyadhama, Lonavla, 2015.

Maheshananda, Sw. et al. (eds & transl.), *Jogapradipyaka of Jayatarama*, Kaivalyadhama, Lonavla, 2006.

Mallinson, J. (ed. & transl.), *Khecarividya of Adinatha*, Indica Books, Varanasi, 2010.

Mallinson, J. (ed. & transl.), *The Gheranda Samhita*, YogaVidya.com, Woodstock, 2004.

Mohan, A.G. (transl.), *Yoga-Yajnavalkya*, Ganesh & Co, Madras.

Mohan, A.G., *Krishnamacharya: His Life and Teachings*, Shambala, Boston & London, 2002.

Mohan, A.G., *Yoga for Body, Breath, and Mind*, Shambala, Boston & London, 2002.

Muktibodhananda, Sw., *Swara Yoga*, Yoga Publication Trust, Munger, 1984.

Muktibodhananda, Sw. (transl. & comm.), *Hatha Yoga Pradipika*, 2nd edn, Yoga Publications Trust, Munger, 1993.

Muller, M. (ed.), *The Sacred Books of the East*, 50 vols, Motilal Banarsidass, Delhi, 1965.

Niranjanananda, Sw., *Prana and Pranayama*, Yoga Publications Trust, Munger, 2009.

Niranjanananda, Sw., *Yoga Darshan*, Sri Panchadashnam Paramahamsa Alakh Bara, Deoghar, 1993.

Radhakrishnan, S. (ed.), *The Principal Upanisads*, HarperCollins Publishers India, New Delhi, 1994.

Radhakrishnan, S. (transl. & comm.), *The Bhagavad Gita*, HarperCollins Publishers India, New Delhi, 2002.

Rama, Sw., *Path of Fire and Light*, vol. 1, Himalayan Institute Press, Honesdale, 1988.

Rama, Sw., *Path of Fire and Light*, vol. 1, Himalayan Institute Press, Honesdale, 1988.

Ramaswami, S., *Yoga for the Three Stages of Life*, Inner Traditions, Rochester, 2000.

Sadhananda Giri, Sw., *Kriya Yoga*, Jujersa Yogashram, Howrah, 2005.

Satyadharma, Sw., *Yoga Chudamani Upanishad*, Yoga Publications Trust, Munger, 2003.

Satyananda Saraswati, Sw., *Moola Bandha*, 2nd edn, Bihar School of Yoga, Munger, 1996.

Satyananda, Sw., *A Systematic Course in the Ancient Tantric Techniques of Yoga and Kriya*, Yoga Publications Trust, Munger, 1981.

Satyananda, Sw., *Asana, Pranayama, Mudra and Bandha*, Yoga Publications Trust, Munger, 1969.

Shrikrishna, *Essence of Pranayama*, 2nd edn, Kaivalyadhama, Lonavla, 1996.

Sinh, P. (transl.), *The Hatha Yoga Pradipika*, Sri Satguru Publications, Delhi, 1915.

Sivananda, Sw., *The Science of Pranayama*, BN Publishing, 2008.

Tiwari, O.P. (publ.), *Hathayoga Manjari of Sahajananda*, Kaivalyadhama, Lonavla, 2006.

Tiwari, O.P., *Concept of Kundalini*, DVD, Kaivalyadhama, Lonavla.

Tiwari, O.P., *Kriyas and Pranayama*, DVD, Kaivalyadhama, Lonavla.

Van Lysebeth, A., *Die Grosse Kraft des Atems*, O.W. Barth, Bern, 1972.

Vimuktananda, Sw. (transl.), *Aparokshanubhuti of Sankaracharya*, Advaita Ashrama, Kolkata, 1938.

Woodroffe, J., *The Serpent Power*, Ganesh & Co., Madras, 1995.

Yoga Mimamsa - A Quarterly Research Journal, Kaivalyadhama, Lonavla, 1924-2004

Yogeshvaranand, P., *First Steps to Higher Yoga*, Yoga Niketan Trust, New Delhi, 2001.

Index

Author Information

Gregor commenced Raja Yoga in the late 1970s and added Hatha Yoga in the early 80s. shortly after that he commenced yearly travels to India, where he learned from various yogic and tantric masters, traditional Indian *sadhus* and ascetics. He lived many years as a recluse, studying Sanskrit and yogic scripture and practicing yogic techniques.

Gregor's textbook series consisting of *Ashtanga Yoga: Practice and Philosophy, Ashtanga Yoga: The Intermediate Series, Pranayama: The Breath of Yoga, Yoga Meditation: Through Mantra, Chakras and Kundalini to Spiritual Freedom, Samadhi The Great Freedom, How to Find Your Life's Divine Purpose and Chakras, Drugs and Evolution* have sold over 100,000 copies worldwide and so far have been translated into eight languages. His blog articles can be found at www.chintamaniyoga.com.

Today Gregor integrates all aspects of yoga into his teaching in the spirit of Patanjali and T. Krishnamacharya. His zany sense of humour, manifold personal experiences, vast and in-depth knowledge of scripture, Indian philosophies, and yogic techniques combine to make Gregor's teachings easily applicable, relevant, and accessible to his students. He offers workshops, retreats and teacher trainings worldwide.

Contact Gregor via:
www.chintamaniyoga.com
www.8limbs.com and
https://www.facebook.com/gregor.maehle.